THE VOLVO TOUR
YEARBOOK

1990

EDITOR **Chris Plumridge**
PHOTOGRAPHIC EDITOR **Charles Briscoe-Knight**
CO-ORDINATING EDITOR **Susan Rose**
CONSULTANT EDITOR **John Hopkins**
DESIGN BY **Chris J. Bailey and Lisa Goldsworthy**
PUBLISHER **Ian Harkness**
EXECUTIVE PUBLISHER **Eddie Thomas**
PRODUCTION MANAGER **Lauri Brill**
PRODUCTION DIRECTOR **John Petty**

THE VOLVO TOUR YEARBOOK 1990 is published by Home and Law Publishing, Greater London House, Hampstead Road, London NW1 7QQ.

Printed by BPCC Paulton Book Limited, Paulton, Avon

Colour origination by Scantrans, Singapore and Hilo, Colchester, Essex.

Typesetting by Maybank, Ilford, Essex.

 ISBN 0-9511918-5-3

INTRODUCTION FROM THE PGA EUROPEAN TOUR

The second year of the Volvo Tour saw a consolidation of European golf's arrival at the very highest levels of international competition. Thirty-four Volvo Tour events produced no fewer than ten first-time Champions.

Ronan Rafferty's overall success as winner of the Volvo Order of Merit required multiple success and there can be no doubt that a worthy new name has joined the celebrated six great players who have monopolised the Harry Vardon Trophy since 1976.

Whereas these successes are vital to the continuing fortunes of European golf, it is also reasonable to reflect on the triumphant note on which our major champions end a decade of unprecedented play. Nick Faldo produced golf of unrivalled quality to add the United States Masters Championship to his 1987 Open Championship and with three Volvo Tour wins, including the Volvo PGA and the Suntory World Match Play (after a sensational final match with 1987 Champion Ian Woosnam) he can lay fair claim to being not only Europe's golfer of the year, but also that of being the best in the world.

Equally, Severiano Ballesteros' three Volvo Tour wins plus inspirational play in the tied Johnnie Walker Ryder Cup Matches ends a decade in which all in Europe can and will claim to be simply the best. Europe's other major champions continued to set a strong pace while young players from around the world, led notably by Craig Parry from Australia, added considerably to spectator enjoyment of the Volvo Tour in 1989.

The third year of Volvo's happy marriage with the PGA European Tour sees a new decade with fresh challenges. Quite simply, everyone's efforts must be stepped up to protect and advance the remarkable achievements of the '80s.

Kenneth D Schofield

KENNETH D. SCHOFIELD

EXECUTIVE DIRECTOR

10
Diners Club
International
hp
VOLVO

CONTENTS

VOLVO
17

New breed moves in

BY MICHAEL McDONNELL

Above all else, the 1989 Volvo Tour delivered ultimate proof, if it were needed, that the rich rewards of success are no longer simply to be shared by a small coterie of superstars.

For a start, there were more young professionals than ever before whose official prize money exceeded £100,000. And even if one makes cautious use of what the Americans call "ball park" figures in assessing overall income, few of these new heroes would have banked less than £200,000 from all sources.

In fact there were around 30 professionals who passed this magical figure and another five or six who were so close to it that the smile on the face of their bank manager would not have wavered for the sake of the few pounds by which they missed it. Indeed this healthy cash flow situation offered substantial evidence of a much more significant development within the European game and one which now must reassure even the pessimists that the good times really will endure.

Hitherto there had been a fear that the great international successes of recent years were somehow part of a random fluke in that a group of great men had all arrived at the same time but once they passed their prime, life would settle back into the humdrum mediocrity that had existed before.

Clearly that is now not the case. The great men still thrive. But the new breed moved in on the scene and for once the battle for the top money spot did not concern a Ballesteros, a Faldo, a Lyle, a Woosnam or a Langer. This time it involved the leading characters of the new generation of star players—Jose Maria Olazabal, Ronan Rafferty and

Craig Parry—and persisted until the last tournament—the Volvo Masters—before it could be resolved.

Moreover, it now emerges that the playing standards have narrowed so finely between the complete troupe of performers who travel week-to-week around Europe, that every one of them really does have the potential to become a winner. They are no longer permanent members of the supporting cast but instead have become a formidable contingent of understudies waiting to take over.

Consider the facts. There were 10 first-time winners on the Volvo Tour in 1989. There had been nine newcomers in the previous season and seven on the 1987 circuit. That makes a total of 26 new faces in the space of three years. It is without question evidence not only that the European game itself is attracting athletes of the highest calibre from all over the world but that the Volvo Tour also has an openess that allows such talent to flourish in a manner that perhaps other professional circuits should try to follow.

There is, however, one curious and unexplained trend to be found among these new winners in that only one of the 1988 newcomers—Mike Harwood—managed to triumph again in 1989. At this time, it may be premature to draw any sombre conclusion about the others or even to consider reasons for this lack of continuity. But if the trend continues, there would be grounds for analysing whether the rich rewards of success have an undermining effect on personal ambition; whether the cosiness of being sure of a Tour place all season instead of working week-to-week has deprived players of an edge; or whether, when all is said and done, the great players will emerge anyway and the others will just settle for what they can.

The Johnnie Walker Ryder Cup matches, for all the high drama and clear proof that Europe remained equal to the best the United States could offer, still contained only one newcomer—Ronan Rafferty—as evidence that, while the new breed possesses the talent to win, they have not yet acquired the consistency that takes them high enough in the money list to secure a team place. That, no doubt, will come and indeed all these cautionary observations are offered by a timid enthusiast who has known the impoverished times of European golf and has become over-sensitive to even the slightest blip that might affect its future.

By far the most heartening aspect of tournament golf in 1989 is the way it touched a wider audience and not just with the Ryder Cup matches which already rank alongside Wimbledon, the Cup Final or the Grand National as one of the truly great sporting

occasions which monopolise public attention. No, this other awareness is much more significant. It becomes the talk in the pubs, the shops, the queues and on trains. It is a topic among people who may not even play the game but have been touched by the achievements of its characters.

One such was Andrew Murray, a first-time winner who captured the Panasonic European Open and unquestionably had the TV-viewing public on his side as he struggled to hold what was to be his first and, if doctors are correct, his last chance of victory. Unless the worsening spondylitis condition in his joints can be slowed—it can never be halted—Andrew knows he will be forced out of tournament golf within a few years. That was the predicament he faced when he suddenly sprung from the pack to take the lead and everybody—perhaps even his rivals—prayed he would hang on to become champion. And while the debuts of the other first-time Tour winners, Ronan Rafferty, Mark Roe, Paul Broadhurst, Gordon Brand, Colin Montgomerie, Australia's Craig Parry, Vijay Singh from Fiji, Eduardo Romero from Argentina and American Mike Allen may have lacked similar poignancy, their effect was to enliven the circuit and offer an inspiring example to other struggling professionals waiting in the wings.

One other measure of a sport's importance is whether its star performers can command front page attention in the national newspapers.

Without doubt, Nick Faldo became a public hero for giving away the £100,000 Suntory World Match-play top prize to children's charities. In truth, he is a man fully aware of his status as a sporting hero and takes that responsibility seriously. It has probably been the most successful year of his career because he followed his US Masters triumph with victories in the Dunhill British Masters and Peugeot French Open before his win at Wentworth. Indeed, a cursory glance at most of our superstars shows that they were ticking over comfortably and maintaining their touch with the occasional win throughout the season. The exception has been Sandy Lyle who unaccountably crashed out of form and gave up his Ryder Cup place. Yet it says much

PING

for his talent, and the faith of others in him, that this miserable period is being regarded a short-term irritation and one that every great golfer, some time in his life, must endure. Sandy will be back.

One last thought. Winning is important. But even more crucial is the style of such triumph in a game that is, after all, public entertainment. It requires men of exceptional flair and ability to deliver exciting stuff for the fans. On that score too, the future looks good. Ronan Rafferty and Jose Maria Olazabal have this priceless gift of making it look so thrilling. In this respect, they follow in the rare tradition of Arnold Palmer and Seve Ballesteros. Rest assured, there is more front page news to come and more new names too.

In the frame in '89

VOLVO ORDER OF MERIT WINNER

The Ronan Conquest

BY ROBERT GREEN

In 1989 Ronan Rafferty had his first child, played in his first Ryder Cup match and won his first 72-hole tournament in Europe. In fact, he won three of them, and in so doing he topped the Volvo Order of Merit. That was another first, of course.

That last achievement put him in exalted company. Since the emergence of Severiano Ballesteros in 1976, and the consequent flourishing in the fortunes of European golf, only seven different men have been awarded the Harry Vardon Trophy which goes to the leading golfer on the Order of Merit at the end of each season. They are Ballesteros, Sandy Lyle, Bernhard Langer, Greg Norman, Nick Faldo, Ian Woosnam and now Rafferty.

So the young Irishman, who turned 25 on January 13, 1989, turns into the 1990s firmly established as one of Europe's best players, with 15 top-10 finishes in the season past and invitations to the US Masters, US Open and USPGA Championship awaiting him in the season ahead. He has also now acquired a 10-year exemption on the Volvo Tour. The future is filled with promise, whereas the past was only filled with potential.

In his first full year on tour, 1982, Rafferty finished 46th on the Order of Merit and won his first tournament as a professional. Admittedly it was only the Venezuelan Open, but everybody has to start somewhere, even if it's in Caracas. Big things were just around the corner. Everybody knew that.

The corner proved to be further away than we all thought. For someone less phlegmatic than Rafferty, the wait might have been enough to drive him round the bend. He inexorably improved his position on the Order of Merit over the next four seasons: to 24th, to 19th, to 17th and then to ninth in 1986, all without actually winning a tournament. But Rafferty was not overly concerned about the lack of trophies coming his way—he may have been on a lot of leaderboards come Sunday evening, but almost invariably that was through shooting a low score on the weekend when he had no chance to win. The result was a load of top-10 finishes—which is the hallmark of his consistency as much as is the fact that the strength of Rafferty's game is not built upon any one great attribute but on the absence of a glaring weakness.

This formula of sneaking up from behind nearly enabled him to snatch one victory over this period when a closing 64 in the 1986 Italian Open took him into a play-off with David Feherty, a fellow-Ulsterman, who had compiled a 68 after entering the final round tied for the lead with Ballesteros. Feherty won the play-off and deserved to. His 68 was, in all the circumstances, a better score than Rafferty's 64. And Ronan knew it.

In 1987, Rafferty retreated to 15th on the Order of Merit despite passing the £100,000 mark for a season's earnings for the first time. But at last he won a tournament, his first for five years. Indeed, the good news was that he won two. The bad news was that they were both on the other side of the world.

Early in the new year, Rafferty completed an Antipodean hat-trick by capturing the Australian Match-play Championship. But all these wins, however worthy, came with asterisks beside them, with a footnote which read: 'Still has not won in Europe'. Come the winter of 1988 he had—twice. All that meant was two more asterisks. The Equity & Law Challenge is a uniquely-scored 54-hole Stableford competition, while Rafferty's $100,000 winner's cheque from the Dunhill Cup was for being a member of the sensationally triumphant Irish team at St. Andrews. The money was marvellous, but Rafferty was expected to come up with a 'proper' tournament victory.

Everyone believed that once Rafferty sampled the taste of winning he would relish it so much that he would quickly be back for more, just as he was for the vast quantities of food he used to demolish indiscriminately during his early years on Tour. But what nobody seriously suggested was that he would go on to end the year as No. 1 on the Order of Merit.

The sceptics always felt that when—if—he made his initial breakthrough it would be via one of his 'no-hope' surges up the field while his rivals were going into reverse. In one respect they were right, because Rafferty finished

the Lancia Italian Open in May with a closing 65 (not unlike '86). But he won the tournament by playing the last four holes in one under par.

It was in the immediate aftermath of that long-awaited victory that it became evident that Rafferty's low key approach to his past frustrations—or, at least, that was how they were perceived by those who were ambitious on his behalf or dubious as to his ability—represented his genuine philosophy on golf, indeed on life. There was no 'two fingers to you all'; no gloating in his glory. Instead he made it clear that he regarded his previous failures to win as an inevitable part of the learning process, during which time he might have been said to have taken a university course in finishing in the frame. And Rafferty was forthright, if cautious, when looking ahead, too.

'To win the Order of Merit I'd need to be playing seriously well,' he said back in May, 'and I don't think I am yet. I'm not in the league of the Seves and the Faldos. I've just won one European tournament; those guys win every three weeks.' In fact, both Ballesteros and Faldo won three official Volvo Tour events in 1989, the same as Rafferty.

His chances of heading the Order of Merit might have been blown away in a remarkable gale at the KLM Dutch Open in July, where he was beaten at the ninth extra hole of a play-off by the 23-year-old Spanish prodigy, Jose Maria Olazabal. It was Olazabal who led the Order of Merit going into the final event of the season, the Volvo Masters at Valderrama. That outcome in Holland then looked likely to be crucial in deciding who would finally top the Order of Merit, but we should have appreciated just how resilient Ronan was—or had become—from the fact that he finished 64-65 to win the Scandinavian Enterprise Open the week after his Dutch defeat. A fortnight later his wife, Clare, gave birth to their son, Jonathan.

The intervening two months—between having a baby and leading the final Order of Merit—were not bereft of incident for Rafferty. In September, his victory over the Open champion, Mark Calcavecchia, in their Ryder Cup singles match was, to rather understate the case, vital. If he hadn't won, Europe would have lost. The next week he beat the US Open champion, Curtis Strange, as Ireland put up a defiant defence of the Dunhill Cup. At the Suntory World Match-play Championship, it was the 1988 US Masters champion, Sandy Lyle, who had to bow to Britain's brightest young star. Finally, at the Volvo Masters it was the defending champion, and reigning US Masters champion, Nick Faldo, who had to settle for second best.

In the perfect climax to an astonishing year, the two chief contenders for the honour of being leading money winner were paired together in the final round of the final event. When it mattered, over the last nine holes of the season, it was Ronan who had the shots and Jose who couldn't find the answers.

Rafferty finished the season with just over £400,000 in official earnings, almost one-third of that being collected from the last, lucrative week in Spain. Olazabal was runner-up on the Order of Merit and Craig Parry of Australia, was third. At the season's end, they were the only three players under 29 years of age who were in the top-30 on the Sony Rankings: Olazabal was ninth, Rafferty 20th and Parry 27th.

Rafferty would be the last man to deny that Olazabal deserves to be ranked where he is, but in 1989 the best young golfer in the world had to be content to be the second best young golfer in Europe.

Moments from
a stunning season

OLAZABAL *erupts in the opener*

After all the gifted performances by Volvo Tour professionals in 1988, it was perhaps appropriate that the following season should begin on a course that is a testament to the genius of man.

Few architects can have ever started with so much chaff and so very little wheat as did Pepe Gancedo, five times Spanish Amateur Champion, when asked to construct Golf Del Sur. The course is situated on the southern tip of Tenerife, on some of its few acres that do not reach up and touch the sky. The basic materials for Gancedo were the entrails of a volcano and the end product caused not a few eruptions among the players who were brought to the Canary Islands for the first time in a professional event.

Many of them got in a lather over the lava-filled bunkers. Or the eccentric design of a couple of the holes. Then there was tournament director John Paramor declaring rock gardens of cactii to be lateral water hazards. The Tour occasionally has to move in mysterious ways, its wonders to perform.

Jose-Maria Olazabal began the week by declaring that if he had known what the course was like he would have brought someone else's clubs. By the end of it he was exceedingly glad he had brought his own. The young Spaniard was the victor by three shots and, suddenly, for one person at least, the course looked more a swan than an ugly duckling. Olazabal, like many of the other top players, had spent the winter at rest. He never touched a club for six weeks. The Tour was so long this year, there was no need for him to go off to warmer climes in February to get ready for the start of the season — the season actually began in February.

THE FIRST EVENT OF THE 1989 SEASON SAW THE VOLVO TOUR BREAK NEW GROUND IN TENERIFE ON A COURSE HEWN FROM VOLCANIC ROCK. BY THE END OF THE WEEK MOST OF THE HEAT HAD BEEN GENERATED BY THE CLUBS OF JOSE-MARIA OLAZABAL AS HE TOOK THE FIFTH TOUR TITLE OF HIS CAREER

He arrived with the intention of using the tournament to play himself back into form. He needed all of the pro-am to do so. Astonishingly, come the start of the event, Olazabal was back in the groove. His play from tee to green was masterly. If his putting had been of its usual standard, he would have won by a street. But Olazabal holed enough to put together four consistently good rounds while all his rivals for the title blew hot and cold.

Many people believe the top professionals to be so good these days they could shoot 64 playing on the M1. Here they did the next best thing. The course built on volcanic rock was reduced to ashes on day one. Golf Del Sur, like many links courses, looks to a sea breeze to afford it protection. In the pro-am it blew so hard many professionals declared the venue unplayable. But on the first day there was no wind at all and Ian Woosnam responded by shooting 65 in his first tournament round for three months. Still he was not leading. As darkness fell, so did Woosnam's briefly-held course record, following a 64 from Canadian Jim Rutledge. All the moaning was now looking decidedly out of place.

Rutledge, a long-hitting 29-year-old from Victoria, British Columbia, was still leading at the halfway stage. But his second round was eight shots worse than his first and now the gap his breathless early pace had opened up had been bridged. The chasing pack were on his heels. One of them, Jose-Maria Canizares, edged alongside him on a total of 136, eight under par.

The weekend however, belonged to the sport's other Jose-Maria. Opening rounds of 69 and 68 had led many to predict a match-play contest between him and Woosnam for the trophy. But while Olazabal shot 68 in the third round, Woosnam was nine shots worse, filing two double bogies on his card. 'File' was the operative word. On the 9th, as he tried to play a shot from a lateral water hazard, ie. solid rock, a piece stuck in the grooves of his club and he had to send for a file to remove it.

Golf del Sur's unusual water hazards

Peter Teravainen, above, and Paul Way, below, go rock climbing on the lava

The final day began with Olazabal one shot in front of Mark Roe. It was a contest for three holes. Roe started with three bogies, the leader all birdies. Now the chase was for second place. That chase was led by the young and unsung, particularly David Gilford, a former English Amateur Champion, who shot 67 to claim the runner-up spot alongside Canizares. Tied for fourth was Spaniard Juan Quiros. Also in the top 20 were two young Frenchmen, Marc Farry and Jean Van de Velde, highlighting the massive Gallic advancement in finding good golfers.

A mention too, for another top 20 finisher, Kevin Dickens, playing in his first European Tour event. The 28-year-old from Northamptonshire made the cut with nothing to spare. He was, therefore, first out in the third round, and was prepared to carry his own clubs when a Dutch Baronness of 14th century lineage, Pauline Van Till, volunteered to do the job for him. It is not everyone who has nobility at their beck and call, and it is not everyone who marks their Tour baptism with a 66. Dickens was certainly king for a day.

As for Golf Del Sur, the popular criteria when courses are talked about are these: is the condition good enough to facilitate good scoring, and is the final result a quality champion? On both these grounds, the only rational answer was an unqualified yes.

Runner-up Jose-Maria Canizares

COURSE: GOLF DEL SUR **YARDAGE: 6,384** **PAR: 72**

POS	NAME	CTRY	1	2	3	4	TOTAL	PRIZE MONEY
1	Jose-Maria OLAZABAL	Sp	69	68	68	70	275	£33330
2	David GILFORD	Eng	72	70	69	67	278	£17360
	Jose-Maria CANIZARES	Sp	70	66	70	72	278	£17360
4	Michael KING	Eng	74	70	69	67	280	£7867
	Philip WALTON	Ire	70	70	68	72	280	£7867
	Juan QUIROS	Sp	70	73	69	68	280	£7867
	Johan RYSTROM	Swe	72	72	68	68	280	£7867
8	Jose RIVERO	Sp	70	72	68	71	281	£4493
	Mark ROE	Eng	68	69	69	75	281	£4493
	Roger CHAPMAN	Eng	74	70	67	70	281	£4493
11	Santiago LUNA	Sp	72	75	70	65	282	£3055
	Jim RUTLEDGE	Can	64	72	72	74	282	£3055
	Marc FARRY	Fr	76	70	67	69	282	£3055
	David JONES	N.Ire	71	70	70	71	282	£3055
	Peter TERAVAINEN	USA	66	73	68	75	282	£3055
	Denis DURNIAN	Eng	68	72	71	71	282	£3055
	Mark JAMES	Eng	71	71	70	70	282	£3055
	Ronan RAFFERTY	N.Ire	72	70	70	70	282	£3055
19	Eamonn DARCY	Ire	73	68	70	72	283	£2344
	David WILLIAMS	Eng	71	70	73	69	283	£2344
	Jean VAN DE VELDE	Fr	70	67	75	71	283	£2344
	Kevin DICKENS	Eng	70	77	66	70	283	£2344
	Malcolm MACKENZIE	Eng	73	71	71	68	283	£2344
24	Bernard GALLACHER	Scot	72	70	70	72	284	£2040
	Juan ROSA	Sp	74	72	69	69	284	£2040
	Martin POXON	Eng	71	71	71	71	284	£2040
	Howard CLARK	Eng	71	71	72	70	284	£2040
	Manuel PINERO	Sp	70	72	71	71	284	£2040
29	Emmanuel DUSSART	Fr	72	72	69	72	285	£1800
	Ronald STELTEN	USA	70	73	69	73	285	£1800
	Jose DAVILA	Sp	74	71	67	73	285	£1800
32	Mike MILLER	Scot	74	72	69	71	286	£1600
	Sam TORRANCE	Scot	73	71	69	73	286	£1600
	Ian WOOSNAM	Wal	65	73	77	71	286	£1600
	Magnus PERSSON	Swe	70	72	70	74	286	£1600
	Charles BOLLING Jnr	USA	75	71	69	71	286	£1600
37	Grant TURNER	Eng	71	72	71	73	287	£1420
	Anders SORENSEN	Den	73	69	77	68	287	£1420
	Mark DAVIS	Eng	72	73	73	69	287	£1420
	Christy O'CONNOR Jnr	Ire	71	74	70	72	287	£1420
41	Eduardo ROMERO	Arg	74	69	72	73	288	£1200
	Bill MALLEY	USA	71	72	74	71	288	£1200
	David LLEWELLYN	Wal	71	74	72	71	288	£1200
	Vijay SINGH	Fij	74	71	67	76	288	£1200
	Philip HARRISON	Eng	69	74	71	74	288	£1200
	Brian WAITES	Eng	75	68	74	71	288	£1200
	Magnus SUNESSON	Swe	71	72	75	70	288	£1200
48	Jamie HOWELL	USA	72	75	72	70	289	£960
	Mats LANNER	Swe	75	71	72	71	289	£960
	Antonio GARRIDO	Sp	71	70	75	73	289	£960
	Michael ALLEN	USA	73	72	72	72	289	£960
	Paul CARRIGILL	Eng	71	76	71	71	289	£960
53	Joe HIGGINS	Eng	74	72	75	69	290	£820
	Andrew SHERBORNE	Eng	76	70	68	76	290	£820
55	Keith WATERS	Eng	73	70	71	77	291	£670
	Alvaro CELLES	Sp	77	70	71	73	291	£670
	Jose CABO	Sp	71	75	71	74	291	£670
	Gordon BRAND Jnr	Scot	71	70	75	75	291	£670
	Barry LANE	Eng	72	72	78	69	291	£670
	Richard BOXALL	Eng	70	75	71	75	291	£670
61	Stephen McALLISTER	Scot	73	73	73	73	292	£560
	Sandy STEPHEN	Scot	73	73	70	76	292	£560
	John O'LEARY	Ire	72	75	72	73	292	£560
64	Gordon J BRAND	Eng	70	77	74	72	293	£301
	Stephen BENNETT	Eng	72	75	73	73	293	£301
	Steven BOTTOMLEY	Eng	70	71	71	81	293	£301
	Francis QUINN	USA	72	75	73	73	293	£301
	John SLAUGHTER	USA	72	72	72	77	293	£301
	Peter MITCHELL	Eng	75	70	72	76	293	£301
70	Ross McFARLANE	Eng	76	71	75	72	294	£192
71	Colin MONTGOMERIE	Scot	73	74	77	71	295	£190
72	Steen TINNING	Den	74	71	77	74	296	£188
73	Daniel LOZANO	Sp	75	72	74	78	299	£186
74	Jimmy HEGGARTY	N.Ire	72	72	80	76	300	£184

GOLF PLUS

JAMES
home in nomad's land

Shimmering on the horizon, in the middle of nomad's land, was what appeared to be a mirror image of a Bedouin encampment. On closer inspection, the tents were of a massive scale and made, not of canvas, but of glass, concrete and sturdy steel.

No mirage. It was the heart of the Emirates Golf Club, seven interconnecting 'tents', serving not only as one of the most original clubhouses in the world but also one of the most outlandish: golf's answer to the Sydney Opera House. The Emirates were offering classic entertainment of a different kind.

The inaugural Desert Classic, on the outskirts of Dubai in the Persian Gulf, represented the Volvo Tour's most adventurous excursion beyond the boundaries of the EEC. The Arabian desert may seem an odd place to detour, especially on the heels of the Tenerife Open which had no sand to boast of but volcanic ash and rocks, and it would have been odder still but for an immaculate course which rewarded those intrepid enough to join the caravan to the Middle East.

'I was amazed to find it in such magnificent condition,' said Tony Jacklin, who was playing in the tournament. 'They spent ages trying to get Muirfield Village in the same condition for the 1987 Ryder Cup.'

Four years ago the course, which measures 7,100 yards, was a pipe dream. The Maktoums, the wheels of the family industries oiled by the black gold beneath the sand, want to develop Dubai as a tourist attraction, hence the golf course. The sheikhs, however, would not sponsor the Desert Classic and the £250,000 prize money

AN IMMACULATE GOLFING OASIS IN THE HEART OF THE ARABIAN DESERT WAS THE VENUE FOR THE SECOND TOURNAMENT OF THE 1989 VOLVO TOUR AND IT WAS HERE THAT MARK JAMES CAME HOME AT THE HEAD OF THE CARAVAN

had to be put up by Karl Litten, the American who designed the complex.

It mattered not to Mark James. The 35-year-old, who was born in Lancashire and lives in Yorkshire, took the £41,660 first prize, beating the unranked Peter O'Malley at the first hole of a sudden-death play-off.

James, clearly at home by the green oasis, led at the halfway stage with rounds of 69 and 68 and his worst score of the week was a par 72 in the third. It left him two shots behind O'Malley's 70 going into the last round but another 68, to O'Malley's 70, took them into extra time on aggregates of 277, 11 under par and three strokes clear of the nearest challenger, Paul Broadhurst.

James and O'Malley returned to the 17th, the first extra hole, and whereas the Australian missed a birdie putt of around 10 feet, the Englishman, who hit a wedge to six feet from 124 yards, struck oil with his putt. It was the score that broke O'Malley's back.

'Whether I am playing for £1 or for £41,000 makes no odds,' said James. 'I don't need any inspiration.' It was James' tenth tournament victory in a career that plumbed the depths two years ago. He underwent a form of rehabilitation, spending hours studying videos of the great swingers of the game, in tandem with his coach, Gavin Christie. 'I haven't given up hope of becoming a world-class golfer,' said James. 'From tee to green I am just as good as anyone in Europe.'

In addition to the cheque, James held aloft the Dalleh, a gigantic silver coffee pot which was the official trophy: coffee-making throughout the Middle East is a way of honouring one's esteemed guests.

O'Malley, who failed to get his Tour card in 1987, won £27,760 which should ensure his presence at far more European events in the years to come. Broadhurst, 25, from Atherstone in Warwickshire, gave an equally astonishing performance to take third place and £15,650. He turned professional last year after winning the silver medal for being the leading amateur in the Open Championship at Royal Lytham. The Desert Classic was his third Tour event.

If there was a criticism of the course it was that the greens were too hard, not in terms of difficulty, but in firmness. They were too hard in both senses for Ian Woosnam. In the absence of Seve Ballesteros, who turned down the offer of considerable appearance money, Woosnam was, as it were, number one seed in the desert. In the first round, on his 31st birthday, he lost his head, or at least the head of his putter, during a 74 and thereafter never really got in a telling blow.

An indication of the course's pedigree is that, in spite of it being in near perfect condition, only 25 players from the field of 120 bettered par in the first round.

To counter the obvious geographical problems the course, which if untended would rapidly revert to desert, is sprayed with up to a million gallons of water a day. The hybrid grass was implanted from Georgia and to keep it alive desalination plants were built. The brine is turned into water and it is pumped 50 miles from the Gulf to the course. To protect the layout from sandstorms, banks of trees were planted around the entire complex. The

The golfing oasis of the Emirates Club

Below, fifth place finish for Magnus Persson

Far left, Peter O'Malley pitches, framed by high tech tents

Left, local interest surrounding the practice ground

Emirates Golf Club, which was officially opened 12 months before the Desert Classic by the late General Zia, charges £1,500 for individual membership and there is a waiting list. 'At the end of the day we hope to have a nation of Arabs playing golf,' said Terry Duffy, English director of operations. That day will be a long time coming. Of 2,000 members, only two are Arabs.

Staunch play from Paul Broadhurst took him to third place

Top, a sign of peace in the Gulf

Above, Mark James' caddie looks towards Mecca?

The influence of St. Andrews comes to bear on the 9th and 18th with a huge double green

Joe Higgins, below, confronts the world's biggest bunker?

COURSE: EMIRATES GOLF CLUB, DUBAI **YARDAGE: 7,100** **PAR: 72**

POS	NAME	CTRY	1	2	3	4	TOTAL	PRIZE MONEY
1	Mark JAMES	Eng	69	68	72	68	277	£41660
2	Peter O'MALLEY	Aus	71	68	68	70	277	£27760
3	Paul BROADHURST	Eng	72	66	70	72	280	£15650
4	Brett OGLE	Aus	77	69	67	69	282	£12500
5	Magnus PERSSON	Swe	67	72	72	72	283	£10600
6	Emmanuel DUSSART	Fr	71	71	72	70	284	£6620
	Barry LANE	Eng	71	73	73	67	284	£6620
	Mike MILLER	Scot	72	74	67	71	284	£6620
	Jim RUTLEDGE	Can	73	70	70	71	284	£6620
	Sam TORRANCE	Scot	70	71	71	72	284	£6620
11	Gordon J BRAND	Eng	77	68	70	70	285	£4450
	Denis DURNIAN	Eng	75	69	68	73	285	£4450
13	Anders SORENSEN	Den	70	71	72	73	286	£4020
14	Alberto BINAGHI	It	68	74	71	74	287	£3522
	David FEHERTY	N.Ire	72	73	72	70	287	£3522
	Joe HIGGINS	Eng	70	72	70	75	287	£3522
	Stephen McALLISTER	Scot	73	74	73	67	287	£3522
	Jean VAN DE VELDE	Fr	76	72	67	72	287	£3522
19	Peter BAKER	Eng	71	74	72	71	288	£2930
	Gordon BRAND Jnr.	Scot	71	71	71	75	288	£2930
	Howard CLARK	Eng	74	69	76	69	288	£2930
	Des SMYTH	Ire	70	72	75	71	288	£2930
	Steen TINNING	Den	66	73	74	75	288	£2930
24	Vicente FERNANDEZ	Arg	75	74	69	71	289	£2550
	Robin MANN	Eng	74	73	76	66	289	£2550
	Martin POXON	Eng	72	71	77	69	289	£2550
	Ronan RAFFERTY	N.Ire	71	72	77	69	289	£2550
	David WILLIAMS	Eng	68	72	76	73	289	£2550
29	Paul CARRIGILL	Eng	73	72	72	73	290	£2150
	Eugene ELLIOTT	USA	71	75	71	73	290	£2150
	Anders FORSBRAND	Swe	71	71	71	77	290	£2150
	John SLAUGHTER	USA	76	70	70	74	290	£2150
	Grant TURNER	Eng	73	73	76	68	290	£2150
	Philip WALTON	Ire	70	76	70	74	290	£2150
35	Mats HALLBERG	Swe	71	76	71	73	291	£1875
	Leif HEDERSTROM	Swe	72	73	74	72	291	£1875
	Wayne STEPHENS	Eng	77	71	73	70	291	£1875
	Peter TERAVAINEN	USA	68	76	76	71	291	£1875
39	Mark DAVIS	Eng	73	74	72	73	292	£1650
	David GILFORD	Eng	74	73	73	72	292	£1650
	Malcolm MACKENZIE	Eng	68	76	75	73	292	£1650
	Chris MOODY	Eng	73	70	77	72	292	£1650
	Eduardo ROMERO	Arg	74	73	75	70	292	£1650
44	Richard FISH	Eng	75	74	70	74	293	£1325
	Mats LANNER	Swe	70	79	72	72	293	£1325
	Bill LONGMUIR	Scot	73	74	76	70	293	£1325
	Ossie MOORE	Aus	73	76	73	71	293	£1325
	Frederic REGARD	Fr	71	74	76	72	293	£1325
	David A RUSSELL	Eng	74	72	72	75	293	£1325
	Johan RYSTROM	Swe	69	79	73	72	293	£1325
	Sandy STEPHEN	Scot	74	73	70	76	293	£1325
52	Andrew CHANDLER	Eng	74	75	69	76	294	£1075
	Ross McFARLANE	Eng	74	75	71	74	294	£1075
54	David LLEWELLYN	Wal	74	75	74	72	295	£925
	Paul MAYO	Wal	75	71	75	74	295	£925
	Ulf NILSSON	Swe	75	73	75	72	295	£925
	David J RUSSELL	Eng	73	76	77	69	295	£925
58	Richard BOXALL	Eng	73	73	76	74	296	£737
	Paul KENT	Eng	75	72	75	74	296	£737
	Bob E SMITH	USA	74	75	73	74	296	£737
	Magnus SUNESSON	Swe	71	73	80	72	296	£737
	Clive TUCKER	Eng	72	74	73	77	296	£737
	Ian WOOSNAM	Wal	74	72	75	75	296	£737
64	Roger CHAPMAN	Eng	75	72	75	75	297	£637
	Carl Magnus STROMBERG	Swe	76	71	76	74	297	£637
66	Michael ALLEN	USA	72	76	79	71	298	£249
	Lee JONES	Eng	73	76	74	75	298	£249
68	Brian MARCHBANK	Scot	74	75	73	77	299	£246
69	John MORGAN	Eng	75	74	76	75	300	£243
	Andrew STUBBS	Eng	70	75	78	77	300	£243
71	Craig McCLELLAN	USA	74	75	76	77	302	£240

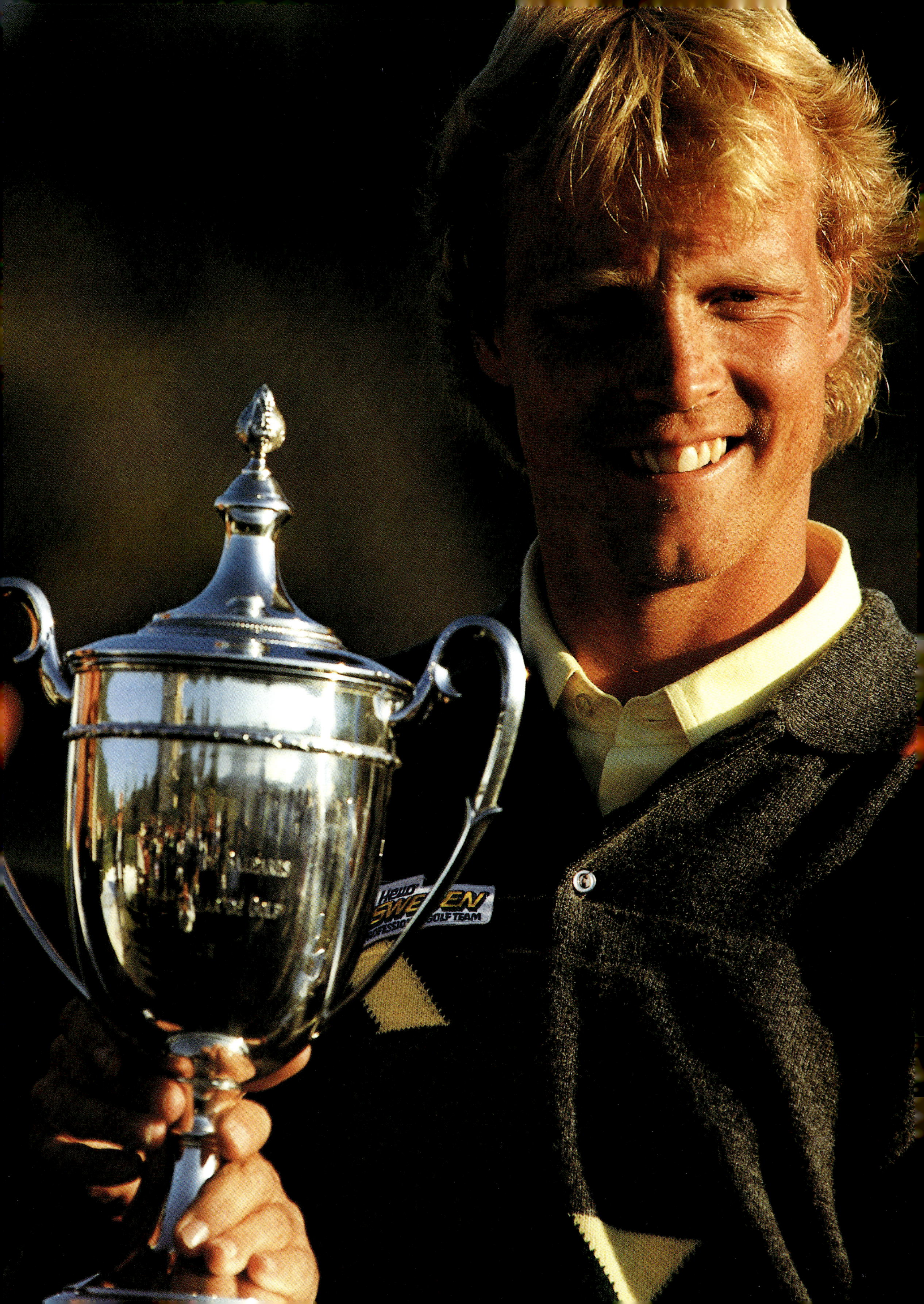
GOLF TEAM

SELLBERG
follows the Faldo example

FOLLOWING A SLUMP IN THE RANKINGS IN 1988, OVE SELLBERG SOUGHT HELP FROM NICK FALDO'S COACH, DAVID LEADBETTER. THE DECISION PAID OFF AS THE SWEDE TOOK THE SECOND EUROPEAN TITLE OF HIS CAREER WITH A DISPLAY OF FALDO-LIKE PRECISION

After starting on an island off the coast of Africa and travelling to an oasis in the middle of the desert in the Arabian Gulf, the caravan that is the contemporary Volvo Tour should have been relieved to get to the relatively familiar territory of Majorca for the Renault Open de Baleares.

Except that is, that the fairways at Santa Ponsa were not as good as they might have been and the greens were not as smooth as they ought to have been. It wasn't the first tournament to have been caught out by frost; and it won't be the last. It *was* early March and anyway, the majority of the best players finished in their rightful places.

What might have been a surprise, though, was that Ove Sellberg won the tournament. Sellberg, the ice-cool Swede who lives in Richmond, Surrey. Sellberg, the 1986 Epson Match-Play champion. Sellberg, who had slumped to 57th in the money list in 1988 after three good years.

He followed the Faldo example and sought counsel from David Leadbetter in Florida and the result in Majorca was almost like Faldo at Muirfield — 17 pars and one birdie in his last round to give him victory by two strokes.

He had to wrest it first from Tony Charnley, who had raced into a three-stroke lead after 36 holes. Charnley, whose Dutch wife Lucienne caddies for him, had been painting his new house for a week before the start of the Tour and it didn't seem to have done his game much harm.

For that matter, nor had the stone in weight that Philip Parkin had put on. The former Amateur champion had been beset by personal problems and his golf had looked like that of a worried and anxious man. But now those problems were behind him and he emerged bigger and stronger than for some years.

Parkin, like so many of the players, wanted to know to whom Emmanuel Dussart had been referring when he alleged in an article in *L'Equipe* in the winter that some golfers took drugs and one in particular was on steroids to beef himself up. 'It's not me,' said Parkin at breakfast on the third day. 'I've put this weight on by working out in the gym. I went to the PGA the other day and said I wanted to be the first player to volunteer for a drugs test.' He grinned and went out to score a 69.

After the third round Sellberg was in the lead on eight under par. He finished his round of 69 with a flourish, the sort of shot that demonstrates just how good the pros are at the short game.

He was faced with a chip from a bare piece of ground 20 yards wide of the last green. There was 12 feet of putting surface, and quite fast putting surface at that, between the edge of the green and the flag. Somehow Sellberg caressed his shot so that it ghosted down the sloping green to within six inches of the hole. Then he flicked a cowlick of hair out of his eyes and walked onto the green as if he did that sort of thing all the time.

By this stage Bill Malley was one behind, Ronan Rafferty, Mark McNulty and Charnley were two behind. Then came Parkin. Ballesteros, suffering from a virus, was nowhere to be seen. His 79 was a score worse than all but two of the 70 players in action that day. He had eight bogies, one birdie and at the end his face was dark with illness. 'I can't remember the last time I took a 79,' he said, and neither could anyone else. It must have been a long time ago.

The Sunday dawned sunny and warm with a refreshing light breeze. Every day, bar Wednesday, the day of the pro-am when Ballesteros had been outscored by his partner, racing driver Nigel Mansell, had been like that.

The questions on everyone's lips were would Sellberg crack? Could Olazabal, who had won the opening Tour event two weeks earlier, make up six strokes? Would everyone stop

Togetherness on the green from Woosnam and Olazabal

moaning about the course?

The answers were no, no, and yes. Sellberg was a model of steadiness in his 71. Olazabal made a brave attempt to catch him, birdieing the last three holes for a 67, but finally had to settle for shared second place with Parkin and McNulty, and yes, at last no-one complained about the greens and the fairways. In the end the best man had won.

Tree trouble at the 16th for Eamonn Darcy

An ailing Ballesteros framed by ruins

COURSE: SANTA PONSA, MAJORCA — YARDAGE: 7,152 — PAR: 72

POS	NAME	CTRY	1	2	3	4	TOTAL	PRIZE MONEY
1	Ove SELLBERG	Swe	68	71	69	71	279	£37500
2	Mark McNULTY	Zim	69	70	71	71	281	£16773
	Jose Maria OLAZABAL	Sp	71	75	68	67	281	£16773
	Philip PARKIN	Wal	71	71	69	70	281	£16773
5	Denis DURNIAN	Eng	71	72	69	70	282	£6523
	Jamie HOWELL	USA	68	74	70	70	282	£6523
	Bill MALLEY	USA	69	70	70	73	282	£6523
	Brett OGLE	Aus	70	70	71	71	282	£6523
	Juan QUIROS	Sp	71	70	71	70	282	£6523
	Ronan RAFFERTY	N.Ire	72	69	69	72	282	£6523
11	Jose Maria CANIZARES	Sp	73	71	70	69	283	£4100
12	Bill LONGMUIR	Scot	73	72	72	67	284	£3890
13	Tony CHARNLEY	Eng	67	69	74	75	285	£3487
	Anders FORSBRAND	Swe	67	73	72	73	285	£3487
	Barry LANE	Eng	74	72	67	72	285	£3487
	Eduardo ROMERO	Arg	69	75	70	71	285	£3487
17	Alberto BINAGHI	It	75	71	71	69	286	£3050
	Ron COMMANS	USA	73	72	72	69	286	£3050
19	Ulf NILSSON	Swe	72	71	72	72	287	£2766
	Jim RUTLEDGE	Can	75	70	72	70	287	£2766
	Mike SMITH	USA	69	74	71	73	287	£2766
22	Juan ANGLADA	Sp	72	75	71	70	288	£2520
	Emmanuel DUSSART	Fr	71	72	74	71	288	£2520
	Mark ROE	Eng	71	73	74	70	288	£2520
25	Eamonn DARCY	Ire	71	72	74	72	289	£2185
	Mark DAVIS	Eng	68	74	72	75	289	£2185
	David FEHERTY	N.Ire	71	73	73	72	289	£2185
	Jerry HAAS	USA	73	73	71	72	289	£2185
	Mats LANNER	Swe	73	69	77	70	289	£2185
	Peter MITCHELL	Eng	72	72	71	74	289	£2185
31	Mariano APARICIO	Sp	71	75	72	72	290	£1776
	Jose CARRILES	Sp	74	73	73	70	290	£1776
	Vicente FERNANDEZ	Arg	72	75	72	71	290	£1776
	Manuel PINERO	Sp	73	71	73	73	290	£1776
	Philip WALTON	Ire	75	69	71	75	290	£1776
	Ian WOOSNAM	Wal	73	71	75	71	290	£1776
37	Antonio GARRIDO	Sp	75	71	73	72	291	£1520
	Joe HIGGINS	Eng	74	73	71	73	291	£1520
	Chris MOODY	Eng	72	75	70	74	291	£1520
	Jose RIVERO	Sp	72	75	72	72	291	£1520
	Peter TERAVAINEN	USA	75	71	71	74	291	£1520
42	Paul CARRIGILL	Eng	72	74	71	75	292	£1320
	Carlos FRANCO	Para	75	71	75	71	292	£1320
	Colin MONTGOMERIE	Scot	70	72	72	78	292	£1320
	John MORGAN	Eng	73	72	72	75	292	£1320
	Wayne STEPHENS	Eng	72	75	71	74	292	£1320
47	Ossie MOORE	Aus	73	70	75	75	293	£1120
	Bryan NORTON	USA	68	77	73	75	293	£1120
	Jesper PARNEVIK	Swe	71	74	74	74	293	£1120
	David A RUSSELL	Eng	74	73	73	73	293	£1120
	Des SMYTH	Ire	74	72	74	73	293	£1120
52	Carl MASON	Eng	72	71	75	76	294	£980
	Mike MILLER	Scot	72	73	77	72	294	£980
54	Severiano BALLESTEROS	Sp	71	74	79	71	295	£840
	Stephen McALLISTER	Scot	73	72	77	73	295	£840
	Jean VAN DE VELDE	Fr	74	73	74	74	295	£840
	Ian YOUNG	Scot	74	71	76	74	295	£840
59	Paul BROADHURST	Eng	73	74	77	72	296	£660
	David JAMES	Scot	73	71	80	72	296	£660
	Magnus PERSSON	Swe	73	74	70	79	296	£660
	Johan TUMBA	Swe	73	72	79	72	296	£660
	David WHELAN	Eng	73	71	76	76	296	£660
64	Alvaro CELLES	Sp	70	77	76	74	297	£555
	Mark MOULAND	Wal	74	70	76	77	297	£555
66	Andrew SHERBORNE	Eng	71	72	76	79	298	£225
67	Mats HALLBERG	Swe	75	72	74	78	299	£223
68	Steen TINNING	Den	73	73	77	77	300	£221
69	Santiago LUNA	Sp	74	72	78	82	306	£219
70	Peter BAKER	Eng	75	71	81	81	308	£217

ROE
leads in old Pals act

Last year the Barcelona Open was held at El Prat, acknowledged as one of the finest courses in Spain. The result was a maiden victory for David Whelan after a four man play-off.

This time there were a few changes The tournament took on a new title, the Catalan Open, a new venue, Pals on the Costa Brava, and a new sponsor, the exotically named fashion company of Massimo Dutti. One thing didn't change, however, there was still a first-time victory.

Mark Roe made it a tournament for celebration and vindication — celebration because he won with a total of 279, 13 under par, and vindication because he proved, not least to himself, that when the going gets tough, the tough win golf tournaments.

Three weeks earlier Roe had gone into the first tournament of the season in Tenerife one shot behind Jose-Maria Olazabal. Within three holes a possible first victory on the Volvo Tour had been whipped from his grasp as his three bogeys were matched by three birdies from the young Spaniard, who went on to win.

The same two players were in the last group on the course in the fourth day's play at Pals. And after going to the turn in 39, Roe must have had an awful sense of *déja vu* as he slipped three shots off the pace. This time, however, there was no holding him as he covered the back nine in an irresistible 32 strokes to complete a round of 71 and snatch victory by one shot from Olazabal, Colin Montgomerie and Gordon Brand Junior.

'After Tenerife, I didn't think I would be tested again so quickly,' Roe said.

HAVING SEEN A CHANCE OF VICTORY EVAPORATE ON THE VOLCANIC DUST OF TENERIFE, MARK ROE WAS IN NO MOOD TO LET ANOTHER OPPORTUNITY PASS BY UNCLAIMED AS HE MADE FRIENDS WITH THE PALS COURSE TO RECORD HIS MAIDEN VICTORY

'But there's only one thing I want to do in this game, and that's win. I know people said I choked in Tenerife, but I knew deep down that I didn't and I wanted to prove that to everybody. It makes me proud to have beaten such a great player as Jose.'

Olazabal was celebrating his Saint's Day but there was no divine intervention on his behalf from San Jose on that final day. He could still have put himself into at least a play-off on the 18th but he hit a 60-yard bunker shot through the green and charged the return five feet past. Roe had two putts for victory from 10 feet and with an outward calmness that he cannot have been feeling inside, took them both.

Roe, aged 26, who had led since the second day, proved that even a person possessed of a personality as excitable as his — he admits to being 'hyper-active' — can keep the nerves under control when the pressure is on.

And pressure there was in abundance. Montgomerie, Rookie of the Year in 1988 after finishing 52nd in the Volvo Order of Merit, had a hole-in-one and finished on 280. Brand Junior mounted another of his familiar late challenges and came in with the same total. Both could have been excused for expecting, at worse, to be involved in a play-off. But behind them Roe was rehabilitating himself after the rocky front nine. He birdied the 12th and 14th but the stroke which did more to win the tournament than anything else was a holed bunker shot for an eagle three at the 15th. After that, anything less than victory just would not do.

The first day had thrown up its share of joy and gloom. The rather unlikely leaders were David Ecob of Australia, a professional for only a few months after a distinguished career as an amateur, and Manuel Calero, who reckoned he was rapidly approaching the other end of his career. Twelve years on the Tour were enough for anybody, he said, and he couldn't wait to get back to his wife, Isabel, and their son, Ivan, in their Barcelona home. Scores of 68 must have encouraged both men to keep trying.

At the other end of the smile spectrum was the rather forlorn figure of young Peter Baker. He had his third competitive 81 in succession: the next day he pulled out of the tournament after only four holes. Quite suddenly, the winner of the 1988 Benson and Hedges International looked far older than his 21 years.

Roe hit the front for the first time with a round of 70 on the second day, which gave him a share of the lead with Grant Turner, another eager student at the Bob Torrance academy for worried golfers. Turner's seven birdies and an eagle convinced him that the Torrance method was beginning to work.

Olazabal became a threatening presence on day three when his 68 put him only one shot behind Roe, who had a 69. Five birdies and only one dropped shot proved that the young man from Derbyshire had the nerve. The next day he won his final battle to keep it.

High finish for Colin Montgomerie

Across the water to the ninth tee at Pals

The winner is anointed in the Press Centre

Olazabal charges in a chip on the 17th

COURSE: CLUB GOLF DE PALS **YARDAGE: 6804** **PAR: 73**

POS	NAME	CTRY	1	2	3	4	TOTAL	PRIZE MONEY
1	Mark ROE	Eng	69	70	69	71	279	£33330
2	Gordon BRAND Jnr	Scot	73	67	70	70	280	£14906
	Colin MONTGOMERIE	Scot	73	68	72	67	280	£14906
	Jose Maria OLAZABAL	Sp	70	71	68	71	280	£14906
5	Denis DURNIAN	Eng	73	68	71	69	281	£8470
6	Howard CLARK	Eng	72	68	70	72	282	£6000
	Peter O'MALLEY	Aus	72	69	69	72	282	£6000
	Grant TURNER	Eng	73	66	70	73	282	£6000
9	Manuel CALERO	Sp	68	76	69	71	284	£4480
10	David ECOB	Aus	68	72	75	70	285	£3840
	Magnus PERSSON	Swe	72	72	71	70	285	£3840
12	Manuel PINERO	Sp	72	71	72	71	286	£3330
	Eduardo ROMERO	Arg	73	69	72	72	286	£3330
14	Vicente FERNANDEZ	Arg	71	72	71	73	287	£2940
	David A RUSSELL	Eng	72	71	72	72	287	£2940
	Jim RUTLEDGE	Can	75	69	71	72	287	£2940
17	Ron COMMANS	USA	72	73	69	74	288	£2428
	John JACOBS	USA	70	70	73	75	288	£2428
	Malcolm MACKENZIE	Eng	70	72	71	75	288	£2428
	John MORGAN	Eng	70	72	68	78	288	£2428
	Jose RIVERO	Sp	72	71	73	72	288	£2428
	Mike SMITH	USA	72	70	75	71	288	£2428
	Sam TORRANCE	Scot	71	73	72	72	288	£2428
24	Ross DRUMMOND	Scot	69	75	71	74	289	£2040
	Neil HANSEN	Eng	72	70	74	73	289	£2040
	Martin POXON	Eng	72	73	70	74	289	£2040
	Ronan RAFFERTY	N.Ire	72	73	72	72	289	£2040
	David WILLIAMS	Eng	72	72	72	73	289	£2040
29	David FEHERTY	N.Ire	74	71	72	73	290	£1720
	David GILFORD	Eng	72	70	74	74	290	£1720
	Leif HEDERSTROM	Swe	71	72	75	72	290	£1720
	Mark McNULTY	Zim	71	74	74	71	290	£1720
	Mark MOULAND	Wal	79	67	71	73	290	£1720
	Peter TERAVAINEN	USA	73	67	76	74	290	£1720
35	Jerry ANDERSON	Can	69	73	73	76	291	£1500
	Emmanuel DUSSART	Fr	72	73	71	75	291	£1500
	Manuel MORENO	Sp	76	71	71	73	291	£1500
	Philip PARKIN	Wal	74	71	70	76	291	£1500
39	Jamie HOWELL	USA	74	72	73	73	292	£1400
40	Gordon J BRAND	Eng	72	71	74	76	293	£1260
	David JONES	N.Ire	72	73	73	75	293	£1260
	Mikael KRANTZ	Swe	76	69	76	72	293	£1260
	Bill LONGMUIR	Scot	76	69	76	72	293	£1260
	Emilio RODRIGUEZ	Sp	72	72	73	76	293	£1260
	Jose ROMERO	Sp	76	70	72	75	293	£1260
46	Steven BOTTOMLEY	Eng	74	73	69	78	294	£920
	Jose DAVILA	Sp	74	71	73	76	294	£920
	Barry LANE	Eng	74	70	74	76	294	£920
	Brian MARCHBANK	Scot	77	68	76	73	294	£920
	Peter MITCHELL	Eng	76	70	73	75	294	£920
	Ian MOSEY	Eng	71	74	75	74	294	£920
	Christy O'CONNOR Jnr	Ire	69	73	76	76	294	£920
	Jose ROZADILLA	Sp	72	72	76	74	294	£920
	Ove SELLBERG	Swe	72	75	72	75	294	£920
	Vijay SINGH	Fij	75	69	76	74	294	£920
	Philip WALTON	Ire	75	71	70	78	294	£920
57	Antonio GARRIDO	Sp	70	74	76	75	295	£635
	Jerry HAAS	USA	74	73	73	75	295	£635
	Miguel Angel MARTIN	Sp	73	71	76	75	295	£635
	Des SMYTH	Ire	75	67	77	76	295	£635
61	Manuel RAMOS	Sp	74	73	74	75	296	£570
	Armando SAAVEDRA	Arg	74	73	74	75	296	£570
63	Mark DAVIS	Eng	72	72	77	76	297	£440
	Philip HARRISON	Eng	74	72	79	72	297	£440
	Mark JAMES	Eng	72	75	75	75	297	£440
	Ossie MOORE	Aus	77	70	73	77	297	£440
67	Bryan NORTON	USA	75	72	74	77	298	£198
68	Wayne RILEY	Aus	74	71	69	85	299	£195
	Andrew STUBBS	Eng	74	72	77	76	299	£195
70	Simon BISHOP	Eng	75	71	79	75	300	£191
	Brett OGLE	Aus	75	72	71	82	300	£191
72	Richard FISH	Eng	75	71	76	79	301	£188

GOLF PLUS
GOLF
PLUS

JAMES
makes it a Spring double

La Grande Motte provided a fascinating new setting for the Volvo Tour in March. It lies two hours west of Marseilles and 15 minutes east of Montpellier, a purpose-built holiday resort with a purpose-built golf complex, the one not a pretty sight with its concrete jungle of holiday apartments, the other a golf course of solid virtues under the delightful name of Flamants Roses (flamingoes).

That graceful bird once held sway on the swampland where Robert Trent Jones was invited to bring his architectural virtues to bear. Yet only four years after the breaking of the ground and 18 months after the opening of this 'masterpiece of ingenuity', as Tony Gray, the Tournament Director, called it, it provided superb fairways, with the few exceptions where local rules were invoked to deal with sea water damage, and greens of velvet texture —if of Machiavellian design.

Not everyone appreciates Trent Jones' creations, with their bunkers of amorphous contours and the proliferation of water hazards, but within the limited space available these features legitimately came into their own as specific defences over a 6,704 yards lay-out. The wind whistling down from the Rhône Valley, too, is a perpetual ally, or at least it should be, but after a gale force earlier in the week there was little more than a zephyr when the tournament opened, quite unusually, on a Friday.

It was a Good Friday for everyone, but a particularly good Friday for Ronald Stelten, a little-known 31-year-old American.

Stelten had won only £6,661 from 17 tournaments in 1988, which left him marooned, 144th in the Volvo Order of

THE IDES OF MARCH BROUGHT NOTHING BUT GOOD FORTUNE FOR MARK JAMES WHO RECORDED HIS SECOND VICTORY OF THE MONTH, PAVING THE WAY WITH A STUNNING RECOVERY SHOT AT THE VITAL MOMENT

Merit, and unable, for physical and emotional reasons, to face six more rounds at the La Manga school. Thus he occupied a place only in category 13, hardly the background for the kind of golf he played in the AGF Open.

He broke Jean Van de Velde's course record of 66 by one stroke on the first day, followed it with a 68 on the second to go 11 under par and stood his ground with a stabilising 72 on the third. He was now moving, he said, into 'uncharted waters' on the final day.

Among the challengers on 68 the first day loomed the enigmatic figure of Sam Torrance, not as consistent as he once was, but with a 67 on the second day he moved to within two shots of Stelten. But another Ryder Cup man, Mark James, was purposefully stalking the two leaders. With rounds of 69 and 67 he was only one shot behind Torrance and three behind Stelten. With another sub-70 round on day three he had drawn level with the American, three ahead of the Scot.

Everyone's money was on James, of course. It seemed improbable that a man of Stelten's moderate achievement could compete with a man of James' vast experience. So it proved. Stelten got a model birdie at the first, from six feet, took three putts at the next and was destroyed at the fourth where he drove into a lake and took six. James rammed home his advantage there by hitting his second to two feet, thus manufacturing a three-stroke swing. Stelten came back with a brilliant second to within 12 inches of the 465 yards sixth but he must have realised at the next that it would not be his day.

James hooked his second at the seventh (558 yards) perilously near a lake and, even having escaped that disaster, he was still faced with no alternative, apparently, to a chip back to the fairway. That was James' first choice, as he later explained, but the more he examined the group of saplings and the bush that impeded his way, the more he became convinced that he might be able to hook the ball round everything and make the green.

Those people standing behind him as he played the shot were amazed to see him strike in the direction of extra

Stelten shot to the top of the leaderboard

cover, 50 yards off line, and still more amazed to follow the ball's fantastic parabola as it boomeranged home. It was the shot of the tournament, maybe the season. Men have been knighted for less. He aggravated a wrist injury in the process but managed to struggle home in par except for three carefree putts in front of a substantial gallery at the 18th.

Stelten's record was subsequently equalled three times – by Grant Turner on the third day and by Mark Mouland and Mariano Aparicio on the fourth. Mouland's spectacular round, set in motion by birdies at the first four holes, launched him into second place with the handsome reward of £15,266. Vijay Singh achieved a flamingo, as the locals would have it, a hole-in-one with an eight iron at the 151 yards 16th. It earned him an £18,000 Volvo 740 GLT.

Mark James strides to the final green

Malcolm Mackenzie goes barefoot in the park

Third round leader Stelten, above, and below, with winner James

COURSE: LA GRANDE MOTTE, MONTPELIER **YARDAGE: 6,704** **PAR: 72**

POS	NAME	CTRY	1	2	3	4	TOTAL	PRIZE MONEY
1	Mark JAMES	Eng	69	67	69	72	277	£22909
2	Mark MOULAND	Wal	72	73	70	65	280	£15266
3	Bryan NORTON	USA	70	70	70	71	281	£8604
4	Vijay SINGH	Fij	73	68	73	68	282	£5408
	Ronald STELTEN	USA	65	68	72	77	282	£5408
	Sam TORRANCE	Scot	68	67	73	74	282	£5408
	Grant TURNER	Eng	73	73	65	71	282	£5408
8	Jamie HOWELL	USA	70	75	70	68	283	£3257
	Andrew SHERBORNE	Eng	72	70	70	71	283	£3257
10	Mariano APARICIO	Sp	74	72	73	65	284	£2327
	Stephen BENNETT	Eng	70	71	71	72	284	£2327
	Michel BESANCENEY	Fr	72	72	70	70	284	£2327
	Juan QUIROS	Sp	69	69	72	74	284	£2327
	Glenn RALPH	Eng	72	71	67	74	284	£2327
	David J RUSSELL	Eng	74	73	66	71	284	£2327
16	Brian EVANS	Eng	72	74	69	70	285	£1933
17	Denis DURNIAN	Eng	71	72	68	75	286	£1718
	Eugene ELLIOTT	USA	72	69	71	74	286	£1718
	David GILFORD	Eng	69	73	70	74	286	£1718
	Armando SAAVEDRA	Arg	69	73	73	71	286	£1718
	Mike SMITH	USA	74	74	67	71	286	£1718
22	Mark DAVIS	Eng	68	70	75	74	287	£1505
	Michael McCLEAN	Eng	70	74	71	72	287	£1505
	Andrew MURRAY	Eng	72	73	74	68	287	£1505
	Wayne RILEY	Aus	73	69	72	73	287	£1505
26	Steven BOTTOMLEY	Eng	73	72	70	73	288	£1319
	Richard FISH	Eng	71	69	76	72	288	£1319
	David JAMES	Scot	76	71	68	73	288	£1319
	Mike MILLER	Scot	75	71	70	72	288	£1319
	Peter O'MALLEY	Aus	74	72	71	71	288	£1319
31	Paul BROADHURST	Eng	72	72	74	71	289	£1129
	Paul CARMAN	Eng	69	74	75	71	289	£1129
	Paul CARRIGILL	Eng	75	70	78	66	289	£1129
	Ron COMMANS	USA	72	70	76	71	289	£1129
	Silvio GRAPPASONNI	It	74	72	69	74	289	£1129
36	Simon BISHOP	Eng	74	71	74	71	290	£1003
	Gordon J BRAND	Eng	74	67	75	74	290	£1003
	Neil HANSEN	Eng	73	73	74	70	290	£1003
	Mark ROE	Eng	72	72	75	71	290	£1003
40	Juan ANGLADA	Sp	73	73	75	70	291	£879
	Mats HALLBERG	Swe	70	72	75	74	291	£879
	John HAWKSWORTH	Eng	70	70	76	75	291	£879
	David LLEWELLYN	Wal	69	75	76	71	291	£879
	Malcolm MACKENZIE	Eng	78	70	67	76	291	£879
45	Tony CHARNLEY	Eng	68	78	75	71	292	£728
	Mike CLAYTON	Aus	74	72	75	71	292	£728
	Marco DURANTE	It	72	75	73	72	292	£728
	Wayne STEPHENS	Eng	73	74	72	73	292	£728
	Johan TUMBA	Swe	76	72	73	71	292	£728
	Philip WALTON	Ire	69	72	75	76	292	£728
51	Michael ALLEN	USA	79	69	74	71	293	£577
	Ross McFARLANE	Eng	73	71	79	70	293	£577
	John McHENRY	Ire	74	74	73	72	293	£577
	Peter MITCHELL	Eng	81	67	72	73	293	£577
	Andrew STUBBS	Eng	71	75	72	75	293	£577
56	Jean VAN DE VELDE	Fr	72	75	76	71	294	£494
57	Jean GARAIALDE	Fr	77	71	73	74	295	£444
	Jerry HAAS	USA	74	74	73	74	295	£444
	Ulf NILSSON	Swe	76	71	72	76	295	£444
60	Emmanuel DUSSART	Fr	71	77	75	73	296	£391
	Vicente FERNANDEZ	Arg	77	70	69	80	296	£391
	Joe HIGGINS	Eng	75	73	70	78	296	£391
	Santiago LUNA	Sp	76	72	70	78	296	£391
64	Chris GRAY	Eng	77	71	75	74	297	£300
	Ossie MOORE	Aus	72	74	75	76	297	£300
	Alfonso PINERO	Sp	73	70	78	76	297	£300
67	Peter COWEN	Eng	73	75	75	75	298	£196
	Philippe PALLI	Fr	75	72	78	73	298	£196
	Ian YOUNG	Scot	78	70	76	74	298	£196
70	Charles BOLLING Jnr	USA	72	74	76	77	299	£190
	Carlos FRANCO	Para	75	71	74	79	299	£190
	Michel TAPIA	Fr	73	73	74	79	299	£190
73	Jose DAVILA	Sp	75	71	70	85	301	£186

Titleist

SINGH
learns his lesson later

THE BURGEONING TALENT OF VIJAY SINGH WAS WELL-KNOWN ON THE SAFARI TOUR BUT AFTER HE BROKE THROUGH TO WIN IN SARDINIA, HE DECIDED IT WAS TIME FOR HIS FIRST GOLF LESSON

A golfer who has his first lesson *after* he has won his first championship is by definition exceptional.

Fiji's Vijay Singh made this back-to-front revelation after his comprehensive victory in the new Volvo Open in Sardinia, the first of four Volvo title sponsorships of the 1989 season.

Singh ran away from the field of Ryder Cup hopefuls at Is Molas with a 12 under par 276, comprising an opening 72 then a trio of 68s. He led by a shot going into the final round and ended three ahead of Australian Peter Fowler. The nearest Britons, Bill Longmuir and Gordon J. Brand were four shots further adrift.

Little doubt, then, that Europe had unearthed a new talent, even if it had blossomed via Australia, Malaysia and most of the compass points of the African Safari Tour. The 26-year-old from the South Seas travelled more than most in his formative years but, amazingly, did not receive a genuine golf lesson until he spent two days with Bob Torrance in Ayrshire after leaving Sardinia victorious.

'I started playing golf when I was eight,' recalled Vijay, 'and I used to caddy for my father. But he did not teach me any of the finer points. He just told me about the grip and, occasionally, if we played together, he would point out defects. But I did not have a proper coach and my father was always too busy to spend a lot of time with me, although he was a very good golfer.'

One of six children, the teenage Vijay was left largely to his own devices, but he was down to scratch at 17 and turned professional the following year. He left Fiji in search of experience in Australia, playing wherever and whenever he was able for two years. It was not easy for this 6ft 3in golfer of Indian stock, but his game improved sufficiently for him to graduate top of the Australian Tour school of 1983.

It was time to head for the Asian circuit where he enjoyed his first victory with the Malyasian PGA title in 1984. Hopes that it would prove a stepping stone to immediate fame proved unfounded. Vijay's form declined and he drifted away from continual tournament play to a club post in Sarawak. His journey from the obscurity of teaching golf in Borneo to the rank of European champion took a little over two years.

'I always wanted to play in the Open Championship,' continued Singh, 'so I set about saving enough to get to Britain and making an attempt to qualify for the 1987 Open at Muirfield. I did not get through, but then I thought I would stay on and have a go at the European Tour qualifying school.'

Singh pre-qualified at Foxhills but failed by two shots to survive the first cut at La Manga in December 1987, and another of golf's avenues had turned into a cul-de-sac. Then came two lucky breaks. Singh gained a sponsorship from the Red Baron oil company, based in Aberdeen and, on the strength of his showing at the school, the Tour authorities at Wentworth allowed him to fill late vacancy on the Safari Tour in spring of 1988.

The tall Fijian, who had modelled his swing on the equally lofty Tom Weiskopf, won the first event, the Nigerian Open in Lagos, after a play-off with Mike Miller. Four top ten finishes in the other four events saw him win over £22,000, and when he graduated second from the school at the end of 1988, a new career was about to commence.

Another stroke of fortune, in the previous week's AGF Open at Montpellier, provided the spark for success in Sardinia. Vijay scored his first ace, won a Volvo car, and tied fourth.

When he found a well-prepared Is Molas suited to his huge, if sometimes wayward hitting, he had discovered the ideal theatre to confirm his class and those who had come expecting to make rapid progress in the Ryder Cup standings saw the lion's share of the spoils snatched away from them.

American Charles Bolling and Britain's Carl Mason were the first day leaders. Mason had arrived direct from the Sunningdale Foursomes with his regular partner, Andrew Chandler, and they were to be the pacemakers after 36 holes, the second round coinciding with Chandler's birthday. The Lancastrian lost his Tour card at the end of 1988 but proved he was no April golf fool by taking first place on a six under par 138 on the first of the month, with two rounds of 69. Singh was two shots back alongside Ronan Rafferty after both had taken advantage of the balmy weather. Rafferty went out in 31 in his 68, while Singh had four birdies in five holes around the turn, almost holing in one again at the 10th.

Bolling, a former US Tour player, had compiled his opening 68 despite a triple bogey seven at the eighth. When he holed a 40-yards pitch for an eagle at the long 15th, he got home in 32 to expose the scoring opportunities on an inward half containing three par fives, all within range of the long hitters.

Singh made merry in his third round with six birdies and almost had another when a greenside bunker shot rattled the flagstick. A slight amendment to his putting method, allied to a tip from Bob Torrance on the practice ground at Pals during the Catalan Open, was giving a daily boost to his confidence. The Scottish senior professional had counselled the Fijian against too much movement of the right knee.

His only serious challenger thereafter was the experienced Australian Peter Fowler, making his first European appearance of the season. He turned in 33 then birdied two of the last three holes for a 68 and a nine under par 279. Despite three putts on the 10th green, Singh was not to be denied. His birdie at the 11th, where he almost drove the downwind green at 393 yards, and another at the 16th, sealed his triumph.

Singh never doubted his ability to hold off the chasing pack. 'I have never lost a tournament from the front,' he said before heading to the West coast of Scotland with his future secure. 'My ambition now is to try and win place on the US Tour, but first I will try and establish myself as a leading player in Europe over the next two seasons.'

Singh swings in scenic Sardinia

Third round leader Carl Mason recovers from sand

Caddie calls for silence for Sellberg in the sand

Serious practise for shirt-sleeved Rafferty

Powerful drive from runner-up Peter Fowler

COURSE: IS MOLAS, SARDINIA **YARDAGE: 7,080** **PAR: 72**

POS	NAME	CTRY	1	2	3	4	TOTAL	PRIZE MONEY
1	Vijay SINGH	Fiji	72	68	68	68	276	£33330
2	Peter FOWLER	Aus	71	69	71	68	279	£22200
3	Gordon J BRAND	Eng	69	72	70	72	283	£11260
	Bill LONGMUIR	Scot	71	69	72	71	283	£11260
5	Charles BOLLING Jnr	USA	68	72	71	73	284	£7735
	Christy O'CONNOR Jnr	Ire	70	72	69	73	284	£7735
7	Massimo MANNELLI	It	73	72	71	69	285	£4870
	Peter O'MALLEY	Aus	72	70	68	75	285	£4870
	Ronan RAFFERTY	N.Ire	72	68	71	74	285	£4870
	David WILLIAMS	Eng	73	72	72	68	285	£4870
11	Mats HALLBERG	Swe	75	69	73	69	286	£3268
	John MORGAN	Eng	70	71	70	75	286	£3268
	Jesper PARNEVIK	Swe	71	70	73	72	286	£3268
	Jacob RASMUSSEN	Den	71	74	72	69	286	£3268
	Jose RIVERO	Sp	74	71	69	72	286	£3268
16	Richard BOXALL	Eng	72	68	72	75	287	£2645
	Vicente FERNANDEZ	Arg	70	70	73	74	287	£2645
	Magnus JONSSON	Swe	72	71	72	72	287	£2645
	Carl MASON	Eng	68	71	70	78	287	£2645
20	Steven BOTTOMLEY	Eng	71	72	72	73	288	£2310
	Mats LANNER	Swe	71	73	70	74	288	£2310
	Malcolm MACKENZIE	Eng	74	72	72	70	288	£2310
	Juan ROSA	Sp	73	70	73	72	288	£2310
24	Giuseppe CALI	It	75	70	71	73	289	£2010
	Andrew CHANDLER	Eng	69	69	75	76	289	£2010
	David GILFORD	Eng	72	72	73	72	289	£2010
	Jamie HOWELL	USA	73	70	71	75	289	£2010
	Frederic REGARD	Fr	70	74	72	73	289	£2010
	Andrew SHERBORNE	Eng	73	71	69	76	289	£2010
30	Mike CLAYTON	Aus	75	73	73	69	290	£1770
	Neil HANSEN	Eng	77	69	73	71	290	£1770
32	Neal BRIGGS	Eng	71	73	72	75	291	£1580
	Andrea CANESSA	It	72	71	70	78	291	£1580
	Eugene ELLIOTT	USA	73	73	73	72	291	£1580
	John HAWKSWORTH	Eng	75	70	71	75	291	£1580
	Ove SELLBERG	Swe	70	74	72	75	291	£1580
	Steen TINNING	Den	72	75	74	70	291	£1580
38	Carlos FRANCO	Para	72	73	73	74	292	£1340
	Gavin LEVENSON	SA	76	70	72	74	292	£1340
	Thomas LEVET	Fr	73	71	72	76	292	£1340
	Colin MONTGOMERIE	Scot	74	72	71	75	292	£1340
	Juan QUIROS	Sp	70	74	71	77	292	£1340
	Peter TERAVAINEN	USA	78	68	70	76	292	£1340
44	Derrick COOPER	Eng	73	72	74	74	293	£1120
	Eamonn DARCY	Ire	70	76	73	74	293	£1120
	Costantino ROCCA	It	73	72	74	74	293	£1120
	Armando SAAVEDRA	Arg	75	72	71	75	293	£1120
	Ian YOUNG	Scot	71	74	75	73	293	£1120
49	Paul CARRIGILL	Eng	77	71	73	73	294	£940
	Bill MALLEY	USA	73	72	74	75	294	£940
	Mike MILLER	Scot	71	72	75	76	294	£940
	Keith WATERS	Eng	73	72	73	76	294	£940
53	Manuel CALERO	Sp	74	73	76	72	295	£780
	Mikael KRANTZ	Swe	73	71	73	78	295	£780
	Robert LEE	Eng	74	74	73	74	295	£780
	Paul WAY	Eng	69	77	70	79	295	£780
57	Laurent LASSALLE	Fr	71	73	74	78	296	£646
	Delio LOVATO	It	73	74	73	76	296	£646
	John McHENRY	Ire	71	77	73	75	296	£646
60	Alberto BINAGHI	It	70	77	72	78	297	£590
	Marc FARRY	Fr	74	74	75	74	297	£590
62	Paul HOAD	Eng	76	71	75	76	298	£540
	Manuel PINERO	Sp	75	72	73	78	298	£540
	Chris PLATTS	Eng	73	75	77	73	298	£540
65	Steven THOMPSON	Eng	72	74	74	79	299	£500

O'CONNOR'S *patience is rewarded*

Patience is a virtue with which Christy O'Connor Junior is amply endowed, which is why his first solo victory in Europe for 14 years, on the clifftop links of La Moye, was such a popular one.

After winning the Carrolls Irish Open and tying with Australian Ian Stanley in the Martini International in 1975, the genial Irishman went on to climb to seventh place in the order of merit. A Ryder Cup baptism that year at Laurel Valley, Pennsylvania, was well deserved and he must have had high hopes of a long Cup run to rival that of his famous uncle, whose tenth and final outing against the Americans had come two years before.

It was not to be. Although he twice partnered Eamonn Darcy to victory in the Sumrie-Bournemouth Better-Ball event, further solo Tour titles and Ryder Cup outings eluded him. Even in 1985, when he played to the very brink of selection, he was to be denied a team spot. He had finished eighth in the Irish Open, joint third in the Open Championship after an opening 64 which shattered Henry Cotton's 51-year-old record, and joint seventh in the Scandinavian Enterprise Open.

Sadly, he missed the cut in the final Cup qualifier and slipped to tenth place in the points table. The top nine made the team automatically but skipper Tony Jacklin plumped for Jose Rivero, Nick Faldo and Ken Brown to fill the final three spots.

But his never-say-die spirit is a model for all and his long-awaited return to the winner's rostrum came in Jersey during a wet and windy week.

The pre-tournament news was made by Brian Barnes, who was making a comeback after retiring from full time

FOURTEEN YEARS HAD ELAPSED SINCE CHRISTY O'CONNOR JUNIOR TASTED VICTORY BUT THE CHEERFUL IRISHMAN STUCK TO HIS TASK AND WAS EVENTUALLY REWARDED

Tour campaigning to concentrate on building his own course at West Chiltington, Surrey. It proved a far from happy return for big Brian, who missed the halfway cut after carding two 77s and suffering a back strain.

Five men shared the lead after round one, which, like round two, teamed pros and amateurs. The leaders included David A. Russell and Peter Mitchell from Kent, Ulsterman David Feherty, Scotland's Colin Montgomerie and American Rick Hartmann, all on 69. Russell, who shed 70lbs to slim down to a respectable 15 stone, shared the lead at halfway on 139 with Welshman David Llewellyn. Llewellyn had opened his round in high style with four successive birdies but then ran up a double bogey six after his ball rolled into a bunker when he removed a rake against which it was resting.

O'Connor made his move in round three when the sun came out on La Moye's spectacular seascape. But his 66 still left him a stroke behind new leader Denis Durnian from Manchester, who was seeking his first victory after finishing second again to Nick Faldo in the 1988 French Open.

Durnian, who had to switch hotels because the thick pile on his bedroom carpet would not accommodate his putting machine, was in hot form on the greens. Birdies at the 12th and 15th in the final round left him tied on 28.

But Christy was to take the title and £24,490 prize money with a par on the first extra hole when Durnian overshot the green to take five. Mats Lanner and former amateur star Paul Broadhurst finished one stroke behind. Des Smyth, Ronan Rafferty, Colin Montgomerie, Bernard Gallacher and Sam Torrance (using a putter over a foot longer than standard tucked under his chin!) tied fifth, one shot further back.

O'Connor claimed he, too, was helped by a switch of putters. 'During the Volvo Open in Sardinia I changed to a J. C. Snead centre-shafted putter and would have finished third but for bogeying the last. I putted beautifully in Jersey after slowing down my stroke.'

Christy was also full of praise for the support of his wife, Ann: 'She's never lost faith in me. I've lost count of the number of near misses I've had and I was starting to wonder if my chance of another win had gone. But Ann has always told me I was good enough.'

Tap-in for Gordon J. Brand

Ronan Rafferty slipped quietly into fifth place

COURSE: LA MOYE, JERSEY **YARDAGE: 6,797** **PAR: 72**

POS	NAME	CTRY	1	2	3	4	TOTAL	PRIZE MONEY
1	Christy O'CONNOR Jnr	Ire	73	70	66	72	281	£24490
2	Denis DURNIAN	Eng	70	71	67	73	281	£16315
3	Mats LANNER	Swe	71	69	70	72	282	£8275
	Paul BROADHURST	Eng	73	69	71	69	282	£8275
5	Des SMYTH	Ire	74	69	71	69	283	£4552
	Colin MONTGOMERIE	Scot	69	75	68	71	283	£4552
	Bernard GALLACHER	Scot	71	70	70	72	283	£4552
	Sam TORRANCE	Scot	72	70	69	72	283	£4552
	Ronan RAFFERTY	N.Ire	74	69	68	72	283	£4552
10	Barry LANE	Eng	76	70	65	73	284	£2822
	Peter FOWLER	Aus	74	71	69	70	284	£2822
12	David J RUSSELL	Eng	73	71	72	69	285	£2381
	David A RUSSELL	Eng	69	70	71	75	285	£2381
	Rick HARTMANN	USA	69	72	75	69	285	£2381
15	Mark ROE	Eng	73	72	70	71	286	£2117
	David JAMES	Scot	71	71	72	72	286	£2117
17	Jesper PARNEVIK	Swe	75	67	70	75	287	£1838
	David FEHERTY	N.Ire	69	72	71	75	287	£1838
	Glenn RALPH	Eng	70	74	76	67	287	£1838
	Magnus PERSSON	Swe	73	69	71	74	287	£1838
	Tony CHARNLEY	Eng	72	72	69	74	287	£1838
22	Wayne STEPHENS	Eng	76	69	70	73	288	£1588
	Paul WAY	Eng	73	74	70	71	288	£1588
	David LLEWELLYN	Wal	70	69	73	76	288	£1588
	Andrew MURRAY	Eng	72	74	72	70	288	£1588
	Ron COMMANS	USA	71	70	71	76	288	£1588
27	Ross McFARLANE	Eng	73	74	70	72	289	£1325
	Carl MASON	Eng	73	69	73	74	289	£1325
	Joe HIGGINS	Eng	76	69	69	75	289	£1325
	David RAY	Eng	74	70	72	73	289	£1325
	Andrew OLDCORN	Eng	71	71	73	74	289	£1325
	Richard BOXALL	Eng	71	73	74	71	289	£1325
	Philip WALTON	Ire	73	71	69	76	289	£1325
34	Sandy STEPHEN	Scot	71	69	73	77	290	£1131
	Paul CURRY	Eng	73	72	68	77	290	£1131
	Gordon BRAND Jnr	Scot	72	71	76	71	290	£1131
	Andrew SHERBORNE	Eng	70	72	73	75	290	£1131
38	Peter MITCHELL	Eng	69	72	75	75	291	£1060
39	Jose Maria CANIZARES	Sp	74	73	70	75	292	£1000
	Paul KENT	Eng	73	70	76	73	292	£1000
	Mark MOULAND	Wal	72	73	73	74	292	£1000
42	Robert LEE	Eng	71	73	73	76	293	£882
	David JONES	N.Ire	72	71	72	78	293	£882
	Marc PENDARIES	Fr	72	76	72	73	293	£882
	Ross DRUMMOND	Scot	77	69	74	73	293	£882
	Martin POXON	Eng	72	74	72	75	293	£882
47	Jerry HAAS	USA	77	70	71	76	294	£705
	Jimmy HEGGARTY	N.Ire	72	76	71	75	294	£705
	Greg J TURNER	NZ	73	70	77	74	294	£705
	John JACOBS	USA	70	70	76	78	294	£705
	David WILLIAMS	Eng	74	73	74	73	294	£705
	Ian YOUNG	Scot	75	72	73	74	294	£705
	Stephen BENNETT	Eng	71	73	75	75	294	£705
54	Peter TERAVAINEN	USA	72	76	76	71	295	£560
	James SPENCE	Eng	76	71	74	74	295	£560
	Bob SHEARER	Aus	73	68	75	79	295	£560
57	Peter O'MALLEY	Aus	73	73	73	77	296	£500
58	Chris MOODY	Eng	72	73	71	81	297	£447
	Mark DAVIS	Eng	73	74	74	76	297	£447
	Armando SAAVEDRA	Arg	74	73	75	75	297	£447
	Gavin LEVENSON	SA	75	72	73	77	297	£447
62	Johan TUMBA	Swe	77	71	73	78	299	£410
63	Leif HEDERSTROM	Swe	72	75	73	80	300	£395
64	Philip HARRISON	Eng	74	72	74	81	301	£375
	Jeff HALL	Eng	74	74	74	79	301	£375
66	Wayne RILEY	Aus	74	74	73	82	303	£200
67	Bill LONGMUIR	Scot	72	72	73	87	304	£198

RIVIERA
rain boosts Broadhurst

Since the age of 12, when he gained his first single figure handicap at Atherstone's nine-hole golf course, Paul Broadhurst has nurtured the ambition to be a successful tournament professional. Yet even he shared the almost universal surprise at the speed with which he made the transition from amateur with high potential to champion on the Volvo Tour.

In only the second event of his debut season the 23-year-old Englishman took third place behind Mark James in the Karl Litten Desert Classic in Dubai. Five weeks later he was again third in the Jersey European Airways tournament, and then in the Credit Lyonnais Cannes Open he led from start to finish, although that finish came prematurely because of a Riviera rainstorm.

Broadhurst turned professional in late August 1988 after gaining amateur international honours with England and Great Britain in the St Andrews Trophy.

His competitive instinct had been honed in the Warwickshire County team, he had won the Lytham Trophy, completed all 72 holes of the Open Championship and had just £120 in his bank account.

When the European season began in Tenerife, Broadhurst had increased his 'working capital' to around £7,000, courtesy of a cross-channel venture to the French domestic tour where, in his first two tournaments in Lyon and Bordeaux, he finished fourth and second. Driving a van, working as a gardener, and in a glass fibre factory, provided additional funds.

Any illusions Broadhurst held were swiftly dispelled by his first skirmish with his future rivals. Like all embryo professionals, he was required to prove his ability at the December Tour school at La Manga. He survived expulsion by the narrowest of margins.

IN THE FIRST FEW MONTHS OF HIS PROFESSIONAL CAREER PAUL BROADHURST HAD ALREADY SERVED NOTICE OF HIS OUTSTANDING ABILITY BUT EVEN HE WAS SURPRISED AT HIS PROGRESS WHICH CULMINATED IN A CURTAILED VICTORY IN CANNES

The successful entrants from the pre-qualifying examination at Kingswood and El Saler in Valencia did not include the name of Broadhurst. Indeed, he was forced to undergo a sudden-death play-off to win a place on the list of reserves for La Manga. Within three months he had joined the exclusive club of Rookie champions, following Jose Maria Olazabal (1986) and Gordon Brand Junior (1982).

Broadhurst had already won his struggle for solvency when he arrived at Cannes Mougins, having banked nearly £26,000 from his remarkable early performances. Each week the field had been getting stronger and now Mark McNulty had arrived to defend his title. Ian Woosnam, Jose Rivero, Sam Torrance and Des Smyth, Peter Senior and Brett Ogle had also arrived with solid aspirations.

Rain and darkness had prevented Broadhurst playing a full practice round, but no-one would have guessed. He began as though he did not have a care in the world, opening with a seven under par 65 and using his putter only 23 times.

Despite steady rain he went out in 32, holing a bunker shot at the ninth for his fourth birdie. Even a lengthy wait at the short 11th, where green staff were waging a valiant battle to prevent flooding of the green, failed to arrest Broadhurst's momentum. A two there and another birdie at the 13th were followed by a third short hole birdie at the 15th. Here the runaway rookie had a stroke of fortune when his seven iron shot rebounded off a tree to within 20 feet of the flag for his seventh birdie.

Richard Boxall, who birdied the last

Water in Cannes

three holes, Barry Lane and Spaniard Juan Anglada got closest, all with 67. Irish first-year professional Stephen Hamill and Sweden's Magnus Persson were among the group on 68.

The weather relented for the second round, although rain was never far away. Broadhurst could not, however, be flushed from the leadership even by a flood of sub-70 returns. Derrick Cooper had 64 while Senior and Manuel Calero both took closer order with 66, and there were second 68s from Hammill and Persson. Broadhurst meanwhile was calmly progressing to nine under par with a 70 that contained five more birdies. Any errors in his long game were more than compensated by his sharpness around the greens.

The cut fell at one over par 145 and Woosnam only just survived after being forced to take a penalty shot in a greenside bunker at the 17th when his ball lodged unplayable under the lip. At halfway he was ten shots adrift and beyond even his recuperative powers, although a third round 68 left the Welshman with an outside chance.

former with one hole of his third round to complete, the latter on the 17th. Ogle then saw his pitch to the last green bounce off the right flank under a bush. He incurred a penalty stroke for an unplayable ball and took a double bogey six. Senior found an awkward lie on the 17th fairway and put his approach into the water fronting the green for a similar result. Both posted 208 and were joined at eight under par by Ulster champion Jimmy Heggarty who shot 67.

Broadhurst had two strokes in hand when he came to the par five 16th but immediately surrendered one of them by driving out of bounds. He then used his driver twice more to reach a greenside bunker in four strokes, before holing from six feet to card a bogey six. Single putts on the last two greens for a par 72 left him one shot ahead on 207.

Broadhurst was as disappointed as his challengers when the elements intervened to make further golf on the saturated course impossible. He needed to subject himself and his game

Paul Broadhurst swept to victory with a flood of birdies

What he and Broadhurst did not realise was that the issue had already been decided. The crucial strokes were played at the last three holes on Saturday, for little more than 12 hours later Mougins was awash.

Ogle and Senior had both made a charge to reach ten under par, the

to the pressures of last day leadership.

'I had already discovered that my record as an amateur meant nothing' he declared. 'But my coach Frank Miller told me just before Cannes that I would win very soon. Now that first win is in the record books, even if it took record rainfall to clinch it for me.'

One shot too many from Jimmy Heggarty

The 18th green at Cannes Mongins

COURSE: CANNES MOUGINS **YARDAGE: 6,786** **PAR: 72**

POS	NAME	CTRY	1	2	3	4	TOTAL	PRIZE MONEY
1	Paul BROADHURST	Eng	65	70	72		207	£34851
2	Jimmy HEGGARTY	N.Ire	69	72	67		208	£15588
	Brett OGLE	Aus	71	68	69		208	£15588
	Peter SENIOR	Aus	70	66	72		208	£15588
5	Ronan RAFFERTY	N.Ire	72	67	70		209	£8829
6	Jean VAN DE VELDE	Fr	71	69	70		210	£5845
	Tony CHARNLEY	Eng	71	68	71		210	£5845
	Mark MCNULTY	Zim	71	70	69		210	£5845
	Derrick COOPER	Eng	73	64	73		210	£5845
10	Des SMYTH	Ire	70	72	69		211	£3671
	Jose RIVERO	Sp	72	68	71		211	£3671
	Manuel CALERO	Sp	70	66	75		211	£3671
	Philip WALTON	Ire	74	71	66		211	£3671
	Magnus PERSSON	Swe	68	68	75		211	£3671
15	Colin MONTGOMERIE	Scot	71	73	68		212	£2905
	Juan ANGLADA	Sp	67	71	74		212	£2905
	Bryan NORTON	USA	70	71	71		212	£2905
	Stephen HAMILL	N.Ire	68	68	76		212	£2905
	Bill MALLEY	USA	69	73	70		212	£2905
20	Mats LANNER	Swe	69	72	72		213	£2527
	Ian WOOSNAM	Wal	72	73	68		213	£2527
22	Eduardo ROMERO	Arg	72	68	74		214	£2134
	Bill GLASSON	USA	71	73	70		214	£2134
	Mark ROE	Eng	75	69	70		214	£2134
	Keith WATERS	Eng	71	73	70		214	£2134
	Richard BOXALL	Eng	67	73	74		214	£2134
	Stephen BENNETT	Eng	70	70	74		214	£2134
	David LLEWELLYN	Wal	69	73	72		214	£2134
	Barry LANE	Eng	67	75	72		214	£2134
	Roger CHAPMAN	Eng	69	72	73		214	£2134
31	Steen TINNING	Den	69	76	70		215	£1627
	Emmanuel DUSSART	Fr	71	73	71		215	£1627
	Paul HOAD	Eng	70	72	73		215	£1627
	David A RUSSELL	Eng	73	69	73		215	£1627
	David WILLIAMS	Eng	73	70	72		215	£1627
	Gordon J BRAND	Eng	71	72	72		215	£1627
	Greg J TURNER	NZ	74	67	74		215	£1627
38	Robert LEE	Eng	70	70	76		216	£1319
	Stephen McALLISTER	Scot	72	68	76		216	£1319
	Emilio RODRIGUEZ	Sp	72	71	73		216	£1319
	Jamie HOWELL	USA	74	69	73		216	£1319
	Rick HARTMANN	USA	70	72	74		216	£1319
	Luis CARBONETTI	Arg	70	73	73		216	£1319
	Ian YOUNG	Scot	71	71	74		216	£1319
	Jesper PARNEVIK	Swe	71	71	74		216	£1319
46	Alberto BINAGHI	It	75	67	75		217	£1022
	Armando SAAVEDRA	Arg	68	77	72		217	£1022
	Sam TORRANCE	Scot	73	71	73		217	£1022
	Jerry HAAS	USA	72	73	72		217	£1022
	Ove SELLBERG	Swe	72	71	74		217	£1022
	Antonio GARRIDO	Sp	74	70	73		217	£1022
	Mark DAVIS	Eng	75	70	72		217	£1022
	Peter TERAVAINEN	USA	69	76	72		217	£1022
54	Marc FARRY	Fr	71	74	73		218	£744
	Bob SHEARER	Aus	73	71	74		218	£744
	David GILFORD	Eng	73	71	74		218	£744
	Mark MOULAND	Wal	71	71	76		218	£744
	Frederic REGARD	Fr	77	67	74		218	£744
	Martin POXON	Eng	74	71	73		218	£744
	Tony JOHNSTONE	Zim	72	70	76		218	£744
61	Ross DRUMMOND	Scot	69	75	75		219	£571
	Laurent LASSALLE	Fr	72	72	75		219	£571
	Andrew MURRAY	Eng	68	75	76		219	£571
	David J RUSSELL	Eng	72	73	74		219	£571
65	Carlos FRANCO	Para	72	73	75		220	£501
66	Wayne STEPHENS	Eng	71	73	77		221	£208
	Neil HANSEN	Eng	71	71	79		221	£208
68	Paul CURRY	Eng	72	73	77		222	£204
	John JACOBS	USA	71	73	78		222	£204
70	David JAMES	Scot	71	74	79		224	£201

BALLESTEROS *levels the score*

There was a time when the Cepsa Madrid Open marked the start of the golf season in Europe. It would come after the US Masters at Augusta and you could almost hear the clanking of the wheels as they started to turn on this side of the Atlantic. How things change. This year the Cepsa Madrid Open was not only the ninth event of the season; it was the fourth to be held on Spanish courses.

Mark James, who had won in Dubai and Montpellier, was in Madrid as was Jose-Maria Olazabal, the winner in Tenerife and runner-up in Majorca and the Catalan Open. Every other 1989 Volvo Tour winner was there too.

So was Seve Ballesteros. A tournament in Spain without Ballesteros would be like a production of Carmen in Madrid without Placido Domingo. Ballesteros hadn't played well in Majorca, his only appearance in Europe so far, and he had won only £840 all year. It was time to show some form. He knew this as well as anybody and didn't repeat the mistake he had made in 1988 when he flew straight from the US Masters to Cannes, lost his golf bag en route and missed the cut. This time he returned to Pedrena and took a week off as he almost always does after major championships. When he arrived at Puerta de Hierro he was relaxed and ready.

The two dominant figures in the recent history of the Cepsa Madrid Open are Howard Clark and Ballesteros. They have won it five times between them (Ballesteros twice, Clark three times). Clark won in 1986 by taking the lead from Ballesteros on the 12th hole of the last round and never surrendering it. This year they fought it out once again and Ballesteros got his revenge on the Yorkshireman, though it wasn't as simple as that might suggest.

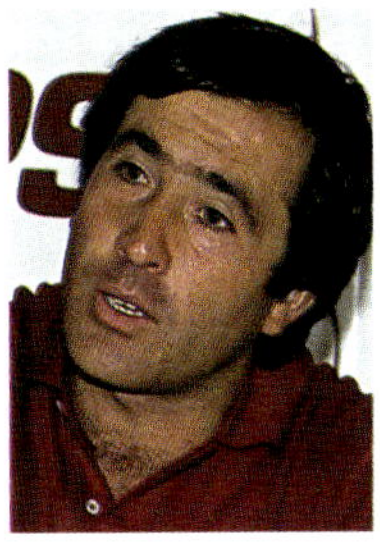

BALLESTEROS HAD NOT ENJOYED A DISTINGUISHED START TO THE SEASON BUT HE SOON SHOWED HIS OLD FORM AS HE CHALKED UP HIS FIRST WIN OF THE 1989 VOLVO TOUR AT THE CEPSA MADRID OPEN, BEATING HIS OLD RIVAL FOR THE TITLE, HOWARD CLARK

Swedes dominated the first round. Magnus Persson had an albatross on the long fifth after holing a 192-yard five iron shot. Persson's two enabled him to reach the turn in 29. His 64, one more than Ballesteros's course record, was equalled by Jesper Parnevik, the winner of the Tour school last December. Parnevik always carries two putters and having missed the cut in three of the previous four tournaments, he needed them both. These two rounds overshadowed a spirited round of 67 by Derrick Cooper, the defending champion.

Soon though, the tournament became the predicted confrontation between Clark and Ballesteros. Clark lay third after the first round, led by one stroke after 36 holes and was tied with Ballesteros with one round remaining. On the 12th Clark couldn't save par. Nor could he on the 14th. And when he birdied the 13th and the 15th, Ballesteros did likewise to keep the lead by two strokes. Clark came at him once more. He birdied the 16th and narrowed the gap to one stroke. Ballesteros responded by holing a 15-foot putt on the 17th to suppress any lingering chance Clark might have harboured. They had 11 birdies between them.

It was Seve's third victory in Madrid, the only one in which all four rounds were less than 70, and his 43rd victory in Europe. His prize money of £37,500 moved him into the top ten on the money list. The Cepsa Madrid Open could have ended there with another Spanish victory as popular with the spectators and organisers as with Ballesteros.

Unhappily, Clark later accused Seve of intimidating behaviour. He claimed that Seve stalked and walked around the green while he was putting. "I like to see Seve playing but I don't like playing with him" snapped Clark.

Clark is not the first player to level this charge at Ballesteros. Bernhard Langer did it during a world match-play championship at Wentworth. And at

the US Masters the American, Tom Kite, once requested Seve to stop practice swinging in his line of vision.

Ballesteros immediately refuted Clark's allegations, saying: "If you watch TV you will see I walk around reading the greens so I am ready to

play when it is my turn. If you want to concentrate well you should not be watching your opponent."

It was another skirmish in the personal golfing battle between Ballesteros and Clark that now stood at three wins each in Madrid.

Supplicatory gesture from Howard Clark as another putt slips by

Singh in a sylvan setting

Old rivals and protagonists: Ballesteros and Clark clashed again

Anguish for defending champion, Derrick Cooper

COURSE: PUERTA DE HIERRO, MADRID **YARDAGE: 6,941** **PAR: 72**

POS	NAME	CTRY	1	2	3	4	TOTAL	PRIZE MONEY
1	Severiano BALLESTEROS	Sp	67	67	69	69	272	£37500
2	Howard CLARK	Eng	65	68	70	70	273	£25000
3	Philip WALTON	Ire	70	67	70	68	275	£14070
4	Mats LANNER	Swe	70	70	68	68	276	£11250
5	Derrick COOPER	Eng	67	72	67	71	277	£9500
6	Tony CHARNLEY	Eng	70	69	70	69	278	£7850
7	Rodger DAVIS	Aus	69	72	70	68	279	£6150
	Magnus PERSSON	Swe	64	70	75	70	279	£6150
9	Emmanuel DUSSART	Fr	69	71	68	72	280	£4370
	Carl MASON	Eng	70	68	71	71	280	£4370
	Mark JAMES	Eng	70	68	68	74	280	£4370
	Mike SMITH	USA	69	72	69	70	280	£4370
13	Jesper PARNEVIK	Swe	64	71	75	71	281	£3487
	Manuel PINERO	Sp	71	68	69	73	281	£3487
	Bob SHEARER	Aus	68	73	71	69	281	£3487
	Richard BOXALL	Eng	69	69	71	72	281	£3487
17	Johan RYSTROM	Swe	70	71	68	73	282	£2702
	Eamonn DARCY	Ire	67	76	69	70	282	£2702
	Jose Maria OLAZABAL	Sp	71	68	70	73	282	£2702
	Ian WOOSNAM	Wal	72	67	72	71	282	£2702
	Antonio GARRIDO	Sp	69	70	68	75	282	£2702
	Chris MOODY	Eng	70	71	69	72	282	£2702
	Colin MONTGOMERIE	Scot	73	69	72	68	282	£2702
	Peter FOWLER	Aus	68	73	72	69	282	£2702
	David WILLIAMS	Eng	70	69	71	72	282	£2702
	Yago BEAMONTE (AM)	Sp	70	70	68	74	282	–
26	Mats HALLBERG	Swe	72	71	68	72	283	£2080
	Neil HANSEN	Eng	71	70	70	72	283	£2080
	Manuel MORENO	Sp	71	71	71	70	283	£2080
	Christy O'CONNOR Jnr	Ire	70	68	75	70	283	£2080
	Vicente FERNANDEZ	Arg	69	67	77	70	283	£2080
	Calvin PEETE	USA	68	72	72	71	283	£2080
	Denis DURNIAN	Eng	75	67	68	73	283	£2080
33	Jose Maria CANIZARES	Sp	69	72	67	76	284	£1668
	Jean VAN DE VELDE	Fr	69	74	71	70	284	£1668
	Mike CLAYTON	Aus	70	74	73	67	284	£1668
	Stephen BENNETT	Eng	71	73	68	72	284	£1668
	Michael ALLEN	USA	69	69	76	70	284	£1668
	Jose DAVILA	Sp	70	72	68	74	284	£1668
39	Mark ROE	Eng	74	70	71	70	285	£1440
	Barry LANE	Eng	70	72	69	74	285	£1440
	Daniel LOZANO	Sp	68	71	73	73	285	£1440
	Philip PARKIN	Wal	73	71	70	71	285	£1440
	Ulf NILSSON	Swe	69	70	69	77	285	£1440
44	Paul CARRIGILL	Eng	72	71	67	76	286	£1880
	Mark MOULAND	Wal	70	71	73	72	286	£1180
	Juan ANGLADA	Sp	69	71	72	74	286	£1180
	Santiago LUNA	Sp	72	71	72	71	286	£1180
	Miguel Angel JIMENEZ	Sp	75	66	72	73	286	£1180
	Ove SELLBERG	Swe	70	74	72	70	286	£1180
	Malcolm MACKENZIE	Eng	72	70	72	72	286	£1180
	Armando SAAVEDRA	Arg	70	71	70	75	286	£1180
52	Alberto BINAGHI	It	71	73	68	75	287	£900
	Sam TORRANCE	Scot	74	70	70	73	287	£900
	Michael McLEAN	Eng	74	70	72	71	287	£900
	Eduardo ROMERO	Arg	72	69	72	74	287	£900
	Juan QUIROS	Sp	70	72	73	72	287	£900
	Paul BROADHURST	Eng	70	72	70	67	78	287	£900
58	Peter TERAVAINEN	USA	67	71	75	75	288	£676
	Gordon BRAND Jnr	Scot	68	73	70	77	288	£676
	Jerry ANDERSON	Can	71	73	76	68	288	£676
	Manuel CALERO	Sp	68	71	76	73	288	£676
	Paul HOAD	Eng	74	69	76	69	288	£676
	Steen TINNING	Den	71	71	75	71	288	£676
64	Ross DRUMMOND	Scot	74	69	72	74	289	£355
	Gordon J BRAND	Eng	75	69	76	69	289	£355
	Mariano APARICIO	Sp	74	70	70	75	289	£355
	Robert LEE	Eng	71	70	76	72	289	£355
	Glenn RALPH	Eng	73	71	72	73	289	£355
69	Stephen McALLISTER	Scot	74	68	71	77	290	£217
	Joe HIGGINS	Eng	71	73	72	74	290	£217
	Grant TURNER	Eng	71	72	76	71	290	£217
72	Peter BAKER	Eng	67	77	75	73	292	£211
	Anders FORSBRAND	Swe	73	66	80	73	292	£211
	Andrew MURRAY	Eng	71	72	77	72	292	£211

MASTER *of El Saler*

FIVE YEARS AGO BERNHARD LANGER PRODUCED THE FINEST ROUND OF HIS CAREER AT EL SALER. ON RETURNING, LANGER ONCE AGAIN SHOWED HIS IRON WILL BY CONQUERING THE FIELD, THE COURSE, AND HIS PUTTING PROBLEMS

When Bernhard Langer took five putts on the 17th green at Royal Lytham in the 1988 Open Championship — trying on every one of them — there were those who feared for his career. Langer, who came onto the Tour in 1976 with the 'yips' and conquered them, had got them again.

Before leaving Lytham for America, Langer told his caddie, Pete Coleman, not to bother making the trip 'because I won't be making any money', and a more thoroughly depressing scene would be hard to imagine. The West German had always been one of the best strikers of the ball in the world and here he was, unable to compete, because he literally could not putt.

But, in addition to his physical disability, Langer is blessed with rare mental strength. 'I have always known,' he says, 'that I have too much ability at this game to let the yips beat me. If I can play the touch shots as delicately as I do, then I must be able to putt.'

It is not a philosophy that would find universal backing for the popular, and awfully applicable, phrase concerning the 'yips' is that once you've had 'em, you've got 'em. They never go away. But Langer went to America, delved deep into his mental reserves, worked on a method that would effectively eliminate the hands from the putting stroke — and practised and practised and practised.

When he got to El Saler for the Peugeot Spanish Open he had evolved a unique way of putting. He had lengthened his putter by two inches and, by placing the left hand at the bottom of the grip and by gripping shaft and arm with his right hand some six inches above the left, he found he was able to make a firm, stiff wristed push at the ball. In fact, so effective was it that briefly, he was 14th in the US Tour statistics for putting.

Langer had been invited by the promoter of the event, none other than Severiano Ballesteros, to play and he needed no further prompting. El Saler had two enormous attractions for Langer — it is one of the best courses in Europe and one that would reward the fine striking of which he is capable. Furthermore, the last time he played it, in 1984, he had gone round in a ridiculous 62 shots, a course record that will probably stand for eternity. It is, and in all probability will remain, Langer's finest round.

The course he found in 1989 was harder, though, than in '84. The tournament was preceded by heavy rain, making the ground soft, the rough uneven, and the greens patchy. There would be no 62s. The weather relented on the eve of the first round and the event was played on four fine days. Bright blue skies and a good strong breeze to temper the heat made for perfection, and obviously the best players would rise to the top, wouldn't they? Well, no. The first round leader was Derrick Cooper, who is a fine uncomplicated striker of the ball but a man who has never finished higher than 32nd in the Volvo Order of Merit. He got round in 66, a round that was the more incredible because he had never set eyes on the course before.

Cooper loathes and detests practice rounds because of the inordinate length of time they take ('Six hours of staring at someone else's backside is not my idea of fun') and deliberately did not arrive until late Wednesday night. He then went out and had eight birdies, two bogies and told us all: 'As long as you can see the fairway and the green, what else do you need to know?' Well, on Thursday, nothing, but the more Cooper got to know the course, the less well he played it and he was not a factor thereafter.

The second day belonged to Paul Carrigill, one of the Tour's journeymen and one of its most pleasant characters, too. As 16th qualifier from the 1988 Tour school he was only a reserve for the tournament at first, but his opening rounds of 70 and 69 gave him the

Flowers frame Sellberg, Olazabal and McNulty

halfway lead at five under par. There were only 18 players out of 146 under par at this stage, a reflection on the difficulty of the course and the testing conditions out there.

Carrigill himself was not unduly optimistic about his chances. He reflected that when players such as himself were in the lead, others would comment that he might be at the top now, but he'll finish at the bottom. 'At least,' added Carrigill, 'they do if it's me.' But his pessimism was unfounded. Carrigill was to play his part right through the Peugeot Spanish Open.

Langer was three strokes behind: by Sunday night he was three ahead of the entire field. His final round was a triumph, not just of golf over course and conditions, but of mind over matter. Langer even 'yipped' a putt, one of only 18 inches at the sixth, but continued to play superlative golf as if it hadn't happened. And, in a way, it hadn't, as Langer proved at his press conference. He was recounting his round, stroke by stroke, and when he got to the sixth said that he had hit his second to 16 feet, missed with his first putt and then missed from; 'A metre, no, a metre and a half.' It was apparent to all those who were there that the putt was certainly not as much as two feet and what we were seeing was a damage limitation and control exercise by Langer's mind — he was exorcising the thought that he might have missed from as little as under two feet.

His golf, thereafter, was remorseless. Carrigill, playing with him and playing in the last group for the first time on the Volvo Tour, kept after him, and by birdieing the long 15th, actually got to level pegging. But Langer, with that quality that only the great players show, came straight back. The 16th was into the wind, needing two big shots to reach it, and Langer was capable while Carrigill was not. Then, just to compound it all, Langer holed — with conventional grip — from 50 feet for a birdie and the tournament was all but decided.

Afterwards Langer confessed that the win was one of the most important of his career. He admitted that he had wondered if he could ever win again and said: 'After what I went through it is hard to believe that you can win again until you do.' But win he did, a victory that represented a triumph of will over one of golf's most dreaded maladies.

Langer and caddie, Peter Coleman, stoop to conquer Below, drivers at dawn for Ballesteros and Woosnam

COURSE: EL SALER, VALENCIA **YARDAGE: 7,092** **PAR: 72**

POS	NAME	CTRY	1	2	3	4	TOTAL	PRIZE MONEY
1	Bernhard LANGER	W.Ger	70	72	67	72	281	£41660
2	Jose Maria CANIZARES	Sp	72	72	70	70	284	£21705
	Paul CARRIGILL	Eng	70	69	72	73	284	£21705
4	Jose Maria OLAZABAL	Sp	70	72	70	73	285	£12500
5	Mats LANNER	Swe	71	72	71	72	286	£10600
6	Gordon BRAND Jnr	Scot	71	73	69	74	287	£8125
	Barry LANE	Eng	72	69	75	71	287	£8125
8	David FEHERTY	N.Ire	70	70	74	74	288	£6250
9	Severiano BALLESTEROS	Sp	75	68	74	72	289	£5300
	Johan RYSTROM	Swe	72	73	72	72	289	£5300
11	Denis DURNIAN	Eng	74	71	71	74	290	£4600
12	Tony CHARNLEY	Eng	73	74	72	72	291	£4160
	Sam TORRANCE	Scot	74	73	69	75	291	£4160
14	Gordon J BRAND	Eng	73	71	75	73	292	£3745
	Derrick COOPER	Eng	66	75	76	75	292	£3745
16	Emmanuel DUSSART	Fr	74	74	71	74	293	£3305
	Paul WAY	Eng	73	75	70	75	293	£3305
	Christy O'CONNOR Jnr	(Ire)	73	73	72	75	293	£3305
	Ronan RAFFERTY	N.Ire	74	74	71	74	293	£3305
20	Brian MARCHBANK	Scot	72	75	73	74	294	£2812
	Jerry HAAS	USA	73	72	76	73	294	£2812
	Mike HARWOOD	Aus	71	75	76	72	294	£2812
	Vicente FERNANDEZ	Arg	75	74	73	72	294	£2812
	Richard FISH	Eng	71	70	80	73	294	£2812
	Antonio GARRIDO	Sp	74	74	75	71	294	£2812
26	David WILLIAMS	Eng	72	75	75	73	295	£2437
	Juan ANGLADA	Sp	77	72	76	70	295	£2437
	Eamonn DARCY	Ire	74	75	75	71	295	£2437
	Howard CLARK	Eng	73	74	73	75	295	£2437
30	Mark MCNULTY	Zim	73	75	73	75	296	£2212
	Frank NOBILO	NZ	73	74	75	74	296	£2212
32	Mark DAVIS	Eng	69	81	75	72	297	£2000
	Ian WOOSNAM	Wal	78	70	73	76	297	£2000
	Manuel PINERO	Sp	75	74	78	70	297	£2000
	Jesper PARNEVIK	Swe	73	73	77	74	297	£2000
	Malcolm MACKENZIE	Eng	72	77	77	71	297	£2000
37	Keith WATERS	Eng	79	71	76	72	298	£1675
	Mike SMITH	USA	74	74	78	72	298	£1675
	Eduardo ROMERO	Arg	71	76	72	79	298	£1675
	Jose DAVILA	Sp	75	74	74	75	298	£1675
	David LLEWELLYN	Wal	74	76	73	75	298	£1675
	Grant TURNER	Eng	73	74	74	77	298	£1675
	Paul KENT	Eng	72	78	76	72	298	£1675
	Jamie HOWELL	USA	73	72	77	76	298	£1675
45	Neil HANSEN	Eng	74	72	77	76	299	£1375
	Manuel CALERO	Sp	71	77	72	79	299	£1375
	Jim RUTLEDGE	Can	73	72	78	76	299	£1375
	Peter MITCHELL	Eng	77	72	71	79	299	£1375
49	Marc FARRY	Fr	70	76	81	73	300	£1175
	Jean VAN DE VELDE	Fr	76	73	77	74	300	£1175
	Philip WALTON	Ire	76	71	76	77	300	£1175
	David JAMES	Scot	78	72	76	74	300	£1175
53	Jose CARRILES	Sp	74	75	77	75	301	£950
	Mariano APARICIO	Sp	69	75	78	79	301	£950
	Vijay SINGH	Fij	70	78	74	79	301	£950
	Andrew SHERBORNE	Eng	74	75	73	79	301	£950
	Alberto BINAGHI	It	74	75	78	74	301	£950
58	Stephen BENNETT	Eng	73	75	77	77	302	£800
	Yago BEAMONTE (AM)	Sp	73	73	81	75	302	–
59	Mark MOULAND	Wal	71	77	79	76	303	£712
	Mark ROE	Eng	73	77	73	80	303	£712
	Philip PARKIN	Wal	74	74	76	79	303	£712
	Santiago LUNA	Sp	73	77	79	74	303	£712
	Ross DRUMMOND	Scot	74	73	78	78	303	£712
	Bill MALLEY	USA	79	71	76	77	303	£712
65	John O'LEARY	Ire	75	73	77	79	304	£625
66	Noel RATCLIFFE	Aus	73	76	81	76	306	£249
	Peter BAKER	Eng	76	69	77	84	306	£249
68	Brian EVANS	Eng	75	74	80	78	307	£246
69	David JONES	N.Ire	75	74	81	80	310	£244

IN PRAISE *of famous men*

AT THE END OF A HOT AND BLISSFUL WEEK AT ST PIERRE THERE WERE FEW DESCRIPTIONS ADEQUATE ENOUGH TO ILLUMINATE THE PLAY OF SEVERIANO BALLESTEROS. HIS MAJESTIC PROGRESS WAS SUMMED UP BY HIS FINAL OPPONENT — 'AWESOME'

Any lover of golf who spent the first week of May in Chepstow was indeed a person blessed. St Pierre, sunshine and Seve provided the ingredients for a tournament of relaxation and pleasure. Senor Ballesteros won the Epson Grand Prix of Europe with a performance of such convincing authority that no other outcome ever seemed likely. Yet if the drama of true competition was played out only among the supporting cast, there was still a magical air about the occasion. There is a tendency to take for granted the talent of the world Number One — awesome, majestic and supreme are the kind of adjectives used to describe him until the words become almost meaningless. When he lives up to his reputation Ballesteros playing golf is an experience not to be missed. He is the Phantom of the Opera, a Beethoven symphony, Elton John in concert and King Lear. So it was at Chepstow.

The crowds turned up in record-breaking numbers, saw plenty of absorbing minor tussles and an exhibition from the maestro. The weather, an unexpected bonus, helped of course. As the sun beat down for almost all four days, putting a smile on everyone's face, St Pierre had never looked better.

Public interest increased in this particular week because, after nearly two months on the road, the Volvo Tour caravan had arrived in Britain. Thus, when Sam Torrance appeared with a putter that nearly reached his chin, pictures of him wielding this wonderful instrument made the front page of one national daily and the back page of most of the other newspapers.

Sam lost to Howard Clark on the final green in the first round, even though his Ryder Cup team-mate insisted that the moustachio-ed Scot had putted admirably. 'Maybe, in a few years time, everyone will be putting like that,' suggested Clark, without confirming where his tongue was in relation to his cheek. The Yorkshireman talked about an iron bar he used to groove his stroke so well that he could putt with his eyes shut. Later in the week he said he had the yips.

Mats Lanner showed that conventional putting is still the best way. He holed from all over the place to be nine under after 12 holes, beating Manuel Pinero eight and six. The philosophical Spaniard reflected ruefully: 'In my country we have a saying "If I ran a circus, all the midgets would grow up",'

His compatriot Jose-Maria Canizares did not need a putter to hole out with the shot of the opening day, a three-wood from 270 yards which rolled into the cup at the 521-yard 12th for an albatross two. It was the longest shot he had ever holed.

On day two Ballesteros made his entrance, beat Australian Mike Clayton four and three and departed with the minimum of fuss. The heroics came from Ian Woosnam and Des Smyth, two veterans of this combat golf. Both arrived at the last tee one down and both survived. Little Woosie, the local favourite, holed a 25-foot putt to take Richard Boxall into extra time and beat him with a birdie at the 19th. How the Welsh loved that.

Irish Des conjured a four-iron shot that came to rest 18 inches from the flag to draw level with Mark Roe. He, too, claimed victory at the first extra hole. So men of experience had beaten two of the young Turks while proving again that it ain't over 'til it's over.

When Ken Brown met the holder Bernhard Langer the following morning some wondered whether it would ever be over. 'We should finish before dark,' chuckled Brown after being informed of the 9am start. The two Ryder Cup players, in their precise, careful manner, slogged it out for four hours before Brown completed a two and one win that continued his rehabilitation from a dreadful start to the year.

Ballesteros had taken half that time to dispose of American Mike Allen by eight and six with superlative golf. He

Epson smash and grab by Ballesteros

Crowds in a reflective mood round the lake at St Pierre

Runner-up Denis Durnian clings on valiantly in the face of a Ballesteros onslaught

was, by this time, compiling statistics that reflected both brilliance and consistency and when he beat Mark Mouland by two holes in the quarter finals, his only testing match of the week, they made impressive reading: forty-four successive holes without dropping a shot and among them 16 birdies and an eagle.

Smyth, one of the four semi-finalists summed up the feelings of the opposition on Saturday night when he said: 'It's wide open — except for Seve. But he's one player you don't mind losing to. Once it used to be Ben Hogan, then came Jack Nicklaus, and now it's Ballesteros.'

The final day confirmed these words. Seve beat Australian Mike Harwood six and five and Denis Durnian four and three to win the £50,000 first prize and go to the top of the Volvo Order of Merit. It was as simple as that. For 73 holes played he was 29 under par: 27 birdies and two eagles, with only two bogeys.

Yet in counting the notes of the rhapsody we may not fully appreciate the tune. As Durnian, who gained widespread publicity for his own surge into Ryder Cup contention, put it: 'I have never seen Seve swinging better. At the moment he's streets ahead of anyone else in the world.'

God was in his heaven, all was well.

St Pierre's dramatic 18th was played as the 16th during the Epson

Ian Woosnam, right, had the measure of Howard Clark in their third round encounter

Spot the player? Mike Harwood veiled in sand, far right

Left, hands across the water as Harwood congratulates Ballesteros

Adulation for the victor

One day, son, all this could be yours

COURSE: ST PIERRE **YARDAGE: 6,859** **PAR: 71**

FIRST ROUND

WINNER	CTRY	LOSER	CTRY	SCORE	PRIZE MONEY
Mike CLAYTON	Aus	Miguel Angel MARTIN	Sp	3 & 2	
Frank NOBILO	NZ	Wayne RILEY	Aus	1 Hole	
Michael ALLEN	USA	Peter SENIOR	Aus	2 & 1	
Jeff HAWKES	SA	Ronan RAFFERTY	N.Ire	2 & 1	
Jose-Maria CANIZARES	Sp	Stephen BENNETT	Eng	at 19th	
Mark MOULAND	Wal	Derrick COOPER	Eng	4 & 2	
Mike HARWOOD	Aus	David WILLIAMS	Eng	at 19th	
Tony JOHNSTONE	Zim	David WHELAN	Eng	5 & 4	
David J RUSSELL	Eng	Peter BAKER	Eng	1 Hole	
Howard CLARK	Eng	Sam TORRANCE	Scot	1 Hole	
Roger CHAPMAN	Eng	Chris MOODY	Eng	3 & 1	First Round Losers won £1,920
Richard BOXALL	Eng	Eduardo ROMERO	Arg	4 & 2	
Philip WALTON	Ire	Mike SMITH	USA	4 & 3	
Gordon J. BRAND	Eng	Anders FORSBRAND	Swe	3 & 1	
Carl MASON	Eng	Barry LANE	Eng	1 Hole	
Gordon BRAND Jnr	Scot	Andrew MURRAY	Eng	5 & 4	
Peter FOWLER	Aus	Colin MONTGOMERIE	Scot .	2 & 1	
Mark ROE	Eng	David LLEWELLYN	Wal	3 & 2	
Mats LANNER	Swe	Manuel PINERO	Sp	8 & 6	
Denis DURNIAN	Eng	Rodger DAVIS	Aus	1 Hole	
Jose RIVERO	Sp	David FEHERTY	N. Ire	1 Hole	
Tony CHARNLEY	Eng	Eamonn DARCY	Ire	2 & 1	
Ken BROWN	Scot	Ove SELLBERG	Swe	3 & 2	
Christy O'CONNOR Jnr	Ire	John MORGAN	Eng	2 & 1	

SECOND ROUND

Seve BALLESTEROS	Sp	Mike CLAYTON	Aus	4 & 3	
Michael ALLEN	USA	Frank NOBILO	NZ	2 & 1	
Jose-Maria CANIZARES	Sp	Jeff HAWKES	SA	1 Hole	
Mark MOULAND	Wal	Masahiro KURAMOTO	Jap	5 & 4	
Mike HARWOOD	Aus	Mark McNULTY	Zim	2 & 1	
Tony JOHNSTONE	Zim	David J. RUSSELL	Eng	4 & 3	
Howard CLARK	Eng	Roger CHAPMAN	Eng	4 & 3	Second Round Losers won £3,450
Ian WOOSNAM	Wal	Richard BOXALL	Eng	at 19th	
Jose-Maria OLAZABAL	Sp	Philip WALTON	Ire	4 & 2	
Gordon J. BRAND	Eng	Carl MASON	Eng	4 & 3	
Peter FOWLER	Aus	Gordon BRAND Jnr	Scot	4 & 3	
Des SMYTH	Ire	Mark ROE	Eng	at 19th	
Mark JAMES	Eng	Mats LANNER	Swe	2 Holes	
Denis DURNIAN	Eng	Jose RIVERO	Sp	2 Holes	
Ken BROWN	Scot	Tony CHARNLEY	Eng	1 Hole	
Bernhard LANGER	WG	Christy O'CONNOR Jnr	Ire	2 & 1	

THIRD ROUND

Seve BALLESTEROS	Sp	Michael ALLEN	USA	8 & 6	
Mark MOULAND	Wal	Jose-Maria CANIZARES	Sp	2 & 1	
Mike HARWOOD	Aus	Tony JOHNSTONE	Zim	1 Hole	Third Round Losers won £5,500
Ian WOOSNAM	Wal	Howard CLARK	Eng	2 Holes	
Jose-Maria OLAZABAL	Sp	Gordon J. BRAND	Eng	4 & 3	
Des SMYTH	Ire	Peter FOWLER	Aus	2 & 1	
Denis DURNIAN	Eng	Mark JAMES	Eng	2 & 1	
Ken BROWN	Scot	Bernhard LANGER	WG	2 & 1	

QUARTER FINALS

Seve BALLESTEROS	Sp	Mark MOULAND	Wal	2 Holes	Quarter Final Losers won £9,900
Mike HARWOOD	Aus	Ian WOOSNAM	Wal	1 Hole	
Des SMYTH	Ire	Jose-Maria OLAZABAL	Sp	1 Hole	
Denis DURNIAN	Eng	Ken BROWN	Scot	3 & 2	

SEMI FINALS

Seve BALLESTEROS	Sp	Mike HARWOOD	Aus	6 & 5
Denis DURNIAN	Eng	Des SMYTH	Ire	4 & 3

PLAY-OFF FOR 3RD & 4TH PLACES

Des SMYTH (£18,370)	Ire	Mike HARWOOD (£14,750)	Aus	1 Hole

FINAL

Seve BALLESTEROS (£50,000)	Sp	Denis DURNIAN (£32,000)	Eng	4 & 3

BRAND
leader at last

Gordon J. Brand is not one to blow his own trumpet, even though he once played cornet concertos in a sauce factory brass band. Yet he took particular satisfaction in leading the Volvo Belgian Open from start to finish to record his first European victory in 13 years.

The Yorkshireman had tied third behind Jose Maria Olazabal the previous year at Bercuit but there had been few signs in the previous weeks to suggest the long-awaited breakthrough was imminent.

Brand had been preoccupied with moving house, from his farm on the moors near Ilkley to a home in the town. His rustic inclinations had led him to acquire a small herd of cows, three horses, and some 50 chickens, as well as a talent for constructing dry stone walls. Driving a tractor around his windswept 30 acres, he had half accepted that, in his mid-thirties, he had already experienced the highlights of his golf career. Despite Ryder Cup, World and Dunhill Cup honours and six wins over eight years on the African Safari Tour, Brand had latterly looked destined to be a permanent member of the supporting cast as far as Britain and Europe were concerned. But with the farm sale arranged and wife Lyn, herself a former professional golfer, and his daughters preparing for the conventional life of suburbia, Brand journeyed to Belgium able to concentrate fully on his golf.

The tournament had returned to its birthplace at Royal Waterloo where Eamonn Darcy had won a rain-curtailed 1987 event. The present La Marache course was opened in 1960, and the modern club now has 45 holes, laid out, for the most part, on the very ground where Wellington changed the face of Europe by stopping Napoleon in his tracks. That engagement did not go according to the script, and neither did the 1989 golf version.

A MULTIPLE WINNER ON THE SAFARI TOUR, GORDON J. BRAND HAD CAMPAIGNED FOR 13 YEARS IN EUROPE WITHOUT VICTORY BUT THERE WAS NO DENYING HIM IN THE VOLVO BELGIAN OPEN

Olazabal, already a winner in Tenerife and runner-up in both the Renault Open de Baleares and Catalan Open, had returned to defend the title which, the previous year, had helped him become the youngest golfer in the top 20 world rankings. Former Masters champion Bernhard Langer had also been recruited to make his Belgian Open debut. This formidable duo were rightly installed as favourites for a £33,330 prize and the accompanying Ryder Cup points.

The latter were of particular interest to the German. He was planning to compete in only seven or eight events before the European team was finalised, and was anxious to earn his place by gaining one of the nine automatic places decreed by officialdom. He had made an excellent start, winning the Spanish Open at El Saler immediately on his return from the US Tour, and reaching the last 16 in defending his Epson Grand Prix of Europe title. In the process Langer had gained another personal triumph in his perennial struggle with what has become fashionably known as the 'putter stutter'.

To universal surprise neither Olazabal or Langer made an impact and both finished outside the leading 20. They failed to come to terms with the soggy fairways of the first two rounds and the variable greens. Langer finished on a four under par 284 to take 21st place, while the Spaniard was two shots further back in 30th position.

The first shots were struck under sombre skies depositing such a surfeit of water that play halted for an hour mid-morning because several greens were immersed. But Brand and Australian Peter McWhinney, recently arrived from hurricane-lashed Queensland, experienced few problems in sharing the opening day lead on 67. Both had taken specialist advice—Brand from his wife, and the Brisbane golfer from the expert technicians of the Volvo Tour's indispensable travelling workshop.

Mrs Brand's most effective stroke in her tournament days was a chip and run with a nine iron. She had been nagging her husband to employ it more often as a stroke-saver around the greens. The wet ground gave Brand the opportunity to demonstrate his wife's wisdom and the nine iron was responsible for three of his six birdies.

McWhinney had worked on his golf clubs at home during the winter and was puzzled that he had played so badly thereafter. "I had not been able to hit my hat with them" he admitted. "By trying to adjust them myself I had put them up to three degrees out of true." The lofts and lies were corrected and the Australian celebrated his return to the straight and narrow by acquiring six birdies in the space of nine holes from the eighth.

Seven players including Darcy, the steadily improving Mark Davis, and Anders Forsbrand of Sweden returned 68, with the French pair Marc Farry and Emmanuel Dussart on 69. It was the latter who revealed the true extent of the support given by the French Federation and French club golfers to their most talented young tournament players who receive 5,000 francs each week towards expenses and are provided with a permanent 'guru' on tour — Henri Frayssineau. The money comes from a levy on the country's 140,000 club golfers who are happy to contribute long term to a scheme designed to produce star players of Ryder Cup status.

In Britain and Ireland such philanthrophy has generally been the preserve of well-heeled club members whose patronage has assisted many an ambitious youngster to become established. One such is Kevin Dickens, a club professional from Cold Ashby in the Midlands of England who made his Volvo Tour debut in Tenerife after scrambling through the winter qualifying school. He finished 19th at Golf del Sur, then missed the halfway cut in his five outings prior to arriving at Royal Waterloo. He had, in the meantime, acquired a sponsorship from an engineering company in Milton Keynes and showed he was back to form in the second round by taking a 67.

By the close of the third round Dickens had moved alongside Brand on a 12-under-par 204, with Richard Boxall ensuring the English ruled the roost by charging to a 66. Peter Baker, who had taken home reserve money from his last two stroke-play tournaments and had also missed four cuts, at last hit form with a course record 65. He had eight birdies but a drive into trees at the 13th, and a five foot putt that escaped at the 18th cost him a special 25,000 ECUs prize for beating 64.

Brand and Dickens were paired at the tail of the field and the latter was accompanied by a sizeable contingent of his club members who had arrived by boat and aeroplane with great expectations.

Brand's tee shot to the par three 15th

McNulty out of the shadows

Runner-up Kevin Dickens

Both players birdied the second, but by the turn Brand, out in 33, was four shots ahead of Dickens and five clear of Boxall. Two birdie putts to start the inward run put Dickens right back in the reckoning, but Brand saved his par four at the 12th after hitting a tree while Dickens hit a wayward shot to the 13th.

Thereafter the Yorkshireman's accuracy through the green and solid putting took him to the 16th tee with a three-shot lead with which to confront the trio of closing par fives. He birdied two of them and won by four shots with a 69. Mark Davis, with an eagle and birdie in the last three holes, snatched third place form Sweden's Jesper Parnevik. Dickens had won £22,000 in only the second European tournament he had completed, but Brand had more than cash to savour.

"I never thought I would not win at some time" he said. "I knew I was as good a player as some of the others who had won this year, but winning is not always about how good your swing is." Brand explained "Many times I have tensed up when I have got into a leading position. Even in the 1986

Winner and caddie celebrate first European victory

Open at Turnberry I got uptight. I had no chance of catching Greg Norman, and I wasn't under pressure for second place. But it was only after I had blown it that I came back. This week I did not get tense and the victory and the way I achieved it gave me more pleasure than the Open. Maybe the older you get the less wound up you get. I know now there is more to life than playing 18 holes of golf."

Brand had also put himself back in the running for a Ryder Cup place and was looking forward to proving to Tony Jacklin that he is now a much better golfer than his 1983 Cup appearance indicated. "I was very disappointed at not getting a game before the singles" added Gordon, who then lost to Bob Gilder. "But I was playing poorly and I couldn't complain. It will be different if I get another chance."

Three weeks after his Belgian triumph Brand proved his point by hopping across the Atlantic to qualify for the US Open with rounds of 71 and 70. He returned to New York a week later to join Nick Faldo, Sandy Lyle and Ian Woosnam in the British challenge for the American title. He no longer needed that middle initial to set him apart from his Scottish namesake. For those who love to unravel the arcane it stands for John.

COURSE: ROYAL WATERLOO GOLF CLUB, BRUSSELS **YARDAGE: 6,803** **PAR: 72**

POS	NAME	CTRY	1	2	3	4	TOTAL	PRIZE MONEY
1	Gordon J BRAND	Eng	67	69	68	69	273	£33330
2	Kevin DICKENS	Eng	70	67	67	73	277	£22200
3	Mark DAVIS	Eng	68	73	70	67	278	£12520
4	Jesper PARNEVIK	Swe	74	70	67	68	279	£10000
5	Richard BOXALL	Eng	69	70	66	75	280	£6190
	Marc FARRY	Fr	69	69	71	71	280	£6190
	Ronan RAFFERTY	N.Ire	70	73	67	70	280	£6190
	Malcolm MACKENZIE	Eng	70	72	71	67	280	£6190
	Derrick COOPER	Eng	71	71	71	67	280	£6190
10	Eamonn DARCY	Ire	68	72	72	69	281	£3480
	Andrew MURRAY	Eng	72	71	69	69	281	£3480
	David WILLIAMS	Eng	71	70	72	68	281	£3480
	Grant TURNER	Eng	74	70	70	67	281	£3480
	Philip WALTON	Ire	75	69	70	67	281	£3480
15	Peter McWHINNEY	Aus	67	74	71	70	282	£2940
16	Peter BAKER	Eng	73	74	65	71	283	£2596
	Mark McNULTY	Zim	71	69	72	71	283	£2596
	Emmanuel DUSSART	Fr	69	72	71	71	283	£2596
	Miguel Angel JIMENEZ	Sp	70	72	72	69	283	£2596
	Mike CLAYTON	Aus	71	72	72	68	283	£2596
21	Bernhard LANGER	W.Ger	73	70	72	69	284	£2310
	Stephen BENNETT	Eng	73	72	71	68	284	£2310
23	David J RUSSELL	Eng	72	69	70	74	285	£2040
	Charles BOLLING Jnr	USA	72	71	71	71	285	£2040
	Carl MASON	Eng	74	70	70	71	285	£2040
	Anders FORSBRAND	Swe	68	74	73	70	285	£2040
	Paul KENT	Eng	73	72	71	69	285	£2040
	Vijay SINGH	Fij	69	76	73	67	285	£2040
	Chris MOODY	Eng	72	75	72	66	285	£2040
30	Santiago LUNA	Sp	68	71	74	73	286	£1648
	Paul CURRY	Eng	74	72	68	72	286	£1648
	Brian MARCHBANK	Scot	70	75	70	71	286	£1648
	Jean VAN DE VELDE	Fr	71	74	73	68	286	£1648
	Gordon BRAND Jnr	Scot	72	75	71	68	286	£1648
	Paul CARRIGILL	Eng	76	71	71	68	286	£1648
	Jose Maria OLAZABAL	Sp	75	71	73	67	286	£1648
37	Steven BOTTOMLEY	Eng	68	76	73	70	287	£1420
	David JAMES	Scot	70	74	74	69	287	£1420
	Neil HANSEN	Eng	70	74	75	68	287	£1420
	Vicente FERNANDEZ	Arg	71	74	74	68	287	£1420
41	Juan QUIROS	Sp	71	76	68	73	288	£1200
	Ken BROWN	Scot	69	72	74	73	288	£1200
	Rick HARTMANN	USA	68	77	71	72	288	£1200
	Mark NICHOLS	Eng	70	74	73	71	288	£1200
	Paul BROADHURST	Eng	68	76	74	70	288	£1200
	Manuel CALERO	Sp	72	72	74	70	288	£1200
	Eduardo ROMERO	Arg	74	73	73	68	288	£1200
48	Tony CHARNLEY	Eng	75	72	69	73	289	£1000
	Bob E SMITH	USA	76	71	70	72	289	£1000
	David A RUSSELL	Eng	71	75	73	70	289	£1000
51	Sandy STEPHEN	Scot	70	77	72	71	290	£920
52	Andrew CHANDLER	Eng	73	73	71	74	291	£840
	Johan RYSTROM	Swe	71	76	71	73	291	£840
	Stephen McALLISTER	Scot	70	75	75	71	291	£840
55	Colin MONTGOMERIE	Scot	70	69	77	76	292	£670
	Kris MOE	USA	71	74	74	73	292	£670
	John MORGAN	Eng	72	75	73	72	292	£670
	Alberto BINAGHI	It	73	71	76	72	292	£670
	Jerry ANDERSON	Can	70	76	75	71	292	£670
	Mariano APARICIO	Sp	71	76	74	71	292	£670
61	Miguel Angel MARTIN	Sp	73	72	74	74	293	£483
	John SLAUGHTER	USA	74	71	74	74	293	£483
	Andrea CANESSA	It	72	74	73	74	293	£483
	Marco DURANTE	It	73	73	74	73	293	£483
	Chris PLATTS	Eng	69	77	79	68	293	£483
	Jeremy BENNETT	Eng	72	74	79	68	293	£483
67	Peter FOWLER	Aus	73	69	75	77	294	£196
	Mats HALLBERG	Swe	75	72	73	74	294	£196
	Greg J TURNER	NZ	76	71	79	68	294	£196
70	Eugene ELLIOTT	USA	69	72	78	76	295	£191
	Torsten GIEDEON	W.Ger	70	75	77	73	295	£191
72	Ruud BOS	Hol	75	72	75	75	297	£188
73	David RAY	Eng	74	72	76	77	299	£186

RAFFERTY *ends title drought*

WITHOUT A MAJOR EUROPEAN TITLE TO HIS NAME IN SEVEN YEARS OF TRYING, RONAN RAFFERTY ERASED THAT UNWELCOME STATISTIC WITH A VICTORY AT MONTICELLO

In the end, it all came down to the 48½ inch putter of Sam Torrance. Five feet of perfect green lay between it and the final hole on the magnificent Monticello course in northern Italy—but the Scot's latest weapon against the 'twitch' failed its ultimate test and Ronan Rafferty, who watched the final moments of drama from the scorer's caravan, won the Lancia Italian Open title, his first major success on the Volvo Tour.

Not that the Ulsterman deserved anything less after firing in a seven birdie final round of 65 for a 15 under par aggregate of 273. He admitted later that he had been jumpy all day and had asked his caddie to talk to him during the round in an effort to relieve the mental strain he felt at being so close to ending his title drought. He had won tournaments on the Australian circuit and last year he took the Equity and Law Challenge at Royal Mid-Surrey. But this was something different. This was worth £42,589, a big promotion on the Volvo Order of Merit and a realistic chance of a Ryder Cup call-up in September. He responded to all the pressures with determination, coolness and skill, picking up two birdies in the last five holes.

The strongly built Ulsterman did not give any early hint of what was to come when he returned an opening round of one under par 71. Well over a dozen players broke the 70 mark and they were led home by the 65 of fellow countryman David Feherty who won the title in 1986 in a play-off with Rafferty. Feherty carded a 72 on the second day and slipped behind Ross McFarlane who improved a stroke on his first round 69.

The biggest surprise, though, was still to come. Paul Carman, not exactly a household name, or even a clubhouse name for that matter, was lined up to partner Seve Ballesteros on the Saturday. Carman is the professional at the Flixby club near Huddersfield and before that was assistant to Denis Durnian. He was told by his friends not to be overwhelmed by the experience of playing Ballesteros. "Just go out and enjoy it," they said. Some four hours later it was clear he had indeed enjoyed himself. What's more, he had shown Ballesteros, who was making his eighth attempt to win the title, the short way around the course with a magnificent 67. That was good enough for him to beat the title favourite by one stroke and to go into the final round in joint second place with Feherty and just two strokes behind Torrance.

On the final day Carman played alongside Torrance and saw the Scot birdie the 10th and 11th holes to go two shots clear of the fast-finishing Rafferty who had reached the turn in 32.

It seemed all over bar the presentation when the experienced Torrance stepped on to the 400-yards 12th but then it all began to go wrong. His putter failed him from eight feet and he dropped another shot at the short 13th where he missed the green.

Rafferty had already birdied the 11th to go 13 under par and he also picked up shots at the 14th and 16th holes. Also still in the hunt was Magnus Persson, 13 under par and in second place after ten holes. He dropped a shot at the 11th where his tee-shot disappeared into a water hazard on the right but still kept Torrance under pressure by returning a 68 for 275.

The rest of the serious challengers had dropped out by then. Carman, Feherty and Andrew Sherborne, all in with a chance at the start of the day, had taken 36 to the turn and hopes of a Ballesteros charge disappeared when he bogied the fifth and eighth holes.

Torrance birdied the 15th to go back to the top of the leader board alongside Rafferty who rifled a three-iron shot 196 yards and saw it lip the same hole and finish five feet behind the pin. And so the Lancia Italian Open moved to its climax with Rafferty home safely with two pars and Torrance needing to match him to force a play-off.

But the pressure finally reached the Ryder Cup-hardened Scot. His tee shot missed the fairway, his second found a

Sam Torrance's putt to tie slips by

bunker and then came the putt that will always feature in his nightmares. He tucked the long shaft of his club under his chin and with a pendulum action sent the ball past the right hand lip of the hole. The crowd gasped, Torrance gave a brave smile, and Rafferty breathed a huge sigh of relief. Then Torrance walked up to Rafferty and echoed everyone's thoughts: "Congratulations", he said, "that's the first of many, I'm sure."

Ruling for José Rivero

Swanning off the 7th tee

COURSE: MONTICELLO **YARDAGE: 6,786** **PAR: 72**

POS	NAME	CTRY	1	2	3	4	TOTAL	PRIZE MONEY
1	Ronan RAFFERTY	N.Ire	71	69	68	65	273	£42589
2	Sam TORRANCE	Scot	69	70	65	70	274	£28371
3	Magnus PERSSON	Swe	66	72	69	68	275	£15995
4	Robert LEE	Eng	66	73	69	69	277	£12772
5	Paul CARMAN	Eng	70	69	67	72	278	£9885
	Andrew SHERBORNE	Eng	72	70	65	71	278	£9885
7	David FEHERTY	N.Ire	65	72	69	73	279	£5915
	Severiano BALLESTEROS	Sp	71	69	68	71	279	£5915
	Luis CARBONETTI	Arg	76	68	67	68	279	£5915
	Frank NOBILO	NZ	71	70	71	67	279	£5915
	Neil HANSEN	Eng	71	72	71	65	279	£5915
12	Mark JAMES	Eng	70	71	69	70	280	£4135
	Philip PARKIN	Wal	74	68	68	70	280	£4135
	Costantino ROCCA	It	69	76	72	63	280	£4135
15	Marc PENDARIES	Fr	72	70	70	69	281	£3674
	Mark HARWOOD	Aus	72	68	73	68	281	£3674
17	Craig PARRY	Aus	70	71	70	71	282	£3193
	Carl Magnus STROMBERG	Swe	69	70	74	69	282	£3193
	Ruud BOS	Hol	70	71	73	68	282	£3193
	Jose DAVILA	Sp	76	68	70	68	282	£3193
	Massimo MANNELLI	It	70	71	74	67	282	£3193
22	Mariano APARICIO	Sp	68	72	70	73	283	£2834
	Russ McFARLANE	Eng	69	68	75	71	283	£2834
	Giuseppe CALI	It	70	70	73	70	283	£2834
25	Gordon J BRAND	Eng	70	72	69	73	284	£2567
	Paul HOAD	Eng	71	72	71	70	284	£2567
	Paul CURRY	Eng	69	74	72	69	284	£2567
	Mark ROE	Eng	68	73	75	68	284	£2567
29	Jesper PARNEVIK	Swe	70	72	69	74	285	£2259
	Roger CHAPMAN	Eng	72	71	68	74	285	£2259
	Noel RATCLIFFE	Aus	72	71	72	70	285	£2259
	Steven BOTTOMLEY	Eng	71	74	72	68	285	£2259
33	Barry LANE	Eng	71	72	68	75	286	£1966
	Jacob RASMUSSEN	Den	71	74	70	71	286	£1966
	Keith WATERS	Eng	71	70	74	71	286	£1966
	Peter McWHINNEY	Aus	71	72	72	71	286	£1966
	Eduardo ROMERO	Arg	71	74	70	71	286	£1966
	Wayne STEPHENS	Eng	74	69	73	70	286	£1966
39	David RAY	Eng	72	73	69	73	287	£1684
	Miguel Angel JIMENEZ	Sp	70	75	70	72	287	£1684
	Jamie HOWELL	USA	73	72	72	70	287	£1684
	Vijay SINGH	Fiji	73	70	74	70	287	£1684
	Peter SENIOR	Aus	72	72	73	70	287	£1684
44	Neal BRIGGS	Eng	70	71	72	75	288	£1404
	Peter MITCHELL	Eng	71	74	70	73	288	£1404
	Baldovino DASSU	It	69	74	72	73	288	£1404
	Delio LOVATO	It	74	71	71	72	288	£1404
	Mark DAVIS	Eng	69	74	75	70	288	£1404
	Jerry ANDERSON	Can	70	75	74	69	288	£1404
50	Michael ALLEN	USA	73	69	75	72	289	£1199
	Jeremy BENNETT	Eng	74	71	73	71	289	£1199
52	Alessandro ROGATO	It	74	69	73	74	290	£1046
	Ronald STELTEN	USA	69	75	73	73	290	£1046
	Brian EVANS	Eng	73	72	72	73	290	£1046
	Andrea CANESSA	It	71	73	76	70	290	£1046
56	Marc FARRY	Fr	69	76	66	80	291	£893
	Thomas LEVET	Fr	68	74	73	76	291	£893
58	John MORGAN	Eng	72	71	74	75	292	£815
59	Alberto BINAGHI	It	72	70	76	75	293	£763
	Jonas SAXTON	USA	72	72	76	73	293	£763
	Paul KENT	Eng	74	71	75	73	293	£763
62	Rick HARTMANN	USA	71	73	73	78	295	£688
	Jose RIVERO	Sp	67	76	78	74	295	£688
	Vittorio MORI	It	75	70	76	74	295	£688
65	Luigi FIGARI	It	75	69	75	77	296	£638
66	Andrew STUBBS	Eng	72	73	76	77	298	£255
67	Lee JONES	Eng	74	71	79	76	300	£253

Signing session for winner Rafferty

FALDO'S *triumphant return*

IN HIS FIRST EUROPEAN APPEARANCE SINCE WINNING THE US MASTERS, NICK FALDO TOOK THE VOLVO PGA CHAMPIONSHIP TITLE IN BRILLIANT FASHION AND THUS CORRECTED A CURIOUS OMISSION FROM HIS RECORD

In 15 years of trying, first as an amateur, then as a professional, and latterly as a member, Nick Faldo had not won so much as a monthly medal round Wentworth's West course. Such a statistic is a mere blemish but the absence of Faldo's name on any silverware pertaining to Wentworth was irritating.

As reigning US Masters champion, Faldo arrived at Wentworth for the Volvo PGA Championship exuding an aura of supremacy. It had taken him time to adjust to the euphoria of his victory at Augusta but he had put in some solid performances in subsequent American events and thus was pretty well prepared for his first foray of the 1989 season on this side of the Atlantic.

This championship, now the flagship of the Volvo Tour, attracted the strongest field of the year, including Europe's Big Five of Ballesteros, Lyle, Langer, Woosnam and Faldo. They were due to play a charity match on the Wednesday prior to the start but a six-hour thunderstorm put paid to that. Even with a torrential downpour soaking the fairways and greens, the course was still burnt and fast, providing conditions that amateurs find flattering and professionals dislike.

The first day, like so many before it, dawned bright and clear but a swirling wind drifting through the tree tops made club selection tricky and the hard ground provided many unpredictable bounces. The upshot of this combination was a pace of play that was almost terminal. Rounds were taking anything up to five hours to complete, PGA European Tour officials and invited referees from the Spanish, Swedish and French Federations, the Australian Tour and St. Andrews were buzzing across the fairways on rule-a-minute errands and players were warned to speed up. Ken Brown and Frank Nobilo didn't and were fined and the entire 18 holes became an exercise in patience.

The chief objective, as Faldo himself put it, was 'to keep the ball down the channel' and he demonstrated how it should be done with another display of exemplary striking coupled with what he considered his best putting round since Augusta — 67 with six birdies.

Joining Faldo on that score was Ian Woosnam, the defending champion, who had not made a particularly auspicious start to the season. The man who appears to change clubs more often than Tommy Docherty was armed with yet another new set of irons which were slightly offset. Woosnam pronounced himself entirely happy with them as they helped him restore the natural draw to his shots. Striking while the irons were hot, he hit every green in par figures, missed a string of putts from under 12 feet, but holed enough to match Faldo's opening round. Tucked in one shot behind were the Australian duo of Brett Ogle and Craig Parry along with Paul Curry. Sandy Lyle enjoyed his best start in weeks with a 70 but still described his game as 'scabby'. Langer and Ballesteros languished six strokes off the pace.

It was Parry who emerged on the second day as the closest challenger to Faldo. The man from Sunshine, Victoria, with the stevedore forearms and the spikey haircut went round in another 68, the basis of which was a first nine of 31. He is an aggressive player who acknowledges his inexperience but still has enough golfing 'nous' to have won in his home country and, more recently, in Japan.

Faldo cruised along relentlessly and looked set for another 67 until an errant tee shot at the 15th cost him a six to pull him back level with Parry. Taking closer order were Mark McNulty, Neil Hansen, Christy O'Connor Junior and Gavin Levenson who joined Woosman three strokes behind the leaders. On the edge of the cut at 147 was Ballesteros while Lyle fell back with a lacklustre 75.

As the current Open champion and winner twice on the Tour already,

Ballesteros, Brand and James on the seventh green

Leftish leanings from Ballesteros

Ballesteros could not have expected to be out first for the third round accompanied by a marker, but this was so. Spurred on by this ignominy he demolished the homeward nine in 31 for a 65 and then made some enigmatic remarks about good prize-money not being the only requirement for a tournament of this stature and a few other things were also important, particularly the condition of the course.Refusing to elaborate any further it can only be assumed that his pride was stung by his anonymous pairing.

Back to the main business of the day, which concerned Faldo and Parry and whether one of them could break free from the field. Parry made the better try and opened up a two-stroke lead on Faldo before impetuousity cost him a six at the 17th. Faldo's birdie made up the deficit and so the two were tied again with Woosnam closing to within two shots.

It was to be Parry's final thrust, for Faldo was in no mood to relinquish that which he had so painstakingly built in the first three rounds. Although caught briefly by Woosnam when the Welshman birdied the 12th, Faldo responded with a run of three birdies from the same hole and arrived on the 15th tee with a three stroke lead. Here he shot the ball out to the right where it came to rest on a layer of leaves close to the tree-line. Unable to see the green, 200 yards away, he would have to bend the ball 40 yards left to right in order to reach the putting surface. It was a shot that only the foolhardy or a man supremely confident in his ability would attempt.

Faldo's mood at the moment was most definitely in the latter category. He selected his three iron, the same club with which he had rifled the ball into the heart of the 11th green in the Masters play-off. At the top of his swing he realised that he hadn't even made a practice swing but it made no difference. The shot was stupendous. The ball came out like a bullet, curved the necessary amount and ran to within five feet of the hole. Down went the putt for a fourth consecutive birdie which moments earlier had looked impossible.

There was a sharp intake of breath on the 17th when Faldo hooked his second and the ball hit a boundary post and bounced back into play, but otherwise it was all plain sailing for the game's most assured player.

Woosnam finished bravely with an

High kicks towards a high finish for Ian Woosnam

Catching practice for Brand's caddie

Anders Forsbrand is ditched at the 15th

eagle at the last to take second place, Ballesteros was round in 66, without a marker this time, and players like Denis Durnian and Christy O'Connor Junior gave their Ryder Cup chances a timely boost. Poor Sandy Lyle finished 28 strokes behind the winner and looked a man in despair as he sought help from sundry gurus, but his fortunes could only improve.

At Wentworth, the Faldo and Lyle show was strictly a one-man performance. Such is the quality of Faldo's striking that it is more surprising when he actually hits a shot off line and there were few occasions when he did that. They simply wound up the mechanical man of golf and sent him clicking round the West course. Four rounds all under 70, a cheque for £58,330 and a handsome silver trophy all belonged to Nick Faldo.

Oh yes, and one other thing, his name will now go up on one of the boards in the clubhouse—Wentworth likes to honour the achievements of its members.

Des Smyth at work with the Apollo Swing Analyser

Lonely walk to recovery for Sandy Lyle

FALDO

Woosnam recovers from trees to set up an eagle three

Faldo drives down the tunnel at the 17th

Two Big Macs and a golf ball . . .

for Mark Mouland . . .

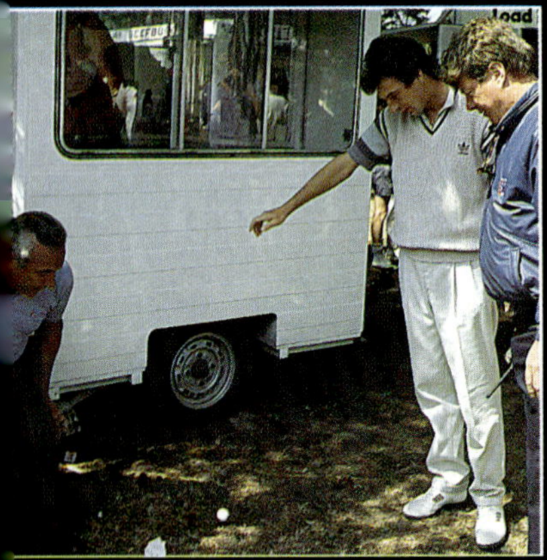

after errant tee shot . . .

. . . at the 10th

Ballesteros and Faldo, Open Champions in triplicate

No play today for Europe's Big Five in the Whyte & Mackay Challenge

Faldo steps into his second shot to the 18th

Nick Faldo finished above the rest at the end of a glorious week

COURSE: WENTWORTH CLUB (West Course) **YARDAGE: 6,945** **PAR: 72**

POS	NAME	CTRY	1	2	3	4	TOTAL	PRIZE MONEY
1	Nick FALDO	Eng	67	69	69	67	272	£58330
2	Ian WOOSNAM	Wal	67	72	68	67	274	£38860
3	Craig PARRY	Aus	68	68	69	71	276	£21910
4	Severiano BALLESTEROS	Sp	73	74	65	66	278	£14860
	Mark McNULTY	Zim	70	69	69	70	278	£14860
	Christy O'CONNOR Jnr	Ire	71	68	74	65	278	£14860
7	Denis DURNIAN	Eng	73	68	69	69	279	£10500
8	Vijay SINGH	Fij	71	70	71	68	280	£7863
	Mark JAMES	Eng	71	75	68	66	280	£7863
	Gordon J BRAND	Eng	74	72	65	69	280	£7863
11	Jeff HAWKES	SA	75	70	66	70	281	£5860
	Jose-Maria OLAZABAL	Sp	72	74	69	66	281	£5860
	Gavin LEVENSON	SA	70	69	69	73	281	£5860
	Neil HANSEN	Eng	69	70	72	70	281	£5860
15	Ronan RAFFERTY	N.Ire	72	69	71	70	282	£5140
16	Jesper PARNEVIK	Swe	72	70	67	74	283	£4930
17	Peter FOWLER	Aus	71	70	74	69	284	£4526
	Paul CURRY	Eng	68	72	73	71	284	£4526
	Eamonn DARCY	Ire	72	71	71	70	284	£5426
20	Brett OGLE	Aus	68	73	70	74	285	£3990
	Sam TORRANCE	Scot	71	75	70	69	285	£3990
	Bernhard LANGER	W.Ger	73	69	68	75	285	£3990
	Eduardo ROMERO	Arg	71	73	70	71	285	£3990
	Glenn RALPH	Eng	72	71	71	71	285	£3990
25	Philip WALTON	Ire	73	70	71	72	286	£3360
	Stephen McALLISTER	Scot	71	74	69	72	286	£3360
	Stephen HAMILL	N.Ire	71	72	70	73	286	£3360
	Michael ALLEN	USA	73	72	73	68	286	£3360
	Gordon BRAND Jnr	Scot	72	74	69	71	286	£3360
	Roger CHAPMAN	Eng	77	69	68	72	286	£3360
	Carl MASON	Eng	69	76	74	67	286	£3360
32	Bernard GALLACHER	Scot	74	73	70	70	287	£2800
	Andrew MURRAY	Eng	70	71	73	73	287	£2800
	Johan RYSTROM	Swe	73	74	67	73	287	£2800
	Malcolm MACKENZIE	Eng	75	71	69	72	287	£2800
	Ross McFARLANE	Eng	70	70	74	73	287	£2300
37	Michael McLEAN	Eng	76	69	75	68	288	£2520
	Howard CLARK	Eng	75	66	74	73	288	£2520
	Mike SMITH	USA	74	73	71	70	288	£2520
40	Magnus PERSSON	Swe	74	72	69	74	289	£2380
41	Ken BROWN	Scot	71	73	69	77	290	£2170
	Philip HARRISON	Eng	76	69	74	71	290	£2170
	Bill LONGMUIR	Scot	69	72	73	76	290	£2170
	Gerry TAYLOR	Aus	72	73	68	77	290	£2170
	Mike HARWOOD	Aus	72	72	70	76	290	£2170
46	Paul KENT	Eng	79	68	72	72	291	£1855
	Ove SELLBERG	Swe	71	73	71	76	291	£1855
	Jerry HAAS	USA	73	73	73	72	291	£1855
	Kevin DICKENS	Eng	74	73	73	71	291	£1855
50	Mike CLAYTON	Aus	74	73	75	70	292	£1610
	Ian YOUNG	Scot	71	75	74	72	292	£1610
	Peter SENIOR	Aus	71	74	73	74	292	£1610
53	David GILFORD	Eng	71	73	78	71	293	£1330
	John MORGAN	Eng	70	75	71	77	293	£1330
	Lee FICKLING	Eng	73	69	76	75	293	£1330
	Anders FORSBRAND	Swe	73	72	80	68	293	£1330
	Anders SORENSEN	Den	71	74	71	77	293	£1330
58	Vicente FERNANDEZ	Arg	72	74	78	70	294	£1067
	Barry LANE	Eng	70	76	73	75	294	£1067
	Michael KING	Eng	72	75	74	73	294	£1067
	Jimmy HEGGARTY	N.Ire	74	71	72	77	294	£1067
62	John JACOBS	USA	76	71	78	70	295	£962
	Paul BROADHURST	Eng	77	69	74	75	295	£962
64	Neil COLES	Eng	75	72	75	74	296	£910
65	Sandy LYLE	Scot	70	75	78	77	300	£875

FALDO'S *scorched earth policy*

Australia's quintuple Open champion, Peter Thomson, used to tell of the American professional who, after a tournament at Oak Hill, was asked if he was going to avail himself of the opportunity to go to Niagara Falls. 'I don't know,' he said, as one who had clearly not given any thought to the matter. 'What's the prize money, anyway?'

The extent to which the more dedicated of professional sportsmen are blinkered is open to exaggeration and certainly, on the first night of the Dunhill Masters at Woburn, No. 10 connoted to Nick Faldo not as a 502-yard par five but as an invitation to dine that evening with Margaret Thatcher and George Bush. As a Big Three gathering, it was not quite the stuff of Yalta and Roosevelt, Stalin and Churchill; far less of Palmer, Player and Nicklaus.

Nevertheless, it was still an occasion fully appreciated by Faldo who, having followed it up the next day with a seven under par record-equalling 65, spoke highly of Downing Street's 1913 Cognac as fuel for golf. Moreover, he had found that President Bush's interest in ballistic missiles included the 1.68. The President, who claimed a 12 handicap, confided that his greatest problem in golf lay '... in keeping my left arm stiff. What is the answer?'

'That's the answer,' responded Faldo, succinctly. 'It shouldn't be!'

Yet, tickled though he was by the whole occasion, which was something neither he nor his wife would ever forget, Faldo was adamant in his hour of victory at Woburn that it did not compare with the sheer thrill of winning: 'Winning golf tournaments, after all, is my purpose in life, what it is about.'

FOR THE SECOND WEEK RUNNING NICK FALDO DEMONSTRATED HIS MASTERY OF FAST-RUNNING CONDITIONS IN COMPLETING A MASTERS TREBLE

In triumphing at Woburn by four strokes from Ronan Rafferty, he completed not only the Transatlantic double in terms of the US Masters and the British Masters but also a hat-trick of such titles in that he had captured the Volvo Masters at the tail-end of the previous season. Once before, in 1983, he had won three European events in succession. Then, which shows the staggering increase in prize-money, the feat had been worth £32,000 whereas this time his three on the trot, if such a phrase can be used of such a painstakingly methodical golfer, had brought bullion amounting to £165,000. Told on the eve of the championship that the bookmakers had made him a 4-1 favourite, Faldo deemed such odds "ludicrous to anyone who knows golf." In his heart of hearts, of course, he probably did see himself as favourite but he was genuinely concerned that the course had been baked rock-hard by weeks of sunshine. Faldo remarked that, in practice, he had "scarcely dared to land a ball on the green. I did so at the short fifth but only by skying a three-iron into the Gods and hoping it would drop soft." That so new a course had not been equipped with fairway watering, he found simply incredible.

Out early on the first morning, Faldo opened with a somewhat uneasy 71. It was already cold and growing colder when he teed off but that did not alter the fact that he felt he should have been five strokes better. By the close of play, Ian Young, the youngest ever to win the Scottish Professional championship, led with a 65 by a stroke from Paul Curry, the former English youth international from Essex. The 31-year-old Peter Mitchell, who had turned professional in 1974 but whose best finish on the Tour had been 11th equal in the 1988 Carrolls Irish Open, was two strokes off the pace and just one ahead of Eamonn Darcy and Stephen McAllister. The latter, having been treated for fallen arches, was discovered two years ago to have rheumatoid arthritis which necessitates his swallowing seven anti-inflamatory pills a day. Had the rain bothered the bespectacled McAllister? 'Rain?' he said, 'It felt more like snow . . .'

Young, over the season, had been earning less than his costs and the contrast with the US Masters champion, whom he led by a handsome six strokes, was not lost on one Sassenach scribe who had gone in search of the surprise first-round leader rather hoping that, with Faldo at Downing Street, Young would be making do with fish and chips. 'Well, actually,' explained Ian, apologetically, 'I'm dining tonight at Woburn Abbey with the Marquess and Lady Tavistock . . .'

Young needed nine strokes more than he had had on the first day, the lead at the half-way mark being shared by Ronan Rafferty and The Man from Uncle, Christy O'Connor, who had six birdies to Faldo's haul of seven, with one of them a collector's piece. At the long fourth, shutting the face of his sand-wedge, O'Connor hooked a pitch round a tree and Bobby Locke could not have done it better.

Rafferty, who had won the Italian Open, had holed out very soundly and used his head shrewdly in his 65 — his feet, as always, encased in rubber-studded Stubert shoes. He has worn them unfailingly for nine years. Though there are corners of the golfing world where you will find folk to tell you that such shoes are liable to damage the greens, Rafferty won't have it: 'You see players all the time having to repair spike marks but tell me when you last saw a player having to repair a Stubert mark? Never.'

Faldo had spoken after his opening round of having had trouble 'getting on to my right side going back.' In the second round, he looked to swing the club beautifully and he himself agreed that it was much better: 'I was obtaining a more powerful coil and the connection with regard to my arm swing was also much improved.'

The most notable casualty of the half-way guillotine was Sandy Lyle who, having shot away 3, 2, against the card of 4, 3, had had a 70 but was still, tantalisingly, one stroke too many. It was the seventh time he had missed the cut in nine tournaments.

A second consecutive 65 gave Faldo the 54-hole lead. He was a stroke ahead of Ronan Rafferty with Peter Mitchell just three strokes adrift after an 8-under-par 64, a new course record. Mitchell had sunk everything in sight, putting with a Taylor Made prototype whose selling point was its particularly soft feel. 'I have never won,' said the player from the Old Kent Road, 'and, obviously, I'm not as great a player as Faldo — but you never know!' He was destined to end eleven strokes to the rear of Faldo but ninth equal was his highest finish and worth £6,080.

As for Faldo, from the moment 'the penny dropped' and he widened his putting stance at the 15th in the first round, he only once dropped a stroke

Crowds surround Rafferty and Faldo on the 11th

Sequence of arboreal problems for Peter Mitchell when his ball became entangled in a tree on the fourth and he was forced to take a penalty drop

Faldo drives from the 12th tee

— at the 16th on the third day as he followed his opening 71 with that brace of 65s and a closing 66. The widening of his stance in his putting stroke had the effect of dropping his hands lower and giving him the sensation of really getting down to the putt, a sensation he liked at once. The Taylor Made TPA XVIII model, which he had used to such dramatic effect in the last round at Augusta, has aiming lines painted on it, a feature which Faldo finds a great help even though he has blacked out all the lines on either side of the central one.

Ronan Rafferty, who played with him in the final round and loved the experience, opined that Faldo was: 'Currently, comfortably the best in the world.' In the course of the Volvo PGA and the Dunhill Masters, Rafferty had played alongside Seve Ballesteros, Bernhard Langer and Sandy Lyle 'and undoubtedly Faldo beats them all in course management.

'He doesn't just blaze away, but always plays the shot in hand with the next in mind,' continued Rafferty. 'Seve, to my mind, would still have the edge as a shotmaker in that he can probably play some shots which Nick couldn't or wouldn't — but, make no mistake, Nick is now a great striker.'

Other players always wanted to play with Sam Snead because they absorbed some of his glorious rhythm and Rafferty felt the same about playing with Faldo. 'Nick has wonderful rhythm as everyone knows and it passed into my own driving. I have always found Woburn an awkward driving course, but even the drive I bunkered at the 15th was well hit.'

Holing from 18 feet for a three at the par four 4th, Rafferty had closed to within a stroke of Faldo and, virtually certain of second place, he had thereafter, to all intents and purposes, nothing to lose and everything to gain — a thought which crossed both their minds. But Faldo recognised that his own drive was likely to be the key stroke of the day and, typically, came up with a beauty. Told that Rafferty had rated him the best golfer in the world, Faldo demurred: 'I still think there are about five or six you cannot really separate and that it would always just depend on whose week it was.'

Dave Leadbetter, the English-born Floridian teaching professional who helped Faldo restructure his swing, had supervised Faldo's warm-up session. His suggestion had been that Faldo concentrate on a more level hip turn on the backswing with the left hip kept up. The outcome was mightily impressive as Faldo, so obviously secure in his technique, bore down implacably on the title.

'These last two weeks,' noted Faldo, 'have represented my best putting for heaven knows how long. It has been no one thing but a combination of several — alignment, rhythm and so forth. I have been working and working on my putting for yonks . . .' He was in a position to poke fun at his own image: 'When I am hitting every green, or almost every green, but missing the putts, I am a boring golfer. When I play exactly the same but the putts start falling, then all of a sudden I'm thrilling!'

Sadly, the first-round leader, Ian Young, signed off with an 81 despite three birdies in the first four holes, while Steve McAllister, another of Thursday's front runners, had a 73. Both tumbled down the prize list — but then, as Sam Torrance always says, determinedly unimpressed by the state of the leaderboard after the early rounds, 'We don't get paid till Sunday.'

Having booked his Ryder Cup debut save for the official stamp, Rafferty, by coming second, also catapulted to the head of the Volvo Order of Merit, but was disposed to keep it very much in perspective: 'These are early days yet.' None the less, he promised that he would give himself every chance. His wife, Clare, was expecting a baby but even for that momentous happening he doubted if he would take a week off. 'What can I do? I've already done it.'

Exemplary style through the hitting area from Christy O'Connor Junior

Ronan Rafferty extends into a shot

Grandstand vista as Faldo and Rafferty finish on the 18th

COURSE: WOBURN **YARDAGE: 6,940** **PAR: 72**

POS	NAME	CTRY	1	2	3	4	TOTAL	PRIZE MONEY
1	Nick FALDO	Eng	71	65	65	66	267	£50000
2	Ronan RAFFERTY	N. Ire	70	65	67	69	271	£33300
3	Christy O'CONNOR Jnr	Ire	69	66	73	68	276	£15493
	Ove SELLBERG	Swe	71	66	70	69	276	£15493
	Mike HARWOOD	Aus	69	70	66	71	276	£15493
6	Ian WOOSNAM	Wal	71	70	70	66	277	£9000
	Rick HARTMANN	USA	70	69	71	67	277	£9000
	Mike SMITH	USA	71	69	66	71	277	£9000
9	Mark JAMES	Eng	69	68	70	71	278	£6080
	Peter SENIOR	Aus	74	66	66	72	278	£6080
	Peter MITCHELL	Eng	67	73	64	74	278	£6080
12	Jose Maria OLAZABAL	Sp	69	71	71	68	279	£4860
	Jose Maria CANIZARES	Sp	69	67	71	72	279	£4860
	Jeff HAWKES	SA	73	65	69	72	279	£4860
15	Gordon BRAND Jnr	Scot	72	73	67	68	280	£4320
	Jose RIVERO	Sp	69	70	71	70	280	£4320
17	Ian MOSEY	Eng	70	73	69	69	281	£3810
	Mike CLAYTON	Aus	72	70	70	69	281	£3810
	Bob SHEARER	Aus	72	71	69	69	281	£3810
	Ross McFARLANE	Eng	72	73	65	71	281	£3810
21	Mark MOULAND	Wal	71	70	72	69	282	£3465
	Peter O'MALLEY	Aus	73	70	69	70	282	£3465
23	Sam TORRANCE	Scot	73	69	68	73	283	£3240
	Richard BOXALL	Eng	71	72	69	71	283	£3240
	Frank NOBILO	NZ	70	75	69	69	283	£3240
26	Mark McNULTY	Zim	72	70	66	76	284	£2880
	Des SMYTH	Ire	70	73	69	72	284	£2880
	Peter FOWLER	Aus	71	67	71	75	284	£2880
	Paul CURRY	Eng	66	76	69	73	284	£2880
	Tony JOHNSTONE	Zim	71	70	70	73	284	£2880
31	Neil HANSEN	Eng	71	70	70	74	285	£2497
	David FEHERTY	N. Ire	71	73	70	71	285	£2497
	Colin MONTGOMERIE	Scot	70	73	70	72	285	£2497
	Carl MASON	Eng	72	70	71	72	285	£2497
35	Eamonn DARCY	Ire	68	70	73	75	286	£2070
	Anders FORSBRAND	Swe	73	71	68	74	286	£2070
	Vicente FERNANDEZ	Arg	73	71	70	72	286	£2070
	Martin POXON	Eng	71	72	70	73	286	£2070
	Manuel CALERO	Sp	72	72	69	73	286	£2070
	Eduardo ROMERO	Arg	74	69	72	71	286	£2070
	Tony CHARNLEY	Eng	70	68	71	77	286	£2070
	Philip WALTON	Ire	71	69	72	74	286	£2070
	Bernard GALLACHER	Scot	77	67	69	73	286	£2070
	Mark ROE	Eng	70	71	70	75	286	£2070
45	Mark DAVIS	Eng	73	71	69	74	287	£1620
	Craig PARRY	Aus	70	73	74	70	287	£1620
	Paul KENT	Eng	71	72	70	74	287	£1620
	Denis DURNIAN	Eng	71	70	76	70	287	£1620
	Ross DRUMMOND	Scot	71	71	74	71	287	£1620
50	Armando SAAVEDRA	Arg	69	71	76	72	288	£1380
	Hugh BAIOCCHI	SA	72	71	71	74	288	£1380
	Keith WATERS	Eng	70	73	70	75	288	£1380
53	Gordon J BRAND	Eng	71	72	70	76	289	£1170
	Andrew SHERBORNE	Eng	72	72	71	74	289	£1170
	Peter McWHINNEY	Aus	74	70	71	74	289	£1170
	John MORGAN	Eng	72	70	72	75	289	£1170
57	Magnus PERSSON	Swe	74	70	73	73	290	£1020
58	Stephen McALLISTER	Scot	68	74	74	75	291	£930
	Ken BROWN	Scot	75	70	70	76	291	£930
	Greg J TURNER	NZ	73	72	75	71	291	£930
61	Philip PARKIN	Wal	73	71	71	77	292	£855
	Stephen BENNETT	Eng	73	71	73	75	292	£855
63	Gavin LEVENSON	SA	75	69	72	77	293	£795
	Ian YOUNG	Scot	65	74	73	81	293	£795
65	Paul WAY	Eng	71	73	75	75	294	£750
66	Juan ANGLADA	Sp	76	69	74	76	295	£300
67	Lyndsay STEPHEN	Aus	74	68	76	79	297	£297
	Neil COLES	Eng	72	73	75	77	297	£297
69	Mats LANNER	Swe	73	72	77	76	298	£294

PARRY
thrusts to the forefront

IT WAS ONLY A MATTER OF TIME BEFORE AUSTRALIA'S CRAIG PARRY RECORDED HIS FIRST VICTORY ON THE VOLVO TOUR BUT THE BREAKTHROUGH CAME THE HARD WAY, AFTER A PLAY-OFF WITH IAN WOOSNAM AT MOOR PARK

Sandy Lyle's bunker shot at the 72nd hole of the 1988 US Masters and the putt that followed prompted the Americans to coin a new golfing phrase. A 'Big Sandy' became their description for holing out in two from a fairway trap.

Craig Parry managed the said 'Big Sandy' at the 72nd hole of the Wang Four Stars at Moor Park. It brought him level with Ian Woosnam and the 23-year-old Australian went on to break his European duck with another birdie when the pair fought out a sudden death play-off.

This was no new face suddenly finding himself in the winner's enclosure, though. In 1987, his second full year as a professional, Parry took the New South Wales Open, South Australia PGA and Canadian TPC titles. He was also only a stroke away from being involved in a play-off at the 1988 Italian Open and Benson and Hedges International and just a fortnight earlier had finished third behind Nick Faldo and Woosnam at the Volvo PGA championship at Wentworth.

As 'Big Sandys' go, Parry's was pretty dramatic. His drive down the 431-yard last caught the edge of the bunker and to play his five-iron second he had to stand with one leg in and one out. Making perfect contact, the ball stopped 15 feet left of the flagstick and the putt dived into the hole. Thus the man from Sunshine, Victoria, birdied three of the last four holes to catch Woosnam on the 15 under par total of 273. His two-putt four on the first extra hole, the 478-yard 17th, was something that the diminutive Welshman just could not match.

Coincidentally, and probably uniquely, he was one of three Australians to win on the same day. Graham Marsh, the player to whom Parry owes most for his early coaching, triumphed in Japan and Wayne Grady captured the Westchester Classic, the last tournament before the US Open.

Woosnam, sponsored by Wang, was the pre-tournament favourite in the absence of man-of-the-moment Faldo and defending champion Rodger Davis, out of action with shoulder trouble. Woosnam looked to be justifying that tag when, following rounds of 67, 72 and 68, he moved from three behind leader Parry into a two-stroke advantage with an outward 32 on the final day. A sixth birdie came when he struck an eight-iron to within 18 inches of the cup on the 13th, but then Woosnam, understandably, was tempted by golf's first £1 million hole-in-one prize — half for the player and half for charity.

The jackpot on offer (only on the Sunday) at the 184-yard 14th in front of the former stately home had nearly been claimed by Australian Brett Ogle and Ireland's Des Smyth, both a foot short, and by American Peter Teravainen, whose tee shot ran over the hole and stopped two feet behind. Woosnam did not even sniff it. He caught the guarding bunker and could do no better than a four. The closing stretch yielded only one more birdie and he knew that might not be enough.

Stoke's Dave Gilford seemed the most likely threat at that moment. Two eagles on the front nine had been cancelled out by four bogies but the 23-year-old, second in the Tenerife Open at the start of the season, then started for home with four birdies in six holes to improve to 15 under.

Up ahead Woosnam had finished on that total and another Australian, Mike Harwood had failed with a 15-footer that would have put him on the same mark. Parry trailed by two with two to play, yet whereas he went four-three, Gilford could only manage five-five, missing the green at the last and leaving his chip 12 feet short.

Harwood, joint third for the second week running, had set the opening day pace with his six-under-par total of 66 but at halfway, the leader was Hertfordshire's David Williams with two successive 68s, one better than a

Telly Savalas tries to get to grips with a pitch, top. The Red Devils swoop in on the prize-giving, above

back-to-health David Jones (he caught a chest infection in Dubai) and a back-to-form Mike McLean.

David Williams had five birdies in this third round 71, but this was the day on which the eagles were flying. Sam Torrance had one in a 64 that was only one outside the composite course record, Woosnam had two, Stephen Bennett had two and Parry had two — the first courtesy of a 30-yard putt on the third and the second at the 17th following on the heels of three birdies in a row.

That took the Australian one ahead with 18 holes to play and the finishing stretch was to be fruitful again, 24 hours later. The player known as 'Popeye' because of his powerful forearms had indeed gone from strength to strength: not on spinach, but on raw talent.

Parry displayed that in large measure in the 'golf and fun' atmosphere of a celebrity pro-am (Kenny Dalglish succeeded Jimmy Tarbuck as the amateur winner) that puts special demands on a player's powers of concentration.

Tournament promoter Bill Mullins and partner Ian Woosnam consider their next move

Christopher Lee cleans up his act

Scenic view of 14th green and clubhouse

Mizuno's Barry Willet adjusts Philip Walton's club

Parry and Woosnam battle out the play-off

COURSE: MOOR PARK, RICKMANSWORTH | **YARDAGE: 6,855** | **PAR: 72**

POS	NAME	CTRY	1	2	3	4	TOTAL	PRIZE MONEY
1	Craig PARRY	Aus	67	71	66	69	273	£32000
2	Ian WOOSNAM	Wal	67	72	68	66	273	£21900
3	David GILFORD	Eng	71	69	65	69	274	£11150
	Mike HARWOOD	Aus	66	72	67	69	274	£11150
5	Barry LANE	Eng	72	68	68	68	276	£7650
	Gordon BRAND Jnr	Scot	72	67	72	65	276	£7650
7	Jerry ANDERSON	Can	70	69	69	69	277	£5800
8	Brian MARCHBANK	Scot	73	69	67	69	278	£3818
	Peter SENIOR	Aus	72	67	68	71	278	£3818
	Bob SHEARER	Aus	69	72	65	72	278	£3818
	Jeff HAWKES	SA	71	70	66	71	278	£3818
	Ross McFARLANE	Eng	68	74	67	69	278	£3818
13	Michael McLEAN	Eng	67	70	73	69	279	£2650
	Anders SORENSEN	Den	73	67	67	72	279	£2650
	Sam TORRANCE	Scot	74	72	64	69	279	£2650
16	Denis DURNIAN	Eng	69	70	68	73	280	£2273
	Michael KING	Eng	75	72	66	67	280	£2273
	Andrew CHANDLER	Eng	69	71	72	68	280	£2273
	Des SMYTH	Ire	73	69	67	71	280	£2273
	David WILLIAMS	Eng	68	68	71	73	280	£2273
	Peter MITCHELL	Eng	70	75	67	68	280	£2273
22	Neil HANSEN	Eng	70	73	68	70	281	£1877
	Mark ROE	Eng	72	70	68	71	281	£1877
	Tommy HORTON	Eng	68	73	71	69	281	£1877
	Paul CURRY	Eng	71	72	69	69	281	£1877
26	Colin MONTGOMERIE	Scot	73	68	72	69	282	£1608
	Jose Maria CANIZARES	Sp	73	70	68	71	282	£1608
	John BLAND	SA	71	71	74	66	282	£1608
	Stephen BENNETT	Eng	71	69	67	75	282	£1608
	Ossie MOORE	Aus	71	73	71	67	282	£1608
	Tony CHARNLEY	Eng	72	70	69	71	282	£1608
	Frank NOBILO	NZ	70	70	70	72	282	£1608
33	Roger CHAPMAN	Eng	72	71	69	71	283	£1380
	Bill MALLEY	USA	70	70	73	70	283	£1380
	Peter FOWLER	Aus	72	72	68	71	283	£1380
	Michael ALLEN	USA	71	74	68	70	283	£1380
37	David FEHERTY	N.Ire	69	72	69	74	284	£1200
	Eamonn DARCY	Ire	72	72	72	68	284	£1200
	Armando SAAVEDRA	Arg	75	68	70	71	284	£1200
	Glenn RALPH	Eng	73	68	74	69	284	£1200
	Bernard GALLACHER	Scot	73	71	68	72	284	£1200
42	Ian MOSEY	Eng	70	75	67	73	285	£965
	Bob E SMITH	USA	71	72	72	70	285	£965
	Stephen McALLISTER	Scot	73	71	72	69	285	£965
	Ian YOUNG	Scot	75	66	70	74	285	£965
	Martin POXON	Eng	70	74	67	74	285	£965
	Paul BROADHURST	Eng	71	68	75	71	285	£965
	Brian WAITES	Eng	69	72	70	74	285	£965
	David JONES	N. Ire	72	65	75	73	285	£965
50	Brian BARNES	Scot	70	74	70	72	286	£820
	Gavin LEVENSON	SA	73	74	72	67	286	£820
	Ron COMMANS	USA	75	72	70	69	286	£820
	Jose RIVERO	Sp	71	75	70	70	286	£820
	Philip HARRISON	Eng	71	72	71	72	286	£820
55	John JACOBS	USA	73	74	68	72	287	£700
	Noel RATCLIFFE	Aus	71	72	73	71	287	£700
	Steven BOTTOMLEY	Eng	72	72	72	71	287	£700
	Jimmy HEGGERTY	N.Ire	70	74	71	72	287	£700
	David A RUSSELL	Eng	76	70	72	69	287	£700
	Hugh BAIOCCHI	SA	71	72	72	72	287	£700
	Mike SMITH	USA	73	70	70	74	287	£700
62	John MORGAN	Eng	73	75	70	70	288	£590
	Lyndsay STEPHEN	Aus	73	69	74	72	288	£590
	Mike CLAYTON	Aus	77	70	70	71	288	£590
	Bill LONGMUIR	Scot	71	73	76	68	288	£590
66	Richard BOXALL	Eng	74	69	68	79	290	£532
	Ross DRUMMOND	Scot	78	70	72	70	290	£532
	Mark MOULAND	Wal	74	73	72	71	290	£532
	Brett OGLE	Aus	73	74	73	70	290	£532
	Peter TERAVAINEN	USA	72	74	75	69	290	£532
	David WHELAND	Eng	76	70	73	71	290	£532
	Carl MASON	Eng	72	70	74	74	290	£532
	David ARMOR	Eng	73	73	71	73	290	£532
74	Vijay SINGH	Fij	72	72	75	72	291	£513
	Philip WALTON	Ire	70	76	73	72	291	£513
	John O'LEARY	Ire	72	76	69	74	291	£513
77	Keith WATERS	Eng	75	71	71	75	292	£500

GOLF PLUS
NM English Open

JAMES
gets first in English

With the biggest names on duty at the US Open there was an opportunity for some of the seasoned players to step into the limelight at The Belfry.

And very important limelight it was too, for the dominating influence throughout a week of soaring temperatures was the prospect of the battle for Sam Ryder's elegant gold chalice three months away. European captain Tony Jacklin was on hand to check out the course, the facilities and maybe pencil in a few names for selectorial consideration. Jacklin had shown his preference for choosing 'horses for courses' when he picked Jose Rivero for the 1985 contest after the Spaniard won over the Brabazon course the previous year. So the winner of the second staging of the English Open Championship, now under the auspices of NM Financial management, would make a very strong claim for a place in the side, even if he failed to gain one automatically. Of course, with all this Ryder Cup jostling, the most likely outcome of the tournament was that someone from the non-aligned countries would sneak in and grab the first prize of £41,660.

And it was one of those players who made the first move. South Africa's Jeff Hawkes, who runs a boat building business in his native land, launched a seven-birdie assault, offset by two bogeys, for a round of 67 and then announced that he no longer had a reactive mind. Kipling actually put it better with his advice to treat those twin imposters of triumph and disaster just the same. But Hawkes' literary guidance came from the less elegant L. Ron Hubbard, of Scientology fame. Two years ago Hawkes read

IN A WEEK OF BLAZING SUNSHINE AT THE BELFRY, MARK JAMES NOTCHED UP HIS THIRD WIN OF THE SEASON AND BOOKED HIMSELF A RETURN TICKET TO THE SAME VENUE IN SEPTEMBER

Hubbard's book on dianetics and resolved to eliminate any negative thoughts that might follow a poor shot.

It was a good day for growing grass and the greens became slower and slower. This did not prevent Craig Parry and Sam Torrance holing a rash of putts: Parry was still riding the crest of his victory the previous week and Torrance supported his score with his extra long putter which could easily double as a crutch. They were both round in 66, a score matched later in the day by Denmark's Steen Tinning.

Defending champion Howard Clark was round in 71 and had a few things to say about the inconsistent growth of the fringes round the greens, as he felt the grass was too long and if it was left like that for the Ryder Cup it would be playing into the Americans' hands. Tony Jacklin agreed and it appeared there wouldn't be any fringe benefits for the Americans in September. There was quite enough other trouble to contend with on a course made hard and fast by the unrelenting sunshine. One unfortunate bounce could lead to disaster, as Gordon Brand Junior discovered on the 17th during the first round when his tee shot kicked away into waist-high rough. He needed seven blows to put the ball back on the fairway and finished with an 11.

A similar fate befell Torrance in the second round when he took an eight on the 15th after tangling with the rough but he was able to maintain close order with half-way leader Hawkes who added a 71 after scrambling round. Ronan Rafferty also joined Torrance, a stroke behind Hawkes after a 67, the best round of a trouble-strewn day.

Mention the 1985 Ryder Cup and one instinctively thinks of Torrance's final putt to seal victory; mention the 1987 contest and the image is of Eamonn Darcy holing a fiendish putt on the 18th to score a vital point. As fate would have it, the two of them finished the day with only a stroke separating them. Torrance put together a 70 with another final hole birdie, while Darcy, who holds the course record of 63, took over the lead with a 67 helped by perhaps the ugliest putter yet devised by man. Darcy referred to this ill-formed lump of metal on the end of a shaft as his 'branding iron' and he certainly made his mark with it.

There were no less than 17 players within five strokes of the lead at the start of the final round so it was anybody's title. From this melee, Mark James emerged as the player with the coolest hand. His first three rounds (72-70-69) had been progressively lower and the man who had won twice in the season already kept his score running with single putts on five consecutive greens, two of them birdies. Ahead of him Parry was racing through the field with a 67 to set the target at eight under par but James, with two further birdies at the 15th and 17th, overhauled the Australian and waited to see if anyone could catch him. Darcy had the most realistic chance and after birdies at the 15th and 17th, he arrived at the final hole needing a birdie to tie. Two shots left him 35 feet from the hole and, brandishing his branding-iron, he left the bail agonisingly poised on the edge of the hole.

James' victory vaulted him to the top of the Volvo Order of Merit. The last time he occupied such exalted heights was after the 1983 Tunisian Open which, as he pointed out with deadpan humour, happened to be the first event of that season. He also made himself a certainty for the Ryder Cup team, having last played in 1981.

The key to his victory? Well, the old adage of 'beware the suffering golfer' applied once again. As a chronic hay-fever sufferer, James had been taking anti-histamine eye-drops every night. The result was a clear head in an extremely tight finish.

Roger Chapman, left, and Sam Torrance, both shot lowest rounds of 66

Gordon Brand Jnr
in an English
setting

Eamonn Darcy pitches to the 10th

Playing it cool down by the lake

Peter Baker and Bob Torrance discuss club selection

Angular pose from Jeff Hawkes after missed putt

Young Master Torrance is up in arms

The Bakers, the Marchbanks and the Jacklins set off to raise money for Birdies and Babes

Sam Torrance in re-run of 1985 Ryder Cup gesture as he birdies the final hole

COURSE: THE BELFRY, BRABAZON COURSE — YARDAGE: 7,202 — PAR: 72

POS	NAME	CTRY	1	2	3	4	TOTAL	PRIZE MONEY
1	Mark JAMES	Eng	72	70	69	68	279	£41660
2	Eamonn DARCY	Ire	70	71	67	72	280	£18636
	Craig PARRY	Aus	66	74	73	67	280	£18636
	Sam TORRANCE	Scot	66	73	70	71	280	£18636
5	Bryan NORTON	USA	74	70	67	71	282	£9675
	John BLAND	SA	69	70	70	73	282	£9675
7	Martin POXON	Eng	69	72	69	73	283	£6450
	Peter TERAVAINEN	USA	71	75	69	68	283	£6450
	Christy O'CONNOR Jnr	Ire	71	73	68	71	283	£6450
10	Jose DAVILA	Sp	68	75	73	68	284	£4235
	Ronan RAFFERTY	N.Ire	72	67	73	72	284	£4235
	Mats LANNER	Swe	72	71	69	72	284	£4235
	Jeff HAWKES	SA	67	71	73	73	284	£4235
	Roger CHAPMAN	Eng	73	72	73	66	284	£4235
	Steen TINNING	Den	66	78	71	69	284	£4235
	Russell CLAYDON (AM)	Eng	72	71	71	70	284	–
16	Jean VAN DE VELDE	Fr	73	70	72	70	285	£3190
	Howard CLARK	Eng	71	75	68	71	285	£3190
	Peter MITCHELL	Eng	74	71	70	70	285	£3190
	Mark DAVIS	Eng	71	69	71	74	285	£3190
	Bill MALLEY	USA	71	72	73	69	285	£3190
	Mark MOULAND	Wal	68	74	69	74	285	£3190
22	Jose-Maria CANIZARES	Sp	71	74	67	74	286	£2700
	Kevin DICKENS	Eng	70	71	72	73	286	£2700
	Brian EVANS	Eng	71	70	71	74	286	£2700
	Alberto BINAGHI	It	74	71	72	69	286	£2700
	Tony JOHNSTONE	Eng	72	72	70	72	286	£2700
27	Tony CHARNLEY	Eng	72	69	73	73	287	£2253
	Ossie MOORE	Aus	70	73	73	71	287	£2253
	David FEHERTY	N.Ire	71	75	69	72	287	£2253
	Keith WATERS	Eng	68	72	74	73	287	£2253
	Manuel PINERO	Sp	73	70	72	72	287	£2253
	Ken BROWN	Scot	71	69	70	77	287	£2253
	Miguel Angel MARTIN	Sp	74	68	74	71	287	£2253
34	Barry LANE	Eng	71	74	70	73	288	£1850
	Ross McFARLANE	Eng	73	71	75	69	288	£1850
	Brian MARCHBANK	Scot	71	74	69	74	288	£1850
	Frank NOBILO	NZ	72	71	70	75	288	£1850
	David RAY	Eng	72	70	74	72	288	£1850
	Peter SENIOR	Aus	74	71	72	71	288	£1850
	Richard BOXALL	Eng	75	70	70	73	288	£1850
41	Michael McLEAN	Eng	72	71	73	73	289	£1600
	David WILLIAMS	Eng	71	73	74	71	289	£1600
	Mark ROE	Eng	70	71	73	75	289	£1600
44	Carl MASON	Eng	74	70	77	69	290	£1425
	Paul HOAD	Eng	71	70	75	74	290	£1425
	Mike SMITH	USA	71	72	74	73	290	£1425
	David A RUSSELL	Eng	75	70	72	73	290	£1425
48	Ross DRUMMOND	Scot	74	71	72	74	291	£1300
49	Ove SELLBERG	Swe	71	73	73	75	292	£1250
50	Brian BARNES	Scot	74	69	73	77	293	£1000
	Bernard GALLACHER	Scot	69	74	72	78	293	£1000
	Bob E SMITH	USA	70	73	75	75	293	£1000
	Robert LEE	Eng	73	72	74	74	293	£1000
	David GILFORD	Eng	73	73	70	77	293	£1000
	Neil HANSEN	Eng	69	72	77	75	293	£1000
	David JONES	N.Ire	70	76	73	74	293	£1000
	Jamie HOWELL	USA	72	74	72	75	293	£1000
	Juan ROSA	Sp	72	68	79	74	293	£1000
59	Wayne STEPHENS	Eng	72	74	74	74	294	£737
	Denis DURNIAN	Eng	74	71	71	78	294	£737
	Anders SORENSEN	Den	74	72	72	76	294	£737
	Mike MILLER	Scot	72	73	77	72	294	£737
	Eoghan O'CONNELL (AM)	Ire	73	70	75	76	294	–
	Stephen DODD (AM)	Eng	72	73	72	78	295	–
63	Stehen HAMILL	N.Ire	75	71	75	75	296	£650
	Marc PENDARIES	Fr	75	69	73	79	296	£650
	Mike CLAYTON	Aus	72	74	74	76	296	£650
66	Marc FARRY	Fr	75	70	78	74	297	£249
	Andrew MURRAY	Eng	72	74	77	74	297	£249
68	Mariano APARICIO	Sp	72	72	74	80	298	£246

WOOSNAM *spoils the party*

*i*t was not as if there was the slightest sense of ungraciousness or begrudgement. Yet when the excitement had died and it began to rain, it was as if tears of sorrow were being spilled for Philip Walton, pipped in a gallant bid to beat Ian Woosnam for the Carrolls Irish Open title in his own backyard.

The long list of great players—defending champion Woosnam included—that have graced the Irish Open down the years are well aware that the Irish public at Portmarnock, far from being biased, are warm and receptive to the deeds of the international visitors. Woosnam himself had savoured that refined enthusiasm the previous year when he conquered the windswept links to coast to a seven stroke victory. So he could readily understand that his brilliantly played birdie three at the first play-off hole—the 18th—was a heartbreak that hapless Walton shared with 30,000 other devastated souls who had willed the local hero in his gallant effort to land the title for Ireland.

Perceptively, for a man with deep-rooted nationalist feelings himself, Welshman Woosnam acknowledged the sensitivity of it all. And the manner in which he publicly delivered consoling words of compensation and encouragement for Walton further endeared him to the locals, whose hearts, in any event, he had won the previous year. 'I accept that the crowds were rooting for the home player—it would be exactly the same in Wales with me. Today, I felt that 10 people clapped for me, but that 10,000 were behind Philip. Everyone wanted an Irishman to win and who could blame them? My only fear was that I would be trampled upon in the excitement of it all'' he said.

THE SCENE WAS SET FOR A FAMOUS IRISH VICTORY AS PHILIP WALTON LED THE WAY AT PORTMARNOCK BUT THEN DEFENDING CHAMPION IAN WOOSNAM CAME ALONG AND FOILED THE CELEBRATION

Mind you, Woosnam had pinpointed a problem because such was the euphoria of the occasion that overstretched stewards, backed up by Gardai, were struggling to maintain control of the record numbers who flocked to the sun-bathed links. It is proudly contended that, other than the Open Championship itself, the biggest collection of golf fans assemble for the annual Carrolls Irish Open.

Of course, the high standards in entertainment value had been set from the start, and from an unlikely quarter: Sandy Lyle. In the doldrums after a succession of missed cuts, the amiable Lyle was delighted to discover an Irish solution when an inspired performance of eight birdies, no bogeys gave him a new course record 64. It finally shattered the barrier of 65 that had first been scored by Gary Player nearly 30 years earlier.

Although Lyle set a scorching pace, he ended up with just a shot to spare from Bill Malley, a Californian adding spice to a great day for the Irish by announcing that his grandparents hail from the 'Old Sod'. It was a tonic for the home brigade as Ronan Rafferty fired 67; amateur Eoghan O'Connell, Christy O'Connor Junior and Philip Walton shot 68, and David Jones and John McHenry joined the sub-70 shooters with 69 apiece. It was interesting to hear Walton reveal that he had passed up the previous week's NM English Open at The Belfry so that he could stay at home in Malahide, a village a mere drive and pitch from the Portmarnock course, 'so that I could relax, have a few beers with the boys, and a lesson from my coach Bob Torrance.'

He certainly hit upon a successful formula because although the fickle weather may have ever so slightly moved the goalposts for the second round (the donning of extra sweaters and movement on the clubhouse Beaufort scale was evidence of a toughening in conditions compared to the sunshine of the previous day) local boy Walton made good with a three-under-par 69 for a two round tally of seven under par 137. Significantly, too, the tenacious Woosnam, desperate to improve upon his runners-up place in the US Open immediately before arriving at Portmarnock, made his move with 67. The pair of them shared the halfway lead with Sandy Lyle, who slipped from his trail-blazing 64 of Thursday to what he described as a 'scruffy' 73.

Perhaps it was in anticipation of Walton bridging the frustrating gap of seven years since John O'Leary last won the title for Ireland, but it was certainly a hot time in Dublin town on Saturday night when the 26-year-old repeated that 69 in the third round to open up a clear two shots lead at 10 under par 206. A double birdie finish to that third round had put the two telling shots between Walton and champion Woosnam, who had taken 71. But a further measure of the merit of the present crop of Irish professionals is that after Mark McNulty on 209, came Ronan Rafferty, Christy O'Connor Junior and Eamonn Darcy, with Mark Davis of England, all on 210, and there was further home brigade back-up with Des Smyth on 211.

As events unfolded amid the quite incredible atmosphere the next day—many impatient followers elected to abandon their cars on the approach roads for fear of traffic chaos and take the gamble of getting across the muddy Estuary in face of the incoming tide. Walton defiantly kept the Irish tricolour flying as the battle narrowed down to a match-play-like contest with the champion. They were to eventually finish four shots clear of Brett Ogle, Rafferty and Mark McNulty.

It had been a cat and mouse confrontation between the last two men left on the crowded course. An indication of the mammoth task facing Walton was provided by the manner in

Langer makes light of heavy rough

Woosnam's tee shot to the 15th on the last day

Spectators from across the water

Youngster sports appropriate hat

Eamonn Darcy drives from the 13th

Leading amateur and Walker Cup hero Eoghan O'Connell

which Woosnam negotiated the 514-yard, par five 16th hole. First he smacked a huge drive, then, drawing gasps of disbelief from the crowds, he allied brawn to brilliance when he pulled out the driver for a second time and, off an uphill lie, sent the ball to within 15 feet of the hole.

Walton failed to match his opponent's effort by pulling a metal three-wood into a bunker and then being incapable of rescuing himself by getting down in two more. Woosnam had made a decisive breakthrough with the lead intact and the odds were suddenly stacked against Ireland's pride, joy and last remaining hope.

Then came the final twist. Woosnam, having shot five birdies and only two bogeys, provided his grateful foe with an unexpected second bite at the cherry when he stumbled with a bogey five, his nine iron approach shot to the 18th green coming up on the apron from where he chipped seven feet past the hole and missed the return. His two under par 70 and Walton's 72 thus had erased the overnight difference between the pair—and it was pistols drawn again as the protagonists returned to the 18th tee to recommence the battle in sudden-death.

The expectant crowds lining the fairway of the 417-yard 18th hole chosen for the shoot out, and the many thousands more riveted to their precious seats that ringed the green, were hushed in anticipation. Two good drives from two capable men gave no advantage. Walton played first and the partisan crowd thrilled to the controlled flight of his soundly-played pitching wedge as the ball was directed to within 25 feet of the hole. Then it was

Peter McWhinney has his footsteps dogged

Woosnam's turn. He had driven to within 93 yards of the green, representing a smack of 324 yards. In golfing parlance he had a 'flick with a wedge' and, with typical dexterity, he brilliantly regained the initiative as he feathered his second shot 12 feet from the hole.

Far beyond the confines of Portmarnock, many an Irishman held his breath tightly. But the audible sigh that broke the silence confirmed that Walton's birdie putt had slipped by and the dream that had endured for 72 holes was shattered in the unscheduled epilogue, when little Ian Woosnam, the small man in the fight, landed the final and killing blow by holing his birdie putt for victory.

Victor and vanquished, Woosnam and Walton

Massive home support behind Philip Walton

Big screen star Walton

Last hole charge engulfs Walton

A pair of happy Woosnams

COURSE: PORTMARNOCK, DUBLIN **YARDAGE: 7,102** **PAR: 72**

POS	NAME	CTRY	1	2	3	4	TOTAL	PRIZE MONEY
1	Ian WOOSNAM	Wal	70	67	71	70	278	£43782
2	Philip WALTON	Ire	68	69	69	72	278	£29159
3	Brett OGLE	Aus	69	69	74	70	282	£13566
	Ronan RAFFERTY	N Ire	67	71	72	72	282	£13566
	Mark McNULTY	Zim	61	76	71	73	282	£13566
6	Sam TORRANCE	Scot	71	70	72	70	282	£7381
	Jose Maria OLAZABAL	Sp	69	70	73	71	283	£7381
	Mark DAVIS	Eng	73	71	66	73	283	£7381
	Peter McWHINNEY	Aus	70	68	73	72	283	£7381
10	Eamonn DARCY	Ire	71	70	69	74	284	£5253
11	Bob E SMITH	USA	69	71	73	72	285	£4527
	Christy O'CONNOR Jnr	Ire	68	71	71	75	285	£4527
	Peter SENIOR	Aus	69	70	76	71	285	£4527
14	Mark ROE	Eng	73	72	70	71	286	£4019
15	Mark MOULAND	Wal	67	73	73	74	287	£3426
	Ossie MOORE	Aus	68	74	75	70	287	£3426
	Mike MILLER	Scot	71	70	75	71	287	£3426
	Bill LONGMUIR	Scot	69	72	72	74	287	£3426
	Sandy LYLE	Scot	64	73	74	76	287	£3426
	Martin SLUDDS	Ire	73	72	69	73	287	£3426
	Ove SELLBERG	Swe	69	72	72	74	287	£3426
22	Manuel PINERO	Sp	70	73	70	75	288	£2797
	Wayne RILEY	Aus	69	72	74	73	288	£2797
	Luis CARBONETTI	Arg	73	71	68	76	288	£2797
	Howard CLARK	Eng	69	70	74	75	288	£2797
	Des SMYTH	Ire	71	72	68	77	288	£2797
	Martin POXON	Eng	69	71	72	76	288	£2797
28	Brian MARCHBANK	Scot	72	71	75	71	289	£2443
	Bernhard LANGER	W.Ger	73	69	70	77	289	£2443
	Gordon BRAND Jnr	Scot	69	71	74	75	289	£2443
31	Christy O'CONNOR	Ire	72	72	70	76	290	£2186
	Magnus JONSSON	Swe	72	69	77	72	290	£2186
	Lyndsay STEPHEN	Aus	71	71	73	75	290	£2186
	Lee JONES	Eng	73	69	73	75	290	£2186
35	Magnus PERSSON	Swe	70	75	73	73	291	£1943
	Richard BOXALL	Eng	69	70	75	77	291	£1943
	Jimmy HEGGARTY	N.Ire	72	73	70	76	291	£1943
	Frank NOBILO	NZ	73	72	71	75	291	£1943
	Wayne STEPHENS	Eng	69	69	76	77	291	£1943
40	David FEHERTY	N.Ire	72	71	74	75	292	£1707
	Sandy STEPHEN	Scot	71	69	74	78	292	£1707
	Andrew CHANDLER	Eng	71	74	70	77	292	£1707
	Kevin DICKENS	Eng	74	68	74	76	292	£1707
44	Paul CARRIGILL	Eng	70	72	73	78	293	£1471
	Jim THORPE	USA	73	71	75	74	293	£1471
	Paul BROADHURST	Eng	72	73	73	75	293	£1471
	David JONES	N.Ire	69	73	71	80	293	£1471
	Andrew SHERBORNE	Eng	72	72	72	77	293	£1471
49	John MORGAN	Eng	73	72	72	77	294	£1208
	David A RUSSELL	Eng	73	72	71	78	294	£1208
	John McHENRY	Ire	69	73	75	77	294	£1208
	Barry LANE	Eng	72	72	74	76	294	£1208
	Bill MALLEY	USA	65	74	78	77	294	£1208
54	Grant TURNER	Eng	71	74	74	76	295	£971
	Jean VAN DE VELDE	Fr	72	70	73	80	295	£971
	John O'LEARY	Ire	74	69	73	79	295	£971
	Philip PARKIN	Wal	72	73	74	76	295	£971
	Eoghan O'CONNELL (AM)	Ire	72	68	75	75	77	295	–
58	Noel RATCLIFFE	Aus	72	71	80	73	296	£801
	Tom WEISKOPF	USA	71	73	75	77	296	£801
	Brendan MCGOVERN	Ire	71	74	73	78	296	£801
	John BLAND	SA	70	69	77	80	296	£801
62	Mike SMITH	USA	72	73	71	81	297	£709
	Greg J TURNER	NZ	71	74	74	78	297	£709
	Ross McFARLANE	Eng	73	71	77	76	297	£709
65	Miguel Angel JIMENEZ	Sp	73	70	76	79	298	£656
66	Leif HEDERSTROM	Swe	72	72	74	81	299	£261
	David WILLIAMS	Eng	72	73	73	81	299	£261
68	Miguel Angel MARTIN	Sp	72	70	79	79	300	£258

PEUGEOT
FRENCH
OPEN

FOUR

out of four for Faldo

Everything was right for Seve Ballesteros. US Tour Commissioner Deane Beman had lifted a five-year-old burden from his shoulders, his swing was showing the glorious rhythm which won the Open Championship at Lytham and a record-equalling fifth Peugeot French Open seemed a formality.

Only one thing was wrong — Nick Faldo was among his 146 rivals. Faldo was on a high and the peak his game had reached proved too much even for a man possessing the rich talent of Severiano Ballesteros. The Spaniard wasn't the only obstacle between Faldo and yet another Volvo PGA European Tour triumph. Ian Woosnam, Bernhard Langer, Jose-Maria Olazabal and the full strength of European golf erected the barricades, but Faldo shattered their defences into fragments of frustration with an exhilarating victory which gave him a Tour record of played four, won four.

This included his final appearance of 1988 at the Volvo Masters at Valderrama when Ballesteros was again unable to break down the fortress Faldo had built around his game. Then the Spaniard had to be content with second place, while at Chantilly he slid into a share of 12th place with 277 behind Faldo's winning seven-under-par 273. Yet on Friday evening the punters had been figuring the odds on Ballesteros' winning margin after he had taken the half-way lead with a new professional course record of 64, with Faldo safely back in the pack after two opening rounds of 70. Ballesteros was at peace with himself and the world after word had filtered through that Deane Beman had finally acceded to his request to cut the minimum tournament rule from 15 to 12. This, of course, would also benefit Faldo, Langer and the absent Sandy Lyle, but it meant far more to Ballesteros, who had won this concession and looked primed to win the battle of Chantilly, insisting the 'old feeling' he had had just before his Open victory at Lytham a year earlier was back, with Aubrey Boomer's five French Open titles his target.

INCLUDING THE VOLVO MASTERS AT THE END OF THE 1988 SEASON, NICK FALDO HAD WON ON EACH OF HIS LAST THREE TOUR APPEARANCES AND AT CHANTILLY HE MADE IT FOUR

But both the experts and Ballesteros had dismissed Faldo too lightly and the US Masters Champion blasted back into contention with a third round 64 which left him just two strokes behind Ulsterman Ronan Rafferty. Ballesteros, with a 71, was still in the hunt but as the final round unfolded he became a supporting act with Rafferty, Faldo, Langer, Mark Roe and Hugh Baiocchi taking centre stage.

Rafferty, heading the Volvo Order of Merit after winning the Italian Open and completing eight top-seven finishes, birdied the second hole from 12ft to move three ahead. It gave him an identical cushion to that which comforted Tom Kite in the US Open a fortnight earlier but, like Kite, he plummeted to earth with back-to-back double bogey sixes as he turned for home. Rafferty failed to find the fairway at the tenth and drove into a bush at the 11th.

This gave Faldo the lead for the first time in the Championship but Rafferty's downfall had breathed fresh life into the chasing pack — Langer burst through with a 66 to set a six-under-par target of 274. The situation called for a cool head and ice-man Faldo fitted the bill superbly — twice saving par when a bogey beckoned before conjuring a winning birdie from a bunker alongside the 18th green. It was a shot every weekend golfer dreads, his ball on an upslope which meant Faldo planting his left foot on the top of the bunker. He executed the shot brilliantly: the ball stopped just a yard short of the flag and the putt dropped to complete a successful defence of the title.

Faldo was more than gracious in victory, offering commiserations to Rafferty and gratitude to his caddie Andy Prodger. 'I felt for Ronan,' he said. 'The pressure really built up mid-way through the round. He played a couple of wayward shots and paid the penalty

Faldo clinches victory from sand on the last hole

for them. I dropped a shot at the ninth and tenth holes and that killed my confidence. It was then that Prodger really earned his corn. If I owe this win to anybody, it is to him. He kept encouraging me all the way home and it was his tip to strengthen my right-hand grip on the putter which made all the difference.'

It was a considerable relief to his rivals that Faldo took the following week off and he couldn't help grinning: 'Maybe they will club together and buy me a new fishing rod to get me off the Tour for a while.'

The tournament which had ended with drama had begun on a tragic note when two well-known caddies — Bill 'Yorkie' Brown and David 'Captain' Kirk — were killed in a car smash on their way to Paris. A wreath, depicting a golf club and ball, stood on the first tee throughout the Championship and all the players readily agreed to donate the £5,000 pro-am money to a trust for their dependants, a fund which would be swelled by another £10,000 from the Monte Carlo and Bell's Scottish Open pro-ams while Ballesteros, himself a former caddie, agreed to donate all proceeds from a special clinic held during the Open Championship.

Are you sitting comfortably?

Ballesteros chews up the course

Ronan Rafferty faltered in the final round

Faldo and final green scene at Chantilly

Bernhard Langer: 'How do I get out of that!'

Palmer-like finish for Ballesteros

Rafferty keeps track of his premier investments

Fruity purchase for Faldo at the counter

'In my day golfers only came up to here!'

COURSE: CHANTILLY, PARIS | YARDAGE: 7,016 | PAR: 70

POS	NAME	CTRY	1	2	3	4	TOTAL	PRIZE MONEY
1	Nick FALDO	Eng	70	70	64	69	273	£52233
2	Hugh BAIOCCHI	SA	69	67	68	70	274	£23359
	Mark ROE	Eng	69	68	67	70	274	£23359
	Bernhard LANGER	W.Ger	70	67	71	66	274	£23359
5	Mark JAMES	Eng	70	70	66	69	275	£10368
	Ian WOOSNAM	Wal	67	70	69	69	275	£10368
	Mike HARWOOD	Aus	68	68	69	70	275	£10368
	Philip PARKIN	Wal	71	68	72	64	275	£10368
9	Ronan RAFFERTY	N.Ire	69	67	66	74	276	£6351
	Mark McNULTY	Zim	70	70	70	66	276	£6351
	Gordon BRAND Jnr	Scot	69	67	69	71	276	£6351
12	Carl MASON	Eng	70	70	66	71	277	£5076
	Severiano BALLESTEROS	Sp	71	64	71	71	277	£5076
	Grant TURNER	Eng	72	67	75	63	277	£5076
15	Richard BOXALL	Eng	69	73	67	69	278	£4237
	Barry LANE	Eng	72	67	73	66	278	£4237
	Jose-Maria OLAZABAL	Sp	66	70	72	70	278	£4237
	Miguel Angel MARTIN	Sp	68	70	71	69	278	£4237
	Des SMYTH	N.Ire	71	70	72	65	278	£4237
20	Jose RIVERO	Sp	72	68	68	71	279	£3525
	Peter MITCHELL	Eng	72	72	69	66	279	£3525
	John BLAND	SA	70	66	71	72	279	£3525
	Miguel Angel JIMENEZ	Sp	69	69	69	72	279	£3525
	Roger CHAPMAN	Eng	73	68	71	67	279	£3525
	Michael ALLEN	USA	67	69	69	74	279	£3525
26	Ian MOSEY	Eng	72	69	68	71	280	£3149
	David WILLIAMS	Eng	71	72	67	70	280	£3149
28	Eduardo ROMERO	Arg	73	70	68	70	281	£2740
	David JONES	N.Ire	72	70	69	70	281	£2740
	Keith WATERS	Eng	70	71	73	67	281	£2740
	Bill MALLEY	USA	75	69	69	68	281	£2740
	Sam TORRANCE	Scot	74	68	67	72	281	£2740
	Andrew MURRAY	Eng	69	73	67	72	281	£2740
	Jeff HAWKES	SA	71	71	68	71	281	£2740
35	Bryan NORTON	USA	69	71	72	70	282	£2225
	Jean VAN DE VELDE	Fr	70	72	73	67	282	£2225
	Howard CLARK	Eng	71	69	73	69	282	£2225
	David FEHERTY	N.Ire	71	68	71	72	282	£2225
	Manuel PINERO	Sp	72	72	69	69	282	£2225
	Jimmy HEGGARTY	N.Ire	71	73	67	71	282	£2225
	Bob E SMITH	USA	74	70	68	70	282	£2225
	Alberto BINAGHI	It	75	67	70	70	282	£2225
43	Vijay SINGH	Fij	75	69	68	71	283	£1880
	John MORGAN	Eng	70	69	69	75	283	£1880
	Magnus PERSSON	Swe	68	73	73	69	283	£1880
46	Mikael KRANTZ	Swe	72	67	71	74	284	£1723
	Luis CARBONETTI	Arg	71	70	70	73	284	£1723
48	Armando SAAVEDRA	Arg	72	69	70	74	285	£1567
	Denis DURNIAN	Eng	70	68	69	78	285	£1567
	Anders SORENSEN	Den	73	67	74	71	285	£1567
51	Colin MONTGOMERIE	Scot	71	67	75	73	286	£1316
	Bill LONGMUIR	Scot	73	70	72	71	286	£1316
	Chris MOODY	Eng	71	71	73	71	286	£1316
	Philip WALTON	N.Ire	73	68	71	74	286	£1316
	Mike SMITH	USA	75	66	71	74	286	£1316
56	Neil HANSEN	Eng	72	72	73	70	287	£1065
	Paul CURRY	Eng	71	72	71	73	287	£1065
	Jerry ANDERSON	Can	72	71	72	72	287	£1065
59	Jean Ignace MOUHICA	Fr	72	64	78	74	288	£877
	David JAMES	Scot	72	72	71	73	288	£877
	Ken BROWN	Scot	71	68	76	73	288	£877
	Brian MARCHBANK	Scot	74	68	72	74	288	£877
	Mark DAVIS	Eng	70	71	76	71	288	£877
	Michael KING	Eng	74	70	73	71	288	£877
	Steen TINNING	Den	71	73	72	72	288	£877
66	Marc Antoine FARRY	Fr	73	70	73	73	289	£312
	Peter BAKER	Eng	74	69	72	74	289	£312
	A VALENZUELA (Am)	Mex	70	70	75	74	289	–
68	Paul MAYO	Wal	72	72	76	70	290	£305
	Derrick COOPER	Eng	77	67	73	73	290	£305
	Andrew SHERBORNE	Eng	75	69	74	72	290	£305
	Johan RYSTROM	Swe	74	69	75	72	290	£305
	Malcolm MACKENZIE	Eng	72	72	67	79	290	£305
73	Paul KENT	Eng	72	72	75	72	291	£297
	Jean Francois REMESY	Fr	68	73	77	73	291	£297
	Giuseppe CALI	It	73	71	74	73	291	£297
76	Jose-Maria CANIZARES	Sp	73	71	71	77	292	£293

Slazenger

McNULTY *in virtuoso mood*

It was hard not to feel some sympathy for Torras. The Spanish-based paper manufacturers had reluctantly pulled out of sponsorship of the Barcelona Open — later to become the Catalan Open — because the tournament found itself in direct opposition to the Tournament Players' Championship in the United States. So when the opportunity arose for the company to put their name to the Monte Carlo Open, they quite naturally jumped at the chance. After all, the tournament had, in a comparatively few years, grown into one of the Volvo Tour's leading events, and they had the added incentive of being sure that Severiano Ballesteros — who holds Monte Carlo residency — would turn up.

Torras's expectations were, therefore, naturally as high as the Mont Agel course which perches 3,000 feet up the mountain above the millionaires' playground with its casinos and wall-to-wall beautiful people. So what did Ballesteros do? He missed the cut by one shot after rounds of 75 and a brave, if ultimately unavailing, 67.

For Ballesteros, snuffling from a nasty cold, it was a salutory experience. It was only the second time in six years that he had failed to complete the four rounds of a tournament. The great Spaniard summed it up succinctly: 'I was physically bad, mentally bad, putting bad, playing bad. It was one of those days you have once in a while.' Enough said. The Spanish press corps and the television crews who flew in to watch their hero take the course and the opposition to pieces were disconsolate. What on earth would they do with the weekend?

Most of them stayed to watch the golf, and were very glad they did as Mark McNulty put on a display of virtuousity, of which even Ballesteros would have been proud, to record his eighth European victory with a total of 261, 15 under par.

IT WAS EXPECTED THAT MONTE CARLO'S MOST FAMOUS GOLFING RESIDENT, SEVERIANO BALLESTEROS, WOULD DOMINATE THE PRINCIPALITY'S OWN CHAMPIONSHIP BUT IT WAS MARK McNULTY WHO DEMONSTRATED THE FINER SKILLS

All week the Zimbabwean espoused the virtue of patience. 'If you get impatient here, this course can jump up and bite you,' he said. He was right. The Mount Agel course, only 6,231 yards long, is short by Tour standards, but cannot be taken for granted. Some did. All paid for it with an early flight home. Joining them was Mark James, who after putting himself in a position from which to challenge on the last two days — rounds of 68 and 70 left him on level par after 36 holes — decided he had had enough of the bright lights and went back home to Leeds. James was perfectly within his rights, a point made clear by Tour officials, but he none the less drew a few sideways looks from the tournament organisers.

There were few complaints, anyway, from two of the Volvo Tour's unsung heroes, Grant Turner and Robin Mann, who with rounds of 63 led by a shot from Jeff Hawkes. Turner had finished the French Open the weekend before with a similar score, while Mann couldn't believe his luck. He got into the tournament as first reserve and only just made it, first discovering he'd had his passport stolen, then being involved in an accident on his way to the airport. A burst of six birdies in the last seven holes made him forget his troubles.

The second day saw McNulty thrusting his way to the top of the leaderboard with a 64, alongside the purposeful figure of Peter Senior, who had his second successive 66. The stubby little Australian, wielding a Sam Torrance-style pendulum putter, rolled them in from all over the place. Two strokes covered the leading 14 players after the second round, but 24 hours later McNulty had opened up a three-stroke lead after a five-birdie round of 64 which, with just a whisker of good luck, could have been a 59. Senior was still in the frame and so, too, was the weather-beaten figure of Jose Maria Canizares, whose 65 contained an eagle and four birdies. The Spaniard in

Picturesque 13th fairway

Poised performance from McNulty

Fifth green at Mont Agel

Nothing narrow about McNulty's vision

pursuit of a fourth Ryder Cup appearance was a stroke in front of the chirpy Londoner, Peter Mitchell, who, armed with a new putter that had taken him to a course record of 64 in the Dunhill Masters the previous month, used it only 26 times in his 67. He did not need it at all on the par-five 16th, where he chipped in from 20 yards from the back of the green.

There was, however, a niggling feeling abroad that now he was in front McNulty would not relax his grip on the £48,000 first prize. The next day, after Mont Agel's legendary low cloud had threatened to put the tournament into a fifth day, he proved it.

'Be patient,' he told himself, and, on

Long putt from long putter exponent, Peter Senior

COURSE: MONT AGEL, MONTE CARLO **YARDAGE: 6,198** **PAR: 69**

POS	NAME	CTRY	1	2	3	4	TOTAL	PRIZE MONEY
1	Mark McNULTY	Zim	68	64	64	65	261	£48285
2	Jeff HAWKES	SA	64	72	67	64	267	£25147
	Jose Maria CANIZARES	Sp	68	66	65	68	267	£25147
4	Peter SENIOR	Aus	66	66	67	69	268	£14485
5	Robert LEE	Eng	68	70	69	64	271	£11202
	Peter MITCHELL	Eng	65	68	67	71	271	£11202
7	Peter FOWLER	Aus	66	72	70	64	272	£7967
	Luis CARBONETTI	Arg	68	66	71	67	272	£7967
9	Gavin LEVENSON	SA	70	70	67	66	273	£5452
	Michael ALLEN	USA	71	67	70	65	273	£5452
	Bernhard LANGER	W.Ger	66	68	71	68	273	£5452
	Jose RIVERO	Sp	67	71	67	68	273	£5452
	Miguel Angel JIMENEZ	Sp	72	64	68	69	273	£5452
14	Mikael KRANTZ	Swe	66	69	70	70	275	£4002
	Andrew SHERBORNE	Eng	65	71	73	66	275	£4002
	Rodger DAVIS	Aus	69	69	69	68	275	£4002
	Jim RUTLEDGE	Can	69	68	66	72	275	£4002
	Neal BRIGGS	Eng	70	69	68	68	275	£4002
	Denis DURNIAN	Eng	71	62	71	71	275	£4002
20	Antonio GARRIDO	Sp	68	70	68	70	276	£3259
	Hugh BAIOCCHI	SA	70	67	70	69	276	£3259
	Miguel Angel MARTIN	Sp	66	67	69	74	276	£3259
	Grant TURNER	Eng	63	70	70	73	276	£3259
	Raymond FLOYD	USA	67	68	70	71	276	£3259
	Craig PARRY	Aus	72	62	78	64	276	£3259
26	Ian MOSEY	Eng	70	71	71	65	277	£2654
	Mark MOULAND	Wal	66	67	68	76	277	£2654
	Jerry HAAS	USA	71	68	71	67	277	£2654
	Alberto BINAGHI	It	67	67	72	71	277	£2654
	Mike SMITH	USA	70	68	72	67	277	£2654
	Paul HOAD	Eng	69	71	72	65	277	£2654
	David WILLIAMS	Eng	72	68	72	65	277	£2654
	Philip PARKIN	Wal	69	69	72	67	277	£2654
34	Paolo QUIRICI	Swi	66	70	71	71	278	£2201
	Ronald STELTEN	USA	70	71	66	71	278	£2201
	Jesper PARNEVIK	Swe	69	72	69	68	278	£2201
	Peter McWHINNEY	Aus	69	71	69	69	278	£2201
	John O'LEARY	Ire	70	70	68	70	278	£2201
39	Stephen McALLISTER	Scot	68	68	73	70	279	£1883
	Robin MANN	Eng	63	70	76	70	279	£1883
	Mike HARWOOD	Aus	71	69	68	71	279	£1883
	Lee JONES	Eng	71	68	69	71	279	£1883
	Paul CURRY	Eng	69	68	69	73	279	£1883
	Stephen HAMILL	N.Ire	74	64	69	72	279	£1883
45	David LLEWELLYN	Wal	66	69	69	76	280	£1593
	Bill MALLEY	USA	70	71	69	70	280	£1593
	Steven BOTTOMLEY	Eng	70	71	73	66	280	£1593
	Jean VAN DE VELDE	Fr	73	67	70	70	280	£1593
49	Silvio GRAPPASONNI	It	69	70	69	73	281	£1361
	Emanuele BOLOGNESI	It	66	69	74	72	281	£1361
	Vijay SINGH	Fij	72	69	73	67	281	£1361
	Jose DAVILA	Sp	66	71	72	72	281	£1361
53	Peter COWEN	Eng	66	73	69	74	282	£1071
	Tim PLANCHIN	Fr	71	70	72	69	282	£1071
	Bob E SMITH	USA	71	70	67	74	282	£1071
	Marc-Antoine FARRY	Fr	69	65	76	72	282	£1071
	Manuel CALERO	Sp	74	65	75	68	282	£1071
	John McHENRY	Ire	70	71	67	74	282	£1071
59	Anders SORENSEN	Den	66	70	74	73	283	£869
	Mitch ADCOCK	USA	71	70	74	68	283	£869
	John GOULD	Eng	71	68	67	77	283	£869
62	Glenn RALPH	Eng	67	74	74	69	284	£796
	Jacob RAMUSSEN	Den	70	70	71	73	284	£796
64	Philip WALTON	Ire	73	68	70	74	285	£738
	Magnus JONSSON	Swe	69	70	74	72	285	£738
66	Benoit DUCOULOMBIER	Fr	72	68	73	75	288	£290
67	John JACOBS	USA	68	67	77	77	289	£288
68	Michel BESANCENEY	Fr	71	70	76	73	290	£286
69	Mark JAMES	Eng	68	70	Retd		138	£284

the front nine, he practised what he had been preaching, grinding out eight pars and a birdie. He became a little more adventurous later on with five birdies and two bogeys from the 11th. By then he could afford to be.

LL'S
sh Open

ALLEN *is a bull market*

It is not being unkind to say that no-one, other than his friends, took any notice of Michael Allen at first in the Bell's Scottish Open at the Gleneagles Hotel. A good many would have been pressed to identify him as an American, for he was the sort of golfer who seldom made even a paragraph, let alone headlines, in the newspapers.

Allen's one prominence was that alphabetically he comes first in the PGA Volvo Tour Guide. Otherwise he had kept what might best be termed a low profile: 91st, 68th and 54th in his three years on Tour after three unsuccessful attempts to obtain his players' card in the States. Nor had things changed as Allen, 30, tousle-haired and six feet in height, made his way up into the Perthshire hills for the Bell's which is now attached by a sort of umbilical cord to the Open Championship since that is the next, and in this case (Royal Troon) fairly adjacent, step along the golfing road.

Allen was 61st in the current money list with seven missed cuts in his 17 tournaments. There was no reason to suppose that this week would be different to any other. He began with a 73, eight strokes behind Ian Woosnam. On the second day Allen perked up with a 66 to halve the difference between himself and the leaders, though a third round of 73 was pretty well back to normal. He was now five strokes behind Gordon Brand Junior, who had moved steadily to the top with all his rounds under 70. Moreover, 12 players stood ahead of Allen going into the last day. It was just another week with the chance of a reasonable cheque provided he did not mess things up.

MICHAEL ALLEN, WHO ONCE TRAINED TO BE A STOCKBROKER, MADE AN UNEXPECTED BID FOR THE BELL'S SCOTTISH OPEN TITLE WITH A DEVASTATING FINAL ROUND THAT WAS MORE THAN HIS RIVALS COULD BEAR

Far from messing things up, Allen played golf the like of which he had never played before, shooting a 63 that catapulted him past all the players who had been ahead of him and, in a daze, into the winner's enclosure where he was presented with a cheque for £50,000, which was more money than he had ever seen in his life.

Every man has his day and Allen certainly had his. He holed two chips, one bunker shot and took only 22 putts. He played the first five holes in one over par (which could have been four over but for his chipping) and the next 13 in nine under. He became the seventh new winner of the season, the fourth from overseas and the first American winner since Mark O'Meara took the Lawrence Batley at Royal Birkdale in 1987. Allen won, not from Brand Junior who collapsed into a tangled heap of 78 poorly executed strokes, but by two from Woosnam and Jose-Maria Olazabal, who always looked as if they were about to pounce but never did. In a way, Allen, who might once have become a stockbroker, gained his victory as much by the failings of others as he did by his own expertise.

Yet though he may not have been under pressure going into the round, he certainly was at the end. He knew he had to set a difficult target for those coming up behind him and it seemed nothing less than a birdie at the last would do, perhaps even an eagle. Though this 525-yard hole had, at times, played ridiculously easily (Woosnam had once reached it with a drive and wedge), it was a slightly tougher proposition on the last day and Allen missed the green on the right, up against the spectator railings. He got a free drop but did not chip too well, some 25 feet beyond the hole, which meant that he was now looking back down the fairway. It also meant that he was looking towards the big leader-board and even as Allen studied his putt, so the numbers changed to show that Woosnam had just birdied the 14th and was now only one behind.

Allen's putt therefore became even more critical since it had to be assumed that Woosnam would probably birdie the 18th. That the American got it in revealed marvellous nerve, though in the end it did not matter. Neither

Woosnam nor Olazabal could do better than par fives at the last hole and so the margin was a comfortable two strokes.

Not the least benefit of victory was that Allen avoided having to qualify for the Open Championship. Five places were available for anyone not already exempt if they also finished in the top 25 in the Bell's and the other lucky four were David Feherty, Richard Boxall, Martin Poxon and Larry Rinker, an American Tour player fully prepared to spend an extra week in Scotland, just for the chance of playing in the Open.

Not that Gleneagles is exactly a hardship! The setting and facilities attracted not only a cosmopolitan field, including the three Ozaki brothers from Japan, but also 100,000 spectators over the four sun-drenched days.

So a lot of people were happy, especially Allen. A member of the Olympic Club in San Francisco, where Scott Simpson won the US Open two years ago, Allen's home is Phoenix, Arizona, with a pad in Surrey. His stockbroker training meant he was able to finance himself as a golfer with a shrewd share purchase or two. Now he can presumably expand his play of the markets.

Woosnam was happy too. He had said right at the beginning that second place would do him very nicely and he got it. It was born of superstition for he had an

Sandy Lyle: 'Nobody knows the troubles I've seen!'

Michael Allen, playing above himself?

Glorious Glen
attracted
c

Blue sky backcloth for Olazabal

idea that if he was second one week, he was likely to win the next and as 'next' was the Open, that would suit him down to the ground. It did not work out that way. Whether sponsors prepared to put up £300,000 in prize money exactly welcome hearing golfers expressing reservations about winning is debatable and Bell's received another kick on the shins when the BBC went on strike, wiping the golf off the screens.

Privately they might even have hoped for a Scottish winner and after three rounds they looked like getting one in Brand. It was not to be, any more than it was with two other Scots who had their moments. Sandy Lyle, who was only just coming out of his longest, darkest night of nine cuts missed in 11 tournaments, had the glens ringing with cheers when he posted a 66 in the second round, two off the lead. The sprint was short-lived as he resumed a more sedate pace with 72 and 71 in the last two rounds.

And then there was Brian Barnes, 44, a keen angler rather than golfer these days though something of his appetite for the latter had been revived when he won the Wilson Club Professionals' Championship at Prince's, Sandwich, the previous week. Two 68s at Gleneagles raised all sorts of fairytale thoughts but fairytales seldom come true — unless your name happens to be Michael Allen.

Gordon Brand Junior led until the last round but finished with a sorry 78

Allen chips in at the 16th during his final round charge

COURSE: KINGS COURSE, GLENEAGLES · YARDAGE: 6,745 · PAR: 71

POS	NAME	CTRY	1	2	3	4	TOTAL	PRIZE MONEY
1	Michael ALLEN	USA	73	66	70	63	272	£50000
2	Jose-Maria OLAZABAL	Sp	67	70	68	69	274	£26040
	Ian WOOSNAM	Wal	65	70	71	68	274	£26040
4	Ronan RAFFERTY	N.Ire	69	67	70	70	276	£13850
	David FEHERTY	N.Ire	71	67	69	69	276	£13850
6	Mark McNULTY	Zim	69	71	67	70	277	£9750
	Eduardo ROMERO	Arg	72	66	70	69	277	£9750
8	Roger CHAPMAN	Eng	69	70	70	69	278	£7110
	Larry RINKER	USA	73	66	68	71	278	£7110
10	Sandy LYLE	Scot	70	66	72	71	279	£5085
	Martin POXON	Eng	68	70	71	70	279	£5085
	Des SMYTH	Ire	67	72	74	66	279	£5085
	Peter FOWLER	Aus	72	69	68	70	279	£5085
	Richard BOXALL	Eng	72	69	69	69	279	£5085
	Peter SENIOR	Aus	71	66	68	74	279	£5085
16	Mark JAMES	Eng	72	69	69	70	280	£3967
	Payne STEWART	USA	72	70	70	68	280	£3967
	Sam TORRANCE	Scot	71	71	69	69	280	£3967
	Howard CLARKE	Eng	72	72	69	67	280	£3967
20	Brian BARNES	Scot	68	68	71	74	281	£3420
	Jeff HAWKES	SA	68	74	73	66	281	£3420
	Jose RIVERO	Sp	74	68	69	70	281	£3420
	Barry LANE	Eng	72	69	72	68	281	£3420
	Nick FALDO	Eng	70	72	72	67	281	£3420
25	Gordon BRAND Jnr	Scot	68	69	67	78	282	£3060
	David WILLIAMS	Eng	75	67	68	72	282	£3060
	Christy O'CONNOR Jnr	Ire	72	70	68	72	282	£3060
28	Gavin LEVENSON	SA	68	71	74	70	283	£2622
	David GRAHAM	Aus	71	70	73	69	283	£2622
	David GILFORD	Eng	68	68	73	74	283	£2622
	Tony CHARNLEY	Eng	70	74	66	73	283	£2622
	Brett OGLE	Aus	70	71	72	70	283	£2622
	Mike CLAYTON	Aus	69	71	73	70	283	£2622
	Hugh BAIOCCHI	SA	71	72	70	70	283	£2622
35	Craig PARRY	Aus	71	69	71	73	284	£2220
	Naomichi OZAKI	Jap	68	67	73	76	284	£2220
	Lyndsay STEPHEN	Aus	73	70	72	69	284	£2220
	Andrew MURRAY	Eng	73	70	70	71	284	£2220
	Vijay SINGH	Fij	70	74	70	70	284	£2220
40	Ove SELLBERG	Swe	73	68	75	69	285	£1890
	Mark DAVIS	Eng	71	71	73	70	285	£1890
	Derrick COOPER	Eng	73	71	70	71	285	£1890
	James WHITE	Scot	72	70	70	73	285	£1890
	John BLAND	SA	74	69	73	69	285	£1890
	Paul MAYO	Wal	73	71	70	71	285	£1890
46	Tommy ARMOUR III	USA	68	73	72	73	286	£1620
	Stephen BENNETT	Eng	72	71	73	70	286	£1620
	Mark ROE	Eng	72	72	72	70	286	£1620
49	Paul WAY	Eng	70	72	70	75	287	£1500
50	Keith WATERS	Eng	73	69	72	74	288	£1410
	Peter McWHINNEY	Aus	72	70	76	70	288	£1410
52	David JONES	N.Ire	71	71	72	75	289	£1290
	Tateo OZAKI	Jap	73	71	74	71	289	£1290
54	Carl MASON	Eng	74	69	75	72	290	£1140
	Eamonn DARCY	Ire	72	70	78	70	290	£1140
	Brian WAITES	Eng	75	69	73	73	290	£1140
57	Neil COLES	Eng	70	72	80	69	291	£990
	Jerry HAAS	USA	71	72	73	75	291	£990
59	Sandy STEPHEN	Scot	74	70	72	76	292	£900
	Brad FAXON	USA	71	71	71	79	292	£900
	Ossie MOORE	Aus	71	73	77	71	292	£900
62	Vincente FERNANDEZ	Arg	69	73	79	72	293	£840
63	Paul BROADHURST	Eng	68	74	77	75	294	£539
	Stephen McALLISTER	Scot	71	70	75	78	294	£539
	Nobuo SERIZAWA	Jap	71	72	77	74	294	£539
	Paul CURRY	Eng	74	68	78	74	294	£539
	Ulf NILSSON	Swe	72	68	75	79	294	£539
	John O'LEARY	Ire	71	71	81	71	294	£539
69	Mark MOULAND	Wal	69	73	83	70	295	£293
	David J RUSSELL	Eng	73	71	72	79	295	£293
71	Rodger DAVIS	Aus	70	70	75	w/d	215	£290

Allen and followers camp round the 15th green

Titleist
FILA

CALCAVECCHIA *fades into history*

In the long and distinguished history of the Open Championship, many illustrious names have claimed the title but none of these have been as long as the 1989 champion, Mark Calcavecchia. Aged 29, born in Nebraska and a professional since 1981, he became one of the more unlikely winners of the world's oldest title in a week which contrived to make it a very un-British Open indeed.

Recent years had certainly lived up to the rugged image that the Championship projects: strong winds, heavy rain and punitive rough were what the Open was all about until it arrived at Royal Troon. At 7,097 yards, the longest on the Championship rota, the course certainly had the muscle to test the best but that was before the weather stepped in with a complete contrast in conditions. Three days of rain in ten weeks had left the old links parched and dry, the rough was thin and wispy and although there were plenty of unpredictable bounces to contend with, the only weapon left was the wind.

As the week began in benign conditions there was a slight air of disbelief among the players. They were all somewhat suspicious of a course that was not showing its true colours. Practice rounds containing a fistful of birdies and eagles were commonplace but what they really wanted was the chance to see the course with a stiff blow coming in off the sea.

This was particularly true of the big names in the field. Ballesteros, Faldo, Watson, Norman, Trevino and Nicklaus all expressed a desire for the wind to blow because they knew they had the extra quality to cope with it. If there was no wind then the field would be very tightly bunched at the top and it would be far harder for any of them to impose themselves on the tournament.

IN THE FIRST THREE MAN PLAY-OFF IN OPEN CHAMPIONSHIP HISTORY, MARK CALCAVECCHIA EMERGED AS THE WINNER OVER AUSTRALIANS GREG NORMAN AND WAYNE GRADY AND PROVED THE SAYING THAT 'YOU CAN TALK TO A FADE BUT A HOOK WON'T LISTEN'

The scoring on the first day bore this out as seven players finished on 68 and eight on 69. The man who set the early pace on 68 was the old links fox himself, Lee Trevino. Revelling in conditions which were made for his low-flying game, Trevino mastered the tougher second nine in 33 strokes, finishing with a birdie on the final hole. Joining him on that score were Americans Fred Couples and Paul Azinger, Argentina's Eduardo Romero, Australia's Wayne Grady and Spaniards Jose Maria Olazabal and Miguel Martin, the latter making the most of his late substitution in the field in place of Jay Haas. One stroke behind lay the formidable presence of Norman and Watson in the group on 69, and those on 70 included Curtis Strange and Tom Kite who, after moving to five under par after 14 holes, had one of his almost predictable collapses with a seven on the 15th. Pre-tournament favourite Nick Faldo had one of his usual Open rounds, 17 pars and only one birdie while Ballesteros only gleaned two birdies, offset by two bogeys, for a 72. Sandy Lyle looked to be rehabilitating himself further when he arrived on the 18th tee two under par but then fate, in the form of a too-strong second shot which ran out of bounds, delivered the sand-filled sock to the base of the skull and Lyle's eventual seven probably finished his Championship there and then.

For the greater part of the day it looked as though 68 would be the best score until, that is, a little piece of Open tradition was maintained. That tradition is founded on the likelihood of an obscure British professional, who has pre-qualified, starting out late and coming in with the lowest round of the day when practically everybody else has left the course. Thus, in the footsteps of Peter Tupling, John Morgan and Bill Longmuir, came Wayne Stephens whose classic story of doubt, debt and despair made the headlines, albeit very late ones. Known as 'Brush' because of his dyed blond hair, Stephens, aged 28, had nearly given up the Tour in 1984 and had made seven visits to the qualifying school. Things had improved a little and prior to the Open he had won over £10,000 for 121st place in the rankings. He had made a swing change six weeks earlier under the eye of Terry Hanson, the professional at Cardiff Golf Club, and at Troon he showed that it was the right move. Out in 32 with four birdies, Stephens did not wilt on the homeward half, holing from 12 feet for a birdie on the 15th and then from 18 feet on the treacherous 17th for another. He completed a round of no dropped shots by chipping and single putting the final hole for a 66 and a piece of instant golfing stardom.

The brutal reality of Stephens' chances was brought home by the bookies' odds of 10-1 on him equalling or beating par in the second round. To his credit, he achieved the former and at one stage the leader-board showed the rhyming triplet of Wayne, Payne and Wayne at the top. The other Wayne was Grady, the 31-year-old Queenslander who had just broken through on the US Tour with victory in the Westchester Classic. He was round in 67 for an aggregate of 135 and a two shot lead over Payne Stewart who set a new course record of 65 on a day when a sprinkling of rain slowed up the course slightly but otherwise had little effect. Moving into joint second place was Tom Watson, still hungry for his record-equalling sixth title.

As Faldo and Ballesteros failed to produce any fireworks, the banner of home hopes was taken up by David Feherty. Round in 67 to lie three strokes off the pace, Feherty made a refreshing change from the norm as he revealed that his preparation for the Championship included listening to tapes of Puccini and Woody Allen. Puccini provided the relaxation and Allen provided the philosophy. Feherty had worked with sports psychologist Alan Fine for many years to improve his mental approach with particular emphasis on visualising a shot before it is hit. Feherty, however, was realistic about his chances, relating them to the Woody Allen warning that 'I've often seen hope disappearing over the horizon with its backside on fire'.

The cut came at two over par which allowed Ian Woosnam and Lyle in by the skin of their teeth and with Ballesteros at one over par the European challenge was looking pretty depleted.

Still the sun shone and still there was no wind as the third round began. There were a few stirrings from the back of the field, a 66 from Larry Mize, 67

Payne Stewart hurdled the field with a course record, above left

Faldo makes one for the home side

British charge from Wayne Stephens and David Feherty

David Feherty came out of the blue on the critical 17th

Above, sun-drenched spectators on the Costa Ecosse

from Tom Kite and Roger Chapman but it was still Grady who set the pace. A solid 69 didn't lose him much ground but it did allow Watson to move a stroke closer and bring back memories of his golden days of the early 1980s. Payne Stewart lay two off the pace and Fred Couples and Mark Calcavecchia, along with Feherty, were three behind to make American domination the main feature of the leader-board.

It is so often said that a Championship doesn't begin until the last nine holes that the expression has become somewhat trite. Whatever its validity, Greg Norman chose to ignore it. Starting the final round seven shots behind Grady and 100 minutes ahead of the final pairing, Norman simply tore tame Troon apart. Six birdies in the first six holes was enough to put the frighteners on anybody and although

Greg Norman leapt to the forefront with a blistering 64 on his last round

he slipped a shot at the Postage Stamp, he reached the turn in 31, five under for the round and was right in the thick of the battle.

One of the great final rounds in the Championship's history was now in the making as he picked up two more birdies on the 11th and 12th and now faced the final four holes with an outside chance of a 64 and a target of 275. He needed to birdie the 542-yard 16th and did so with a stupendous second shot from the fairway with a driver which sent the ball 277 yards onto the green. The momentum was nearly halted on the 223-yard 17th, the hole that played the hardest all week, as Norman missed the green on the left, pitched too long, but then ran in a little sand-wedge chip for a saving par. Par at the last gave him that 64 — a total of 13 under par and the opportunity to return to his hotel room and watch how his challengers were faring.

Couples and Stewart had faded, Watson had gone through a sticky patch round the turn, Feherty was clinging on, Calcavecchia was steady and Grady, was as solid as a rock. Grady, in fact, moved to 15 under after the 11th but three putts on the 14th meant he had to play the last four in level par to win. If you were looking for

Beach-crashers witness Watson birdie the 6th

Faldo's caddy goes underground

Tom Watson faces the wilderness from the 18th

Aerial view of Royal Troon on the final day

omens as to who would emerge then Calcavecchia was the man to provide them. On the 11th he hacked down the left-hand side of the gorse but then holed a putt of 40 feet to save his par. Boosted by this, he then missed the green on the left of the 12th, pitched hard at the flag and watched in delighted amazement as the ball struck the pin three feet up and dropped in the hole. It was then he knew he was back in the hunt. A driver from the fairway at the 16th set up a Norman-type birdie and Calcavecchia came to the last hole needing another to tie with the Australian. He got it via a huge drive which stopped just short of an unnoticed bunker 325 yards from the tee and an eight iron which finished five feet from the hole.

Watson's hopes all but vanished when his birdie putt on the 16th looked in the hole but stayed out and Grady still had the world on his shoulders as he stepped on the 17th tee needing two pars to win. The hole had troubled him all week and this was no time to hit the ball short and into a bunker 40 yards from the flag. That, however, was where Grady's ball finished and although he played the bravest of recoveries his par putt slid agonisingly by. At the last he made par with a chip and single putt from the back of the green and so the first four hole play-off involving three men came about with the lowest stroke-play aggregate over those four holes being the winning score. Any further tie would mean sudden-death.

The holes selected were the first and second and the 17th and 18th. Norman carried on from where he had started earlier in the day with two successive birdies, the latter one being matched by Calcavecchia with a putt of 30 feet. Grady was pretty well drained by his

Everyone can dream . . .

History in the making with the first three man play-off in the Open

efforts and managed two pars. On to the 17th where Calcavecchia found the green, Grady found another bunker on the right and Norman found the fringe rough on the back of the green. Grady played a marvellous recovery to around eight feet, Calcavecchia putted up dead but Norman's ball flew too much and finished 12 feet away. He missed and so did Grady.

From the 18th tee, Calcavecchia struck a wild tee shot into the crowd on the right but the ball landed safely enough in the rough. Norman then unleashed his fatal shot, a drive which started down the left and then faded back across the fairway, bounded on and ran destructively into that unnoticed bunker 325 yards away. Thus when Calcavecchia struck his second to within eight feet of the hole the Championship was virtually his. Norman could not reach the green from the bunker and Grady was two shots behind. Norman's recovery trickled into another bunker well short of the green and from there he hit the ball out-of-bounds. Calcavecchia rolled in his putt to become the first American winner for six years and Norman departed the scene, yet again the victim of some outrageous bad fortune which, yet again, he bore with the utmost good grace and dignity.

For Calcavecchia it was a moment of disbelief. The man who arrived on the US Tour with only a big hook and a lot of guts had changed his game round to become a fader of the ball with a magnificent touch around the greens. His swing is certainly not the most elegant but there was no denying the depth of emotion he felt as he clutched the old claret jug.

It must also have been quite a moment for the Royal and Ancient's engraver as he sat in a small office beside the 18th green. As he started to carve that 12 letter name on the trophy he must have been grateful that a certain S. Ballesteros was not also involved in that play-off. But with the almost total eclipse of the European challenge there had been very little danger of that.

Having lead since the second round, Wayne Grady needed to hole this chip on the 18th for outright victory

Return of the warrior

Perhaps it was the emotional warmth of his reception that got to him but, by his own demanding standards, he started rather falteringly. But then he did a simple, majestic thing. He tossed away his notes, stood erect and spoke from the heart. And there was not a sound, a movement even, until the room rose as one man to accord him an ovation he will not forget.

It was Arnold Palmer's valedictory address at the Association of Golf Writers' dinner on the eve of the Open at Royal Troon. Aged 59, irritated by encroaching deafness, he had, his wife revealed, worried about that speech. This was not another off-the-cuff chat to a few corporation presidents back home in America. This was to be a statement about the meaning, his love for and the condition of the game of golf in the home of golf. And as soon as he had thrown the yardages away the birdies and the eagles flowed. 'Revere this game, protect it from the erosion of good manners, of lowering of standards', was what he said in essence, 'for there is none other like it.'

Well, Arnie promptly went out and shot 82-82 over the scorched links of Royal Troon to miss the half-way cut by miles. But he will not forget the inward holes of that second round. His score was an irrelevance as he came to the 18th tee. As he came down through the valley formed by the towering stands either side of that final fairway, everyone was standing and applauding. The subject of their veneration gravely raised first left arm, then right, head modestly bowed in acknowledgement of their affection. The hair is greying now, the lines deeply chiselled into the gladiator's face, but Arnold Palmer remained dignity incarnate as he walked away from his last competitive round at Troon.

Palmer's magnetism made that cliche word of the sports pages, charisma, redundant. It wasn't calculated charm school imagery he exuded, it was genuine. Palmer didn't just arrive for big championships. He

TIME HAD TAKEN ITS TOLL, BUT IT HAD NOT ERODED THE DEEP AFFECTION THAT GOLFERS EVERYWHERE FEEL FOR THE MAN WHO SET THE STANDARDS FOR THE MODERN GAME

was put ashore by the US Marine Corps. You didn't follow Arnie because he was necessarily going to win. You joined the thousands-strong gallery of Arnie's Army because the chances were that you were about to witness the Art of the Impossible solved.

He was the antithesis of the cautious percentage play of so many of the professional sports from the 1950s onwards. He was the John Wayne of the golf course, resembling him in speech and political persuasion. Arnie was not just American, he *was* America.

A mere three years after emerging from the amateur game he had conferred upon him the equivalent of the British knighthood: a front cover of Time Magazine all to himself. He had taken by storm a sport that until then had been scarcely more than some esoteric pursuit. Every professional golfer the world over owes a debt to him for what he did, and Palmer would require nothing more from them that, in triumph or adversity, they simply sustained the game's dignity. He was silently outraged, for example, when Mark Calcavecchia went out to receive the Open trophy on the 18th green at Royal Troon without a jacket.

Silently, too, he was seething at his own performances there. 'He was absolutely disgusted with himself for playing so badly', said Winnie, the wife of 35 years, who has followed his every major round throughout their marriage from outside the ropes. 'The point is, you see, that he still convinces himself every time that he is capable of winning.' He clearly had only a matter of three weeks later when, exactly one month short of his 60th birthday, he shot an opening round 68 at the United States PGA Championship.

He would have preferred that wonderful round, however, at Royal Troon as a final tribute to Scotland. Instead he left with an 82 and it was only very late that evening, over almost the last of many drinks, that the full extent of the wound was revealed. Never once, in public, had he showed even a flicker of dismay.

The next morning he drove down the coast to play Turnberry. He had a sandwich and a beer with club members and a few visitors in the tiny house restaurant when his round was over. He could have been any other tourist just in from the course until, that is, you noticed the reaction his presence evoked.

One member, leaving, said: 'Did you enjoy your round, Mr Palmer?' Mr Palmer flashed a smile and replied: 'Very much, thank you.' End of conversation. The room began talking again. It was intensely civilised, indeed precisely what Arnold Palmer referred to when he threw his notes away and talked, from the heart, about golf.

Final green scenes as Calcavecchia clinches victory, above, and then displays the spoils of victory, right

Vanquished Australians Norman and Grady console each other

COURSE: ROYAL TROON			**YARDAGE: 7,097**					**PAR: 72**
POS	NAME	CTRY	1	2	3	4	TOTAL	PRIZE MONEY
1	Mark CALCAVECCHIA	USA	71	68	68	68	275	£80000
2	Wayne GRADY	Aus	68	67	69	71	275	£55000
	Greg NORMAN	Aus	69	70	72	64	275	£55000
4	Tom WATSON	USA	69	68	68	72	277	£40000
5	Jodie MUDD	USA	73	67	68	70	278	£30000
6	Fred COUPLES	USA	68	71	68	72	279	£26000
	David FEHERTY	N.Ire	71	67	69	72	279	£26000
8	Eduardo ROMERO	Arg	68	70	75	67	280	£21000
	Paul AZINGER	USA	68	73	67	72	280	£21000
	Payne STEWART	USA	72	65	69	74	280	£21000
11	Nick FALDO	Eng	71	71	70	69	281	£17000
	Mark McNULTY	Zim	75	70	70	66	281	£17000
13	Philip WALTON	Ire	69	74	69	70	282	£13000
	Howard CLARK	Eng	72	68	72	70	282	£13000
	Steve PATE	USA	69	70	70	73	282	£13000
	Roger CHAPMAN	Eng	76	68	67	71	282	£13000
	Mark JAMES	Eng	69	70	71	72	282	£13000
	Craig STADLER	USA	73	69	69	71	282	£13000
19	Larry MIZE	USA	71	74	66	72	283	£8575
	Derrick COOPER	Eng	69	70	76	68	283	£8575
	Tom KITE Jnr	USA	70	74	67	72	283	£8575
	Don POOLEY	USA	73	70	69	71	283	£8575
23	Vijay SINGH	Fij	71	73	69	71	284	£6733
	Davis LOVE III	USA	72	70	73	69	284	£6733
	Jose Maria OLAZABAL	Sp	68	72	69	75	284	£6733
26	Stephen BENNETT	Eng	75	69	68	73	285	£5800
	Lanny WADKINS	USA	72	70	69	74	285	£5800
	Chip BECK	USA	75	69	68	73	285	£5800
	Scott SIMPSON	USA	73	66	72	74	285	£5800
30	Jeff HAWKES	SA	75	67	69	75	286	£4711
	Gary KOCH	USA	72	71	74	69	286	£4711
	Jack NICKLAUS	USA	74	71	71	70	286	£4711
	Peter JACOBSEN	USA	71	74	71	70	286	£4711
	Brian MARCHBANK	Scot	69	74	73	70	286	£4711
	Miguel Angel MARTIN	Sp	68	73	73	72	286	£4711
	Ian BAKER-FINCH	Aus	72	69	70	75	286	£4711
	Masashi OZAKI	Jap	71	73	70	72	286	£4711
	Mark DAVIS	Eng	77	68	67	74	286	£4711
39	Mike HARWOOD	Aus	71	72	72	72	287	£4100
	Tommy ARMOUR III	USA	70	71	72	74	287	£4100
	Jeff WOODLAND	Aus	74	67	75	71	287	£4100
42	Mark O'MEARA	USA	72	74	69	73	288	£3725
	Lee TREVINO	USA	68	73	73	74	288	£3725
	Raymond FLOYD	USA	73	68	73	74	288	£3725
	Jose RIVERO	Sp	71	75	72	70	288	£3725
46	Mark McCUMBER	USA	71	68	70	80	289	£3550
	Sandy LYLE	Scot	73	73	71	72	289	£3550
	Naomichi OZAKI	Jap	71	71	69	78	289	£3550
49	Johnny MILLER	USA	72	69	76	73	290	£3400
	Ian WOOSNAM	Wal	74	72	73	71	290	£3400
	Christy O'CONNOR Jnr	Ire	71	73	72	74	290	£3400
52	Brett OGLE	Aus	74	70	76	71	291	£3100
	Mark ROE	Eng	74	71	73	73	291	£3100
	Tateo OZAKI	Jap	75	71	73	72	291	£3100
	Michael ALLEN	USA	74	67	76	74	291	£3100
	Tony JOHNSTONE	Zim	71	71	74	75	291	£3100
	Emmanuel DUSSART	Fr	76	68	73	74	291	£3100
	Richard BOXALL	Eng	74	68	73	76	291	£3100
	Gene SAUERS	USA	70	73	72	76	291	£3100
	Ben CRENSHAW	USA	73	73	74	71	291	£3100
61	Curtis STRANGE	USA	70	74	74	74	292	£2675
	David GRAHAM	Aus	74	72	69	77	292	£2675
	Ken GREEN	USA	75	71	68	78	292	£2675
	Paul HOAD	Eng	72	71	77	72	292	£2675
	Bob TWAY	USA	76	70	71	75	292	£2675
	Ronan RAFFERTY	N.Ire	70	72	74	76	292	£2675
	Mike REID	USA	74	72	73	73	292	£2675
	Wayne STEPHENS	Eng	66	72	76	78	292	£2675
69	Luis CARBONETTI	Arg	71	72	74	76	293	£2425
	Sandy STEPHEN	Scot	71	74	71	77	293	£2425
	Russell CLAYDON (AM)	Eng	70	74	74	75	293	–
71	Colin GILLIES	Scot	72	74	74	74	294	£2400
72	Brad FAXON	USA	72	72	75	76	295	£2400
	Peter TERAVAINEN	USA	72	73	72	78	295	£2400
74	Emlyn AUBREY	USA	72	73	73	78	296	£2400
75	Martin SLUDDS	Ire	72	74	73	78	297	£2400
76	Severiano BALLESTEROS	Sp	72	73	76	78	299	£2400
	Robert KARLSSON (AM)	Swe	75	70	76	78	299	–
77	Gavin LEVENSON	SA	69	76	77	79	301	£2400
78	Bernhard LANGER	W.Ger	71	73	83	82	309	£2400

OLAZABAL *survives the marathon*

Jose Maria Olazabal will always have extra special memories of the KLM Open at Kennemer. The young Spaniard eventually gained his fifth Volvo Tour victory on the links where Severiano Ballesteros had recorded his first, 13 years previously.

But Olazabal's win was a long time coming, for it took a nine hole play-off, the longest in the history of European professional golf, to separate him from Ireland's Ronan Rafferty after they had tied on a three-under-par 277 for the regulation 72 holes.

England's Roger Chapman had also finished on the same score, but was eliminated at the first extra hole, acclaimed for a gallant effort by a gallery who stoically endured another eight holes in driving wind and rain before the title was decided.

Such a finale was as surprising as the chilling front that sped up the English Channel to halt the heatwave on Holland's North Sea coast. The tournament had begun with the field enjoying perfect weather for links golf; warm sunshine and the brand of brisk sea breeze that the Open Championship had craved at Royal Troon.

Ballesteros certainly appreciated it, although the course which faced him was not the one on which, in 1976, he had gained the first of his three Dutch titles. An extra nine holes have since been added to the Kennemer Country Club's lay-out and the organisers had decided that the new loop should form the first half of the Open test. Eyebrows were raised, for some of the best holes in Dutch golf were turned into temporary car parks and one of the least impressive became the sixth; a sharply descending, right-angled dog-leg.

AFTER A GRUELLING NINE HOLE PLAY-OFF IN ATROCIOUS CONDITIONS, JOSE MARIA OLAZABAL EMERGED VICTORIOUS AT KENNEMER FOR HIS SECOND TITLE OF THE YEAR

Two-irons and wedges were the most widely used clubs on the fast running links, but the clever way to play the swooping 355-yard sixth was to hit a five-iron from the tee in order to stay on what fairway could be seen, then a six-iron over a wilderness of scrub to the green. Ballesteros did just that in his first round 67 and walked off with a birdie three, but there were numerous players who put their faith in fortune and found themselves in the bushes.

Among those who charted a straight course through the "fiddly" stretch from the fourth to the seventh were Scotland's Gordon Brand Junior and Ireland's Eamonn Darcy who opened with 65 and 66 respectively. Two years previously, Brand had won the Dutch title at Hilversum, triumphed again the following week in Stockholm, and waltzed straight into Europe's Ryder Cup team to perform great deeds at Muirfield Village.

Despite a disappointing Open, in which he never got going after he had driven into seven bunkers in the outward half of the opening round, Brand was now in a justifiably optimistic mood. He had played himself into a winning position in the recent Bell's Scottish Open before falling back, but his form was good as he entered the decisive stages of this year's Ryder Cup qualifying programme. Darcy came home in 30 to put himself at four under, one ahead of a group which included Olazabal, with Mark Roe and Philip Walton in the batch on 68. Twenty-six players beat the card.

Quite the most remarkable second rounds came from Michael Allen, the American who had won so dramatically at Gleneagles a fortnight before, and the other major championship winner in the strong field—Sandy Lyle. Allen had shot 63 with only 22 putts in the final round to scoop the Scottish title from under the noses of the Europeans. At Kennemer he returned 64 with only 25 putts. Lyle, having started with a 71, took six at the short third to be four over and heading for an early exit. His ball hit a spectator, rolled into a footmark and from there he struck it into a bush and lost it. But Sandy then collected seven birdies in the next 13 holes and handed in a 67 to put himself in the title reckoning.

Rafferty began with two birdies and had a pair of twos in the last four holes of his 66 to move alongside Lyle, while there were notable advances by Craig

Parry (65) and Peter Baker (67). The Englishman had been through a wretched year since his 'double-eagle' defeat of Nick Faldo to win the 1988 Benson and Hedges International Open. There were 11 missed cuts in his 18 previous outings of 1989. But perseverance on the practice ground under the tuition of Bob Torrance and a recent change back to a favoured old set of clubs had brought Baker back to the fore, and fourth place, three shots behind Brand and Olazabal. Ballesteros meanwhile had become palindromic, reversing his first round figure of 67, after fighting a losing battle with a hook.

Rafferty made his big move in the third round with a 66 which put him alongside Parry but could not prevent Olazabal taking a three shot advantage in the final round. Everything looked cut and dried with the 23-year-old from San Sebastian a warm favourite for the title. Jose Maria had dropped only one shot in 54 holes of accomplished stroke-play and even with Rafferty as his last round partner there was little cause for alarm.

However, by the time the leaders

Storm clouds gather round Ronan Rafferty

Peter Baker drives from the 10th

Olazabal chips to the 18th in the rain-lashed play-off

Play-off protagonist Roger Chapman

took to the course the storm had broken, scattering sunshades and advertising hoardings among the sandhills and turning golf into an Outward Bound survival trek. Only five golfers beat par on that wild final day, and the finest golf came from Ballesteros. His week had begun with a clinic for Royalty—Prince Bernhard of the Netherlands had also appeared in the pro-am—and there was some regal golf in his closing 67. He could easily have been two or three shots better, for several putts around the four foot range slid by the hole.

It was the difficulty of holing such putts in a gale that caused Olazabal problems in the afternoon. He had created additional anxiety for himself by taking eight at the long second where he was in bushes and incurred a penalty stroke. Rafferty took seven thereafter and, though he did not know it, Baker, who began with two birdies, went into the lead, if only for the time it took to play the short third. He later took ten at the 10th and was disqualified for forgetting to sign his card.

Olazabal then fell victim to an epidemic of three-putting. He arrived at the 18th needing a par four for victory

Olazabal ends his round in tiers

over Rafferty and Chapman. The Spaniard pushed his first putt six feet wide of the hole and missed the next to ensure a triple play-off for the second Sunday in a row.

Sudden-death it duly was for Chapman, but for Rafferty, who had shot 73 to Olazabal's 76, it was a lingering torture as they went three times round the par four 16th, short 17th and par four 18th. The first four holes were shared in par, the next four in bogeys as the exertions of European golf's longest day took their toll in the gathering gloom. Each had gilt-edged chances, but after nearly six hours out in the cold, wind and rain, errors were inevitable.

Olazabal missed from 18 inches to take six and sat crestfallen on his golf bag with his head cradled in his hands as Rafferty considered a four foot putt for the £46,000 title. But it was downhill and downwind and he hit it five feet past the hole—and missed the return to take a triple bogey seven.

"I was just a bit luckier than Ronan," said the Spaniard. "It was never easy to putt and they were some of the worst conditions I have ever played in." But golf can also be wild in north-west Spain and Ollie's experience and temperament had come to his aid when he needed it most. He had won his second title of the season and earned a third—Europe's "Marathon Man."

Intensive care for Philip Harrison from fiancée Nurse Louise Stewart

Siren call from Tournament Director, Andy McFee

COURSE: KENNEMER, HOLLAND **YARDAGE: 6,634** **PAR: 73**

POS	NAME	CTRY	1	2	3	4	TOTAL	PRIZE MONEY
1	Jose Maria OLAZABAL	Sp	67	66	68	76	277	£45830
2	Roger CHAPMAN	Eng	70	67	71	69	277	£23875
	Ronan RAFFERTY	N. Ire	72	66	66	73	277	£23875
4	Jesper PARNEVIK	Swe	69	67	72	70	278	£13750
5	Gordon BRAND Jnr	Scot	65	68	74	72	279	£11665
6	Sam TORRANCE	Scot	69	70	72	69	280	£8937
	Craig PARRY	Aus	69	65	70	76	280	£8937
8	Des SMYTH	Ire	71	68	70	72	281	£6180
	Miguel Angel MARTIN	Sp	68	71	71	71	281	£6180
	David FEHERTY	N. Ire	72	69	68	72	281	£6180
11	Severiano BALLESTEROS	Sp	67	76	72	67	282	£5050
12	Peter FOWLER	Aus	70	70	68	75	283	£4483
	Eamonn DARCY	Ire	66	73	76	68	283	£4483
	Carl MASON	Eng	68	71	69	75	283	£4483
15	Mark ROE	Eng	68	72	70	74	284	£3891
	Christy O'CONNOR Jnr	Ire	71	69	68	76	284	£3891
	Michael KING	Eng	69	73	68	74	284	£3891
18	David JONES	N. Ire	70	70	71	74	285	£3560
19	Sandy LYLE	Scot	71	67	71	77	286	£2967
	Tony CHARNLEY	Eng	70	74	72	70	286	£2967
	Stephen McALLISTER	Scot	74	68	69	75	286	£2967
	Michael ALLEN	USA	75	64	70	77	286	£2967
	Lyndsay STEPHEN	Aus	67	70	74	75	286	£2967
	David WILLIAMS	Eng	69	70	79	68	286	£2967
	Barry LANE	Eng	70	68	73	75	286	£2967
	Colin MONTGOMERIE	Scot	67	72	72	75	286	£2967
	Philip HARRISON	Eng	69	69	77	71	286	£2967
	Bryan NORTON	USA	70	71	70	75	286	£2967
	Eduardo ROMERO	Arg	71	68	77	70	286	£2967
30	John WOOF	Eng	70	69	71	77	287	£2300
	Andrew SHERBORNE	Eng	72	70	73	72	287	£2300
	Jamie HOWELL	USA	73	69	73	72	287	£2300
	Glenn RALPH	Eng	70	74	72	71	287	£2300
	Sandy STEPHEN	Scot	76	68	71	72	287	£2300
	Mike MILLER	Scot	70	69	71	77	287	£2300
36	John O'LEARY	Ire	70	73	70	75	288	£1990
	Vincente FERNANDEZ	Arg	73	70	72	73	288	£1990
	Philip WALTON	Ire	68	74	71	75	288	£1990
	Anders SORENSEN	Den	72	71	74	71	288	£1990
40	Bob SHEARER	Aus	71	73	70	75	289	£1618
	Lee JONES	Eng	74	69	76	70	289	£1618
	Andrew MURRAY	Eng	73	69	74	73	289	£1618
	Mike COLANDRO	USA	72	67	78	72	289	£1618
	Jonas SAXTON	USA	75	68	74	72	289	£1618
	Jimmy HEGGARTY	N. Ire	72	68	73	76	289	£1618
	Grant TURNER	Eng	74	70	72	73	289	£1618
	Paul CARMAN	Eng	67	72	75	75	289	£1618
	Wayne RILEY	Aus	69	70	73	77	289	£1618
49	Steen TINNING	Den	73	66	75	76	290	£1235
	Magnus PERSSON	Swe	70	71	74	75	290	£1235
	Marc PENDARIES	Fra	69	73	74	74	290	£1235
	Leif HEDERSTROM	Swe	72	71	72	75	290	£1235
	Marc Antoine FARRY	Fr	70	71	72	77	290	£1235
	Bob E SMITH	USA	70	70	73	77	290	£1235
55	Alberto BINAGHI	It	68	72	76	75	291	£985
	Rick HARTMANN	USA	72	71	73	75	291	£985
	Magnus JONSSON	Swe	68	72	73	78	291	£985
	Charles BOLLING Jnr	USA	71	73	78	69	291	£985
59	Richard BOXALL	Eng	71	73	72	76	292	£835
	Keith WATERS	Eng	72	70	76	74	292	£835
	Juan QUIROS	Sp	72	72	72	76	292	£835
	Stephen BENNETT	Eng	71	72	71	78	292	£835
63	Paolo QUIRICI	Swi	70	74	75	74	293	£730
	Manuel MORENO	Sp	72	69	78	74	293	£730
	Johan RYSTROM	Swe	69	74	72	78	293	£730
66	Ronald STELTEN	USA	73	68	80	73	294	£274
	Juan ANGLADA	Sp	73	71	71	79	294	£274
68	Santiago LUNA	Sp	69	72	75	79	295	£269
	Kyi HLA HAN	Bur	71	71	72	81	295	£269
	Andrew CHANDLER	Eng	71	73	73	78	295	£269
71	Paul WAY	Eng	71	73	73	79	296	£265
72	Ross DRUMMOND	Scot	72	70	75	80	297	£263
73	Peter BAKER	Eng	69	67	69	Disq	205	£261

CHARLES *completes Open double*

Bob Charles proved himself to be a man for all seasons, all continents and all-comers in the £150,000 Volvo Seniors British Open at Turnberry Hotel.

The tall, slim 53-year-old New Zealander, justifiably proud to be exactly the same weight as he was 10 years ago, did not take the lead in this championship of varied conditions until the sixth hole in the final round. But once he was in front there was only one winner. At the end of a week during which the distinguished international field experienced rain, flat calm, sunshine, moments stolen from a later season and a different wind every day, the most successful left-hander golf has ever known won by seven shots from former US Open and Masters champion, Billy Casper.

It was Charles' fifth victory of the season — three of them in the United States and one in Japan — and the 52nd of his career in professional golf, while the £25,000 champion's cheque brought his earnings in three years as a senior to around £950,000. Considering Bob made only £328,000 in 23 years on the regular US Tour, it was easy to understand why Lee Trevino was counting the days until he could board the over-50s 'gravy train' on December 1, 1989.

Charles' was an unexpectedly large margin of victory after Casper had looked ready to win for the first time in Britain and others had threatened in the early rounds.

The most unforeseen challenge on the first day came from Agim Bardha, an American citizen with a hairdressing salon in Birmingham, Michigan. But there was considerably more to Bardha than clipping hair in America and trimming Turnberry's Ailsa course to 70 shots. It transpired that he escaped the clutches of the Albanian communists in 1953, fled over the mountains to Greece with his mother and three brothers, and spent the next 18 months in a concentration camp before moving to West Germany, where he worked for two years in a car factory. Eventually he made it to America, discovered an aptitude with the scissors and later with golf clubs before a friend persuaded him to turn professional at the age of 50. Now here he was at 52 outscoring his heroes, and, incidentally, two of his customers, Arnold Palmer and Gary Player, in a championship. However, it was Casper who held the clear lead with a three under par 67, three clear of Bardha, Neil Coles and Bob Charles.

VICTORY AT TURNBERRY MEANT THAT BOB CHARLES RECORDED HIS SECOND BRITISH OPEN WIN — 26 YEARS AFTER HIS FIRST

On day two an old friend emerged to threaten Casper, Charles, Player and another American, Larry Mancour, all of whom broke 70 in the tricky and constantly changing wind. That old friend was Bert Yancey. It was Bert's first visit to Britain since the 1973 Open Championship at Troon, and the first real indication that the man who so nearly won the Masters and the US Open in the late 1960s and early '70s, had recovered completely from manic depression. Yancey revealed that he had been to hospital on 16 different occasions for treatment and that it was only in 1983 that the correct drug to control his illness had been discovered. Since then he had been preparing for the US Seniors' Tour, and while he expressed disappointment at his failure to win a tournament thus far, his eventual equal 10th place finish promised a great deal.

But 58-year-old Casper was still in the lead. Only Charles, Mancour, Player and Bryant Hiskey remained in sight, although the race for the title was beginning to look like one between two players. Hiskey might have expected to make up the leeway when the next day he went round the Ailsa in 65, coming home brilliantly in 31. Astonishingly, he did not gain a single stroke. Casper and Charles, playing together, responded to each other and shot 65s as well. But with Casper and Charles nine under and seven under respectively,

Billy Casper faded in the last round

Co-ordination in colour and swing from Doug Sanders

most observers were convinced the title would be won by Billy or Bob.

And so it transpired. Charles went three shots behind when he bogeyed the second hole, but he covered the remaining holes in five under par for a 66 and an 11-under-par winning aggregate of 269. Casper, five years older than the New Zealander and less sharp competitively, faltered under the bombardment of birdies, double-bogeying the 5th and 6th holes and the 16th for a 75 and the consolation of the £16,400 runners-up prize. Hiskey, who for a time must have felt like Hubert Green when he finished third behind Tom Watson and Jack Nicklaus in the 1977 Open at Turnberry, made up some ground to end up only three strokes adrift of Casper.

Later, Charles was disappointed to learn that he would have to change his putter to defend at Turnberry the following year because the Royal and Ancient and the USGA have banned the moulded "Griprite" grips he has been using for 30 years. But for the moment he was happy enough to savour his British 'double', having been Open champion at Royal Lytham 26 years earlier.

Coombe Wood's David Butler, in his 'rookie' year, had the honour of being leading Briton, sharing fourth place with the ever-determined Gary Player.

Those who attended this final day of the Volvo Seniors British Open will tell you the moment they relished most of all was when Arnold Palmer and

First tee scene at Turnberry

Turnberry's famous landmark highlights a Charles chip

Leading British player David Butler

Christy O'Connor walked on to the last green together. Their combined ages totalled 123 years. But here they were recalling their great days, O'Connor at 64 going round in 68 for seventh place and the over-60s prize of £2,000, and Palmer, at 59, finishing with an eagle and a birdie for 70 and eighth spot. Finally, there was Kyle Burton who, at 64 and in difficult conditions, failed to equal his age by only two strokes. He did not register a single bogey. Truly, this is a game for all ages.

Another British Open trophy for Bob Charles

COURSE: AILSA COURSE, TURNBERRY **YARDAGE: 6,480** **PAR: 70**

POS	NAME	CTRY	1	2	3	4	TOTAL	PRIZE MONEY
1	Bob CHARLES	NZ	70	68	65	66	269	£25000
2	Billy CASPER	USA	67	69	65	75	276	£16400
3	Bryant HISKEY	USA	71	71	65	72	279	£9150
4	Gary PLAYER	SA	74	68	69	71	282	£6750
	David BUTLER	Eng	72	74	67	69	282	£6750
6	Neil COLES	Eng	70	74	70	69	283	£5100
7	Christy O'CONNOR	Ire	76	70	70	68	284	£4340
8	Arnold PALMER	USA	74	72	70	70	286	£3610
9	Anthony GRUBB	Eng	73	72	70	73	288	£3235
10	Bert YANCEY	USA	75	68	71	75	289	£2716
	Larry MANCOUR	USA	72	68	73	76	289	£2716
	Doug DALZIEL	USA	72	76	71	70	289	£2716
13	Ross WHITEHEAD	Eng	7,3	73	68	76	290	£2430
14	Jack O'KEEFE	USA	76	74	71	70	291	£2200
	Art SILVERSTRONE	USA	73	74	73	71	291	£2200
	Agim BARDHA	Alb	70	77	69	75	291	£2200
17	Austin SKERRITT	Ire	76	70	74	72	292	£1870
	George WILL	Scot	72	72	70	78	292	£1870
	Kyle BURTON	USA	75	78	73	66	292	£1870
	Mohamed MOUSSA	Egy	73	73	71	75	292	£1870
21	Hugh BOYLE	Ire	77	74	69	73	293	£1640
	Frank RENNIE	Scot	73	72	76	72	293	£1640
	Paul KELLY	USA	73	75	74	71	293	£1640
	Michael PLUMBRIDGE	Eng	74	72	72	75	293	£1640
25	Allan BALDING	Can	77	71	76	70	294	£1540
26	Doug SANDERS	USA	78	72	72	73	295	£1480
	Alec BICKERDIKE	Eng	72	74	73	76	295	£1480
28	Lou GARRISON	Can	75	76	70	75	296	£1340
	Al JOHNSTON	USA	74	77	73	72	296	£1340
	Roger FIDLER	Eng	74	76	69	77	296	£1340
	Ernie JONES	N.Ire	73	71	73	79	296	£1340
	Douglas BEATTIE	Scot	79	72	72	73	296	£1340
33	David SNELL	Eng	76	70	74	77	297	£1200
	Jimmy KINSELLA	Ire	76	77	68	76	297	£1200
35	Charles MEHOK	USA	72	73	74	79	298	£1080
	John TAYLOR	Can	74	73	75	76	298	£1080
	Dean REFRAM	USA	73	76	75	74	298	£1080
	Hedley MUSCROFT	Eng	77	74	73	74	298	£1080
39	Terence WESTBROOK	SA	78	75	77	69	299	£960
	Frederick BOOBYER	Eng	77	70	74	78	299	£960
	Charles GREEN (Am)	Scot	80	71	75	73	299	–
	Gordon CLARK (Am)	Eng	76	74	74	75	299	–
41	Paddy SKERRITT	Ire	73	77	77	73	300	£841
	Norman DREW	N.Ire	75	75	73	77	300	£841
	Peter BUTLER	Eng	72	79	75	74	300	£841
	Robert WATSON	USA	77	74	73	76	300	£841
	Michael MURPHY	Ire	74	74	76	76	300	£841
46	Derek CRAIK	Eng	80	74	72	75	301	£740
	Maurice MOIR	Scot	73	76	80	72	301	£740
	Jack WILKSHIRE	Eng	76	77	74	74	301	£740
49	John PHELP	Scot	80	71	76	75	302	£700
50	Robert PRESTON	Eng	75	75	76	77	303	£670
	Bryan CARTER	Eng	73	80	74	76	303	£670
52	Derek STRACHAN	Eng	77	73	78	77	305	£600
	Stuart MURRAY	Scot	75	79	76	75	305	£600
	Peter GILL	Eng	80	73	73	79	305	£600
	Denis HUTCHINSON	SA	76	77	76	76	305	£600
	Jim McALISTER	Scot	71	75	86	73	305	£600
57	James CHESTNUT	USA	74	77	80	75	306	£530
	John LITTLE	Eng	78	73	77	78	306	£530
59	John GOODWIN	Eng	78	76	80	75	309	£480
	David BONTHRON	Scot	76	76	78	79	309	£480
	Ron NICOL	USA	80	72	83	74	309	£480
62	Francis RABAIN	Ber	74	79	75	82	310	£440
	Frank CAMPBELL (Am)	USA	81	74	78	77	310	–
63	Bill LARGE	Eng	77	77	76	81	311	£420
64	Tony MANZONI	USA	75	78	75	84	312	£400

RAFFERTY
is the pacemaker

The second victory that proved his first owed nothing to fortune arrived in convincing style for Ronan Rafferty in Stockholm. The Irishman wasted little time in self-recrimination following his Dutch Open play-off defeat the previous weekend by adding the Scandinavian Enterprise Open to the Italian title he won in May.

If Monticello marked Rafferty's breakthrough to the ranks of Volvo Tour winners, Drottingholm stamped him as a confident champion who wants to make a habit of winning. Rounds of 70 and 69, then 64 and 65 at the weekend were hugely impressive but it was the way in which he held off American Michael Allen to get to the winning post that most pleased Rafferty and his many admirers.

Ronan candidly admitted that too often in the past he had backed off when in a winning position. 'But all week in Sweden I was determined to be positive and hit the shots necessary for victory' he said. 'I won the way you want to win, by leading at the start of the last round and then shooting a low score.'

Rafferty certainly needed to produce positive golf of the highest quality because the 30-year old Allen made it one of the season's most exciting shoot-outs by also returning a last round 65. The San Fransican golfer had elbowed aside some of Europe's biggest names, as well as fellow American Payne Stewart, with his closing 63 to take the Bell's Scottish Open at Gleneagles. In Stockholm he claimed five birdies in the last six holes to keep Rafferty alert until the final putt. Allen's 30-foot eagle putt at the 18th was inches from falling and imposing real pressure on an opponent who had

IN CLAIMING HIS SECOND TITLE OF THE SEASON, RONAN RAFFERTY REALISED THE IMPORTANCE OF BEING SELECTIVE IN HIS TOURNAMENT APPEARANCES AND PACING HIMSELF MORE CAREFULLY

found greenside sand with his approach to the par five. Rafferty, however, was more than equal to the task and a good recovery and two putts took him to the top of the Order of Merit by a two stroke margin.

Rafferty had arrived in the Swedish capital to find that Seve Ballesteros had declined to defend the title and that Sam Torrance was the centre of attraction. The Scot was on the brink of becoming the sixth European golfer to top £1 million prize money. Ballesteros, Nick Faldo, Sandy Lyle, Ian Woosnam and Bernhard Langer had already reached that milestone: Torrance needed to finish first or second to join them. He subsequently went home at the halfway point, as did Denis Durnian, another of the front runners in the Ryder Cup campaign which was then in full swing. Former US Masters champion Craig Stadler and the Australian Rodger Davis were also eliminated after two rounds. Davis had just returned to the tournament fold after eleven weeks' absence with an injury to the shoulder.

Torrance and Durnian saddled themselves with opening rounds of 74, ten strokes more than the record-equalling pacemakers Peter Senior and Philip Harrison. Senior's career has been saved by his adoption of the extra-long shaft which Torrance had made fashionable. He has suffered for ten years with the 'yips' but since he plucked up the courage to use the 'broomhandle' putter at the Dunhill British Masters, his golf has prospered. The Australian started with two birdies, had four more in five holes around the turn and got his ninth with a putt of 40 feet at the 17th to match the course best set by rival Australian Craig Parry the previous year.

Harrison had enjoyed his highest finish of a disappointing season the previous week in Holland. A car crash in South Africa during the winter had been responsible for his indifferent golf, for the golfer from Carlisle had suffered whiplash when his vehicle was hit from behind. At one stage he needed two hot baths and massage before he could play and six months later was still undergoing physiotherapy. But there was nothing wrong with his putting as he harvested six birdies in the first 11 holes, and then joined Senior at the head of affairs by sinking a 60 foot eagle putt at the 18th.

Texan John Slaughter, another convert to the king-sized putter employed by Torrance, Senior, and England's Andrew Murray, were among four players to return 67 on the blustery second day when Senior held a one-stroke halfway lead over Harrison. Johan Tumba, son of the ubiquitous Sven, Sweden's 'Mr Sport', was the best of the home contenders of a five under par 137.

Rafferty and Allen were respectively five and four shots off the lead but dramatically changed the shape of the tournament on Saturday afternoon. It was evident that the Irishman was taking a much more relaxed approach to the serious business of tournament golf. Instead of pounding balls on the practice ground he loosened up with a few chips and putts and relaxed by watching videos. Rafferty said he was beginning to learn how to pace himself: 'I wish I had listened to advice five years ago and not played 40 tournaments a year,' he said. He certainly looked relaxed as he reached the third round turn in only 30 strokes.

Gordon Brand Junior who had won the title after a play-off in 1987 was another to make a significant move. The Scot also birdied six of the first nine holes, going on to a 66 for a 206, joining Harrison and the Fijian, Vijay Singh, winner of the Volvo Open in Sardinia, in third place after 54 holes.

Rafferty made only one mistake on the homeward half, driving too far at the 12th and reaching the rough at the angle of the fairway. But three birdies more than repaired the setback and his 64 for a 13 under par 203 gave him a two shot lead over Allen. The American was again succeeding in his philosophy for successful golf — taking the emotion out of the game. 'It sounds a contradiction in terms,' said Allen. 'I still get excited and disappointed during a round but it is all under control because my concentration is so good.' A third round 67 took him to second place, a shot clear of Brand Junior and company and setting the stage for a last round attack.

Any thoughts he or the field entertained of overhauling Rafferty lasted for only as long as it took the latter to play the first nine holes. The Irishman put the parkland course to the sword, waltzing to the turn in 31 and into a five stroke advantage for what is more often than not the decisive period of the week. This time it was over before it began, even though Allen, to his great credit, refused to accept the inevitable. He was still five shots adrift of Rafferty when they reached the 15th tee but the American birdied the last four holes to keep the large galleries buzzing.

He, too, had shot 65 for an 18-under-par 270, which would have won him the title the previous year. But Rafferty was in no mood to be denied in the finale, although he was unable to match Allen's imperious three-wood to the home green. He had no need to be alarmed with a three shot lead playing the last, and settled for the par which brought him his second European title and underlined his right to a Ryder Cup

debut the following month.

'The iron shots I hit at the first five holes of the last round were my best of the year' he enthused. 'It was a great feeling to play as well as that.'

Ireland's 'iron man' had discovered another meaning to the term and also understood why players like Ballesteros, Norman and Lyle limit themselves to around 25 tournaments a year. Consistent top quality golf does not come from constant competition, but from an intelligent assessment of when and where to play. They plan their year around major events and Rafferty will in future be doing the same.

Sunshine and shadows envelop spectators

Poised finish from new champion Rafferty

Johan Tumba, son of SEO founder Sven, blasts from a bunker

The 14th green at Drottingholm

Close examination of the Rafferty swing by interested spectators

COURSE: DROTTINGHOLM, STOCKHOLM | **YARDAGE: 6,747** | **PAR: 72**

POS	NAME	CTRY	1	2	3	4	TOTAL	PRIZE MONEY
1	Ronan RAFFERTY	N. Ire	70	69	64	65	268	£55810
2	Michael ALLEN	USA	67	71	67	65	270	£37180
3	Peter SENIOR	Aus	64	70	73	67	274	£20970
4	Gordon BRAND Jnr	Scot	70	70	66	69	275	£15475
	Vijay SINGH	Fij	69	70	67	69	275	£15475
6	Brett OGLE	Aus	68	70	70	68	276	£10887
	Derrick COOPER	Eng	70	70	69	67	276	£10887
8	David WHELAN	Eng	68	73	72	64	277	£7526
	Mark MOULAND	Wal	70	71	67	69	277	£7526
	Jerry HAAS	USA	71	68	68	70	277	£7526
11	Joakim HAGGMAN	Swe	70	73	69	66	278	£5962
	Mats LANNER	Swe	68	72	72	66	278	£5962
13	Philip HARRISON	Eng	64	71	71	73	279	£4939
	Alberto BINAGHI	It	70	69	70	70	279	£4939
	Johan TUMBA	Swe	67	70	71	71	279	£4939
	Ossie MOORE	Aus	72	71	66	70	279	£4939
	David FEHERTY	N. Ire	72	70	71	66	279	£4939
18	Magnus JONSSON	Swe	71	71	68	70	280	£3886
	Bob SHEARER	Aus	72	70	71	67	280	£3886
	Paul HOAD	Eng	69	69	71	71	280	£3886
	Grant TURNER	Eng	69	69	73	69	280	£3886
	Ove SELLBERG	Swe	69	70	71	70	280	£3886
	Andrew MURRAY	Eng	74	67	70	69	280	£3886
	John SLAUGHTER	USA	73	67	68	72	280	£3886
	Jose Maria CANIZARES	Sp	72	68	72	68	280	£3886
26	Anders SORENSEN	Den	73	69	71	68	281	£3025
	Richard BOXALL	Eng	69	70	72	70	281	£3025
	Marc Antoine FARRY	Fr	71	70	71	69	281	£3025
	Peter TERAVAINEN	USA	67	72	72	70	281	£3025
	Carl MASON	Eng	69	69	72	71	281	£3025
	Andrew SHERBORNE	Eng	70	71	70	70	281	£3025
	Eamonn DARCY	Ire	71	69	68	73	281	£3025
	Jesper PARNEVIK	Swe	69	73	72	67	281	£3025
	Christy O'CONNOR Jnr	Ire	70	73	66	72	281	£3025
35	Mark DAVIS	Eng	71	69	74	68	282	£2445
	Magnus PERSSON	Swe	71	70	73	68	282	£2445
	Philip WALTON	Ire	72	68	71	71	282	£2445
	Des SMYTH	Ire	72	68	71	71	282	£2445
	Juan ANGLADA	Sp	68	70	74	70	282	£2445
	David LLEWELLYN	Wal	73	70	70	69	282	£2445
41	Andrea CANESSA	It	69	73	70	71	283	£2110
	Jon HEIMER	Swe	69	71	74	69	283	£2110
	Frank NOBILO	NZ	70	70	72	71	283	£2110
	Mike HARWOOD	Aus	72	69	70	72	283	£2110
45	Leif HEDERSTROM	Swe	69	72	70	73	284	£1809
	Brian MARCHBANK	Scot	68	74	72	70	284	£1809
	Marc PENDARIES	Fr	70	69	73	72	284	£1809
	Gary KOCH	USA	71	71	68	74	284	£1809
	Manuel CALERO	Sp	70	73	73	68	284	£1809
50	David JAMES	Scot	68	70	72	75	285	£1474
	Rick HARTMANN	USA	72	70	73	70	285	£1474
	Mariano APARICIO	Sp	75	67	71	72	285	£1474
	Magnus GRANQVIST	Swe	68	72	72	73	285	£1474
	Mark ROE	Eng	73	69	68	75	285	£1474
55	Mats HALLBERG	Swe	70	68	80	68	286	£1172
	Mikael HOEGBERG	Swe	68	73	69	76	286	£1172
	David RAY	Eng	72	70	72	72	286	£1172
	Miguel Angel JIMENEZ	Sp	70	73	72	71	286	£1172
59	Stephen HAMILL	N. Ire	74	69	76	68	287	£1005
	Silvio GRAPPASONNI	It	75	67	71	74	287	£1005
	Peter FOWLER	Aus	70	73	73	71	287	£1005
62	Richard FISH	Eng	71	72	75	70	288	£922
	Malcolm MACKENZIE	Eng	73	69	73	73	288	£922
64	David GILFORD	Eng	67	76	75	71	289	£870
65	Sandy STEPHEN	Scot	71	72	76	71	290	£840
66	Mikael KRANTZ	Swe	75	68	71	77	291	£334
	Daniel WESTERMARK	Swe	68	74	75	74	291	£334
68	Don KLENK	USA	72	70	73	77	292	£330
	Glenn RALPH	Eng	72	69	76	75	292	£330
70	Tony JOHNSTONE	Zim	71	72	76	75	294	£327

BRAND *marks Fulford finale*

It was a tearful farewell. After a hugely successful marriage, marred only by one brief separation, the time had come for the final break. This three-way partnership of Benson and Hedges, Fulford Golf Club and a faithful Yorkshire golfing public was dissolved in champagne on the evening of Sunday, August 13, 1989. And the toast was: "Thanks for the golfing memories."

After nearly 20 years of good times and happiness, Benson and Hedges, sponsors of one of Europe's most popular tournaments, announced they were leaving Fulford, lovely suburb of historic York, and setting up camp in Cornwall. The decision was made with regret, necessitated by a need to secure a tournament date on the increasingly busy calendar which did not coincide with the four major championships of the world. That meant switching from a traditional August date to May as from 1990, and the sponsors felt that was too early in the year to expect good greens in the North of England. So it was that Benson and Hedges said goodbye to Fulford and headed for St Mellion, which staged the tournament in 1979, the only time it had previously ventured out of Yorkshire.

It was sad news for Yorkshire golf fans, who had supported the tournament year in, year out, through rain or shine. Many even booked their annual holidays to coincide with the event, such was its popularity. The sponsors had spared nothing to make their tournament one of the best on the Volvo Tour and they brought many of the world's top professionals to Fulford, as the roll call of winners over the years will testify—Jack Newton, Graham Marsh (twice), Lee Trevino, Tom Weiskopf, Greg Norman, Sam Torrance and Sandy Lyle, to mention but a few. Indeed, the Benson and Hedges tournament got away to the best possible start in 1971 when Tony Jacklin, very much the hero of British sport, scored an eagle three at Fulford's final hole to tie with Peter Butler and then win the play-off.

GORDON BRAND JUNIOR PROVIDED A FITTING END TO BENSON AND HEDGES' 18-YEAR ASSOCIATION WITH FULFORD WITH A MEMORABLE FINAL ROUND ON A COURSE THAT ALWAYS ENCOURAGED THE DRAMATIC

Now Len Owen, who masterminded each of the 18 tournaments there, had arranged a special dinner in a York hotel and invited many of the people who had been associated with the event over the years, including some of the past captains of the club. At the dinner, Benson and Hedges managing director John Taylor sprang a pleasant surprise. He presented the delightful gold trophy, worth several thousand pounds, to the club. It will be played for annually and the winners' names will be engraved alongside those of the tournament winners, making it a unique trophy in British club golf. Not only that, but John Taylor also handed over a cheque for £5,000, the interest from which will be used to provide the competition prizes.

The 1989 tournament was, as usual, a resounding success and blessed with superb weather and a fine winner in Gordon Brand Junior, his success sealing his place in Europe's Ryder Cup team to play the Americans at The Belfry the following month. Ryder Cup captain Tony Jacklin returned to the scene of his 1971 triumph to cast an eye over some of the players on the fringe of selection. He also played in the tournament, though not with any great aspirations. He explained: 'I'd rather be playing than hanging around.'

The former British and US Open champion still has many followers and they were delighted to see him score a 68 in the first round, not that it put him into any sort of contention because a chirpy and little-known Australian by the name of Bradley Hughes equalled Ian Woosnam's course record of 62 with ten birdies and eight pars.

It was an astonishing performance by 22-year-old Hughes because he did not possess a PGA Tour player's card and could only play in European events with sponsors' invitations. The last time he had played in a tournament was in May, in Canada, and he had been living in Britain for the previous ten weeks, just waiting for his chance to play in the Benson and Hedges, the only sponsors prepared to give him a chance. 'I've been staying with friends in Scotland and living off my savings,' said Hughes. 'I knew I was capable of a score like this, but I'm surprised to have done it after not having played for so long. It's good to show Benson and Hedges they were right to give me an invitation to play in their tournament.' The affable Aussie went on to score 71, 71 and 74 to finish joint ninth, six shots behind the winner, and scoop a handsome £6,360.

Another Australian, Peter Senior, came in with a first round of 64 and Jose Maria Canizares started his charge for a Ryder Cup team place with a 65. But there was little joy for Sandy Lyle. He had a 77—only two players fared worse on the opening day—and his hopes of regaining his form in time for the Ryder Cup were finally shattered.

Bradley Hughes was still at the top of leader board after the second round and he was joined by one of the 'fringe' men of the Ryder Cup year, Derrick Cooper, a relaxed Lancastrian with a happy knack of making big cheques week after week.

Malcolm Mackenzie stepped smartly to the fore with opening rounds of 66, 68 and he greatly impressed those who had not noticed him before. Indeed, the BBC TV commentators regularly remarked on Mackenzie's striking resemblance to Jacklin, not just in his purposeful walk and cheery waves to the crowds but in his aggressive style of play. It proved to be a good week, indeed, for Mackenzie, who had a large following from his home town of Sheffield, and he achieved his best result as a professional by claiming third place to win £18,780.

Also hoping for a big cheque was Danish golfer Steen Tinning, 26, who had won only £14,000 on the Tour thus far. His hopes were dashed when he hit four consecutive shots out-of-bounds at the 438-yard second, three of them with a three iron, the last with a four iron, to card a 13.

'When I kept hitting my second shot out of bounds I just had to smile in the end,' he said. 'I could see the funny side of what was happening. The worst score I can ever remember for one hole was an 11 when I was 12 years old.' Fortunately for Tinning, a steward found all four balls and handed them back. 'I had only seven golf balls in my bag at the start of the round and I was getting worried,' said Tinning.

Third place for Yorkshire's Malcolm Mackenzie

Feherty and Canizares were looking for Ryder Cup spots

Hole-in-one man Steen Tinning

First round leader
Bradley Hughes

Two hours later, however, he was smiling again when he scored a hole-in-one at the 14th and won a £15,000 Volvo 440 car.

Meanwhile, back at the leader-board, Howard Clark and Brand Junior were within sight of Derrick Cooper, who had established a three-stroke lead over Bradley Hughes after three rounds.

Both Clark and Brand desperately needed that cheque to leap into the top nine of the Ryder Cup points table and secure a Belfry berth. In the event, Clark struggled with his putter in the final round, needing 35 putts in a level par score of 72, but Brand steamed into first

Derrick Cooper plays to a packed crowd on the 18th

place with a brilliant last round of 64.

It was a case of finishing as he had begun. Brand opened with a 64, performed only moderately in the second and third rounds with 72s and then made up seven shots on Cooper to push the Lancastrian into second place. Clinching his place in the Ryder Cup was as big a thrill as winning the tournament. 'If I hadn't made the team, my year wouldn't have been worth talking about,' said Brand. 'I got such a buzz from playing last time and it was important to me to be in the side again. Winning at Fulford is very special for me and I'm sad we won't be coming back.'

The Anglo-Scot—he was born in Fife and brought up in Bristol—joined an impressive list of past winners who had scored an eagle three at Fulford's 480-yard finishing hole to snatch victory. He achieved it by hitting a three iron from the tee, a three iron onto the green and holing a putt of 18 feet. Golfers who have played Fulford's 18th may find it difficult to imagine anybody covering those 480 yards with two three irons but Brand later explained that he was so 'pumped up' that he feared he would hit a two iron tee shot too far.

'On the 16th, I'd hit a two iron 275 yards and that sort of distance would have put me in trouble on the 18th,' he said. 'So I hit the three iron for safety and it was perfect, just 237 yards down the middle of the fairway and an easy three iron distance from the green.'

For some people, it's just a different game.

Gordon Brand Junior got the drop on his rivals with his eagle putt on the 18th

COURSE: FULFORD GOLF CLUB, YORK **YARDAGE: 6,807** **PAR: 72**

POS	NAME	CTRY	1	2	3	4	TOTAL	PRIZE MONEY
1	Gordon BRAND Jnr	Scot	64	72	72	64	272	£50000
2	Derrick COOPER	Eng	67	66	68	72	273	£33300
3	Malcolm MACKENZIE	Eng	66	68	71	69	274	£18780
4	Jose Maria CANIZARES	Sp	65	72	70	69	276	£15000
5	Craig PARRY	Aus	68	72	67	70	277	£9925
	Howard CLARK	Eng	69	67	69	72	277	£9925
	Ian MOSEY	Eng	69	67	69	72	277	£9925
	John BLAND	SA	67	68	70	72	277	£9925
9	Peter FOWLER	Aus	69	71	70	68	278	£6360
	Bradley HUGHES	Aus	62	71	71	74	278	£6360
11	Des SMYTH	Ire	67	73	69	70	279	£5520
12	Philip HARRISON	Eng	71	69	70	70	280	£4747
	Jose RIVERO	Sp	69	72	68	71	280	£4747
	Gary PLAYER	SA	69	67	73	71	280	£4747
	Eamonn DARCY	Ire	67	72	71	70	280	£4747
16	Andrew OLDCORN	Eng	72	71	66	72	281	£4140
	Brett OGLE	Aus	72	69	68	72	281	£4140
18	Peter SENIOR	Aus	64	72	72	74	282	£3730
	Jerry HAAS	USA	67	72	72	71	282	£3730
	Antonio GARRIDO	Sp	70	70	70	72	282	£3730
21	David JONES	N.Ire	73	69	70	71	283	£3375
	Gavin LEVENSON	SA	69	74	70	70	283	£3375
	Emmanuel DUSSART	Fr	66	72	73	72	283	£3375
	Tony JOHNSTONE	Zim	73	69	69	72	283	£3375
25	David WILLIAMS	Eng	71	71	69	73	284	£2925
	John O'LEARY	Ire	68	74	70	72	284	£2925
	Peter BAKER	Eng	68	75	67	74	284	£2925
	Richard BOXALL	Eng	70	71	70	73	284	£2925
	Andrew MURRAY	Eng	72	69	69	74	284	£2925
	Andrew STUBBS	Eng	70	72	68	74	284	£2925
31	Philip WALTON	Ire	71	65	75	74	285	£2466
	David A RUSSELL	Eng	69	73	69	74	285	£2466
	Carl MASON	Eng	69	74	71	71	285	£2466
	Bernard GALLACHER	Scot	67	72	74	72	285	£2466
	Ross DRUMMOND	Scot	72	68	72	73	285	£2466
36	Bob E SMITH	USA	70	72	72	72	286	£2100
	Joe HIGGINS	Eng	71	71	69	75	286	£2100
	Peter ALLAN	Eng	72	71	73	70	286	£2100
	Rick HARTMANN	USA	67	68	78	73	286	£2100
	Peter MITCHELL	Eng	68	72	74	72	286	£2100
	Ross McFARLANE	Eng	66	74	71	75	286	£2100
	Ken BROWN	Scot	69	69	76	72	286	£2100
43	Mark ROE	Eng	71	72	71	73	287	£1740
	Mark McNULTY	Zim	66	73	76	72	287	£1740
	Ignacio GERVAS	Sp	72	69	70	76	287	£1740
	Neil HANSEN	Eng	71	70	73	73	287	£1740
	David J RUSSELL	Eng	70	73	74	70	287	£1740
48	Armando SAAVEDRA	Arg	71	70	73	74	288	£1500
	Mike CLAYTON	Aus	71	72	75	70	288	£1500
	Chris MOODY	Eng	69	69	76	74	288	£1500
51	Bryan NORTON	USA	66	73	75	75	289	£1320
	Gordon J BRAND	Eng	66	73	75	75	289	£1320
	Paul MAYO	Wal	69	69	74	77	289	£1320
54	Martin POXON	Eng	71	69	76	74	290	£1080
	Stephen BENNETT	Eng	71	70	71	78	290	£1080
	Mark MOULAND	Wal	67	68	76	79	290	£1080
	David FEHERTY	N.Ire	68	70	72	80	290	£1080
	Sandy STEPHEN	Scot	68	71	77	74	290	£1080
59	Marc PENDARIES	Fr	72	70	72	77	291	£915
	David GILFORD	Eng	71	71	78	71	291	£915
61	Lee JONES	Eng	70	73	71	78	292	£855
	David RAY	Eng	72	70	74	76	292	£855
63	Manuel MORENO	Sp	67	76	74	76	293	£780
	John JACOBS	USA	68	75	76	74	293	£780
	Steen TINNING	Den	71	69	72	81	293	£780
66	Steven BOTTOMLEY	Eng	70	69	79	77	295	£300
67	Anders FORSBRAND	Swe	70	73	77	77	297	£298

Wolsey
Wolsey

HARWOOD'S *eagle lands title*

AUSTRALIA'S PETER SENIOR APPEARED TO HAVE MATTERS WELL UNDER CONTROL AT BOKSKOGEN UNTIL THE FINAL TWO HOLES WHEN COUNTRYMAN MIKE HARWOOD SNATCHED THE TITLE WITH A DRAMATIC FINAL HOLE BUNKER SHOT

At six foot and four inches Mike Harwood is difficult to overlook. The lofty man from Sydney had already shown his rivals the folly of disregarding him when he snatched the Portuguese Open at Quinta do Lago from Eamonn Darcy to record his first Volvo Tour success early in 1988.

Harwood holed a bunker shot on his way to becoming Portuguese champion and there were striking similarities in his success in the PLM at Bokskogen. His title-winning shot in Sweden was a 15-metre sand recovery which dived into the 72nd hole for an eagle three. It meant that rival Australian Peter Senior and Scotland's Sam Torrance literally had to take it on the chin. The two devotees of the long putter were knocked out by Lady Luck, and what a spectacular show she provided.

The event's switch from the holiday peninsular at Falsterbo to coincide with Malmo's Fairs week was a huge success. Not only did the crowds flock to the parkland course in blissful weather but also the sponsors secured a quality field. It says much for Harwood's golf that he was able to immunise himself against Ryder Cup fever and eclipse a line-up which included Ian Woosnam, Bernhard Langer, Jose Maria Olazabal and Ronan Rafferty, as well as Torrance and Howard Clark.

All the drama came in the last two holes of the final round. Harwood had started three strokes behind pace-setting Senior and even when, at the 17th, he cut the gap to one, Harwood still looked an unlikely champion because both Senior and Torrance had a clear birdie or eagle chance at the 540-yard 18th. But Senior's last two drives found rough and at the 18th he took three shots to reach the same greenside bunker from which Harwood pitched into the hole. A par five was just good enough to keep him ahead of Torrance, for whom third place secured his Ryder Cup spot at The Belfry. For Torrance, it was an emotional finale. When he holed from eight feet at the last for a 15-under-par 273, his return to the Midlands course was certain.

Gordon Brand Junior had claimed his Cup place the previous week at York and when Torrance followed suit, Scotland was assured of a strong Ryder hand. The long and short of Sam's success in reaching his goal was the king-sized putter he put into service back in the spring. Since he first used the 'broomhandle' club for all four rounds in the Jersey European Airways Open, Torrance's hesitancy on the greens had disappeared. Gone were the 'yips' that had so troubled him in 1988 and, as the birdies and eagles arrived, the confidence spread to the rest of his game.

Senior, too, had profited from a stretched putter and Denis Durnian, who partnered Torrance in the Sweden v Volvo Tour PLM Cup match at the start of the week, is another. The Swedes won the match to retain the trophy they took in the inaugural contest the previous year. The Tour's only winning pair were Langer and Olazabal and the next day the latter shot a record eight under par 64 in the pro-am, clipping one shot off Tony Jacklin's course best set 15 years previously.

England's Barry Lane, making a belated charge for a Ryder Cup place, also had 64 in the first round of the main event, putting left hand below right for the first time and being rewarded with nine birdies. Harwood was no slouch either, getting out in 31 and sharing second place with Martin Poxon on 66, one ahead of Irish crack-shot Philip Walton and the erratic Swede Anders Forsbrand.

By the end of the second round Langer, whose putting problems have filled many a magazine page, was reproducing his own brand of eccentricity on the greens. Clamping the shaft of his club against his left forearm like a splint, he ran down six birdies to take himself to a ten-under-par 134 at

Mike Harwood came out of the blue to win

halfway. He had a shot to spare over Senior and Johan Rystrom, with Harwood and Spaniard Manuel Moreno on 136. Another Swede, Leif Hederstrom, excited the large, enthusiastic galleries with a 66, while Torrance and Rafferty were in close attendance.

The pace was hectic, for already 58 players had bettered par and by the end of the third day Senior had led them to a 16-under total of 200. The Brisbane golfer had begun with five successive birdies but Torrance claimed eight in a matching 65 to share second place on 203 with Harwood (67) and Langer (69). Moving up fast were the Irish pair Rafferty and Walton who both had 66. The Dublin golfer had so far recorded an eagle and 21 birdies and was running away with the Tour's Equity and Law Challenge league. But the bogeys were almost as abundant and were once again to prove his downfall.

The last leg was billed as the battle of the long putters. Torrance clipped one stroke off Senior's advantage by the final turn. Senior responded with a birdie at the 11th and there seemed little threat to his serene progress to a second PLM title, even when Harwood closed to within a single stroke with birdies at the 14th and 15th. Senior gave himself a two-shot cushion by holing from ten feet at the 16th and Torrance did the same to join Harwood two behind.

The glorious uncertainty of golf was once again demonstrated in the next few strokes. Almost as soon as Senior found rough with his drive at the dog-leg uphill 17th, Harwood walked off the green with a par four. When Senior missed the target with his approach and dropped a shot, Harwood recognised his chance. He had enjoyed four top five finishes in 1989 so far and another was already certain. He cracked two solid woods up the rolling final fairway to find the trap guarding the entrance to the 18th green. His final stroke was greeted by a roar that conveyed a sickening signal to Torrance and Senior back on the tee.

The eagle landed with a £50,000 thump in Harwood's pocket and stayed there as Senior carved his final drive into rough and then beat a zig-zag path to the last flag. 'That last hole was amazing,' said Harwood. 'I had driven the ball badly all week and I was really under pressure on the tee. But I hit a straight long ball and when I walked into the bunker I just had a premonition I would hole the sand shot. It was a good lie and I could see the stroke to be played so clearly.'

The golfer the Volvo Tour's Australian contingent call 'Laughing Timber' was still chuckling at his smash-and-grab act as he headed back to his British base for the impending birth of his first child.

Mats Lanner, top Swedish finisher

Final green drama as Harwood plays from the bunker . . .

. . . exults as the ball goes in the hole . . .

. . . and shares the moment with his caddie

COURSE: BOKSKOGEN, MALMO, SWEDEN **YARDAGE: 6,889** **PAR: 72**

POS	NAME	CTRY	1	2	3	4	TOTAL	PRIZE MONEY
1	Mike HARWOOD	Aus	66	70	67	68	271	£50000
2	Peter SENIOR	Aus	68	67	65	72	272	£33300
3	Sam TORRANCE	Scot	71	67	65	70	273	£18780
4	Mats LANNER	Swe	70	68	69	67	274	£13850
	Bernhard LANGER	W.Ger	68	66	69	71	274	£13850
6	Ronan RAFFERTY	N. Ire	69	69	66	72	276	£9750
	Philip WALTON	Ire	67	72	66	71	276	£9750
8	Ove SELLBERG	Swe	69	73	65	70	277	£7110
	Leif HEDERSTROM	Swe	71	66	70	70	277	£7110
10	Manuel MORENO	Sp	68	68	73	69	278	£6000
11	Jose Maria OLAZABAL	Sp	70	70	70	69	279	£4790
	Derrick COOPER	Eng	69	71	68	71	279	£4790
	Mike CLAYTON	Aus	68	73	67	71	279	£4790
	Jeremy BENNETT	Eng	70	70	68	71	279	£4790
	Roger CHAPMAN	Eng	69	71	67	72	279	£4790
	Frank NOBILO	NZ	71	71	67	70	279	£4790
17	Howard CLARK	Eng	69	71	70	70	280	£3960
	Barry LANE	Eng	64	74	70	72	280	£3960
19	Robin MANN	Eng	70	70	71	70	281	£3610
	Ruud BOS	Hol	67	72	72	70	281	£3610
	Jose RIVERO	Sp	73	67	69	72	281	£3610
22	Lyndsay STEPHEN	Aus	68	73	71	70	282	£3150
	Ian WOOSNAM	Wal	69	72	68	73	282	£3150
	Wayne RILEY	Aus	71	70	71	70	282	£3150
	Mark ROE	Eng	70	74	70	68	282	£3150
	Johan RYSTROM	Swe	69	66	72	75	282	£3150
	Mark JAMES	Eng	73	71	69	69	282	£3150
	Rodger DAVIS	Aus	71	71	70	70	282	£3150
29	Clive TUCKER	Eng	69	69	71	74	283	£2580
	Craig PARRY	Aus	71	72	72	68	283	£2580
	Daniel LOZANO	Sp	71	71	73	68	283	£2580
	Kevin DICKENS	Eng	70	73	66	74	283	£2580
	Anders FORSBRAND	Swe	67	75	72	69	283	£2580
	Grant TURNER	Eng	70	69	73	71	283	£2580
35	Peter BAKER	Eng	69	70	71	74	284	£2250
	Vijay SINGH	Fiji	73	70	71	70	284	£2250
	Magnus SUNESSON	Swe	71	69	72	72	284	£2250
	Gordon BRAND Jnr	Scot	71	71	70	72	284	£2250
39	Neil HANSEN	Eng	69	71	70	75	285	£1920
	David ECOB	Aus	72	72	72	69	285	£1920
	Fredrik LINDGREN	Swe	69	73	71	72	285	£1920
	Jean VAN DE VELDE	Fr	72	71	70	72	285	£1920
	Ronald STELTEN	USA	72	72	67	74	285	£1920
	Steven BOTTOMLEY	Eng	69	71	73	72	285	£1920
	Paul HUNSTONE	Eng	72	70	71	72	285	£1920
46	Joakim HAGGMAN	Swe	69	74	77	66	286	£1620
	Jerry HAAS	USA	72	70	71	73	286	£1620
	Denis DURNIAN	Eng	70	70	73	73	286	£1620
49	Christy O'CONNOR Jnr	Ire	72	71	72	72	287	£1350
	Mark DAVIS	Eng	67	73	74	73	287	£1350
	Tony CHARNLEY	Eng	71	73	70	73	287	£1350
	Magnus JONSSON	Swe	69	71	72	75	287	£1350
	Ossie MOORE	Aus	72	70	72	73	287	£1350
	Stephen McALLISTER	Scot	70	73	73	71	287	£1350
55	Anders GILLNER	Swe	72	71	73	72	288	£1080
	Ian YOUNG	Scot	70	73	71	74	288	£1080
	Peter TERAVAINEN	USA	71	72	75	70	288	£1080
58	David CURRY	Eng	73	67	71	78	289	£930
	David LLEWELLYN	Wal	70	71	73	75	289	£930
	Martin POXON	Eng	66	74	73	76	289	£930
	Mathias GRONBERG (AM)	Swe	73	70	72	74	289	–
61	Ulf NILSSON	Swe	70	72	73	75	290	£840
	Juan ROSA	Sp	71	73	75	71	290	£840
	Jimmy HEGGARTY	N. Ire	72	66	77	75	290	£840
64	Jose DAVILA	Sp	72	72	74	78	296	£780
65	Francis QUINN	USA	68	76	79	80	303	£750

THE GERMAN OPEN

PARRY
makes it a double

CHUNKY AUSTRALIAN CRAIG PARRY TOOK HIS SECOND TITLE OF THE SEASON WITH VICTORY IN FRANKFURT BUT THE MAIN DRAMA OF THE WEEK CONCERNED THE FINAL MAKE-UP OF THE JOHNNIE WALKER RYDER CUP TEAM

Like all really good dramas, the German Open at the Frankfurter Club had the advantage of a sub-plot. As the final qualifying tournament to count towards what are still quaintly referred to as Ryder Cup points and not Ryder Cup pounds, the German Open was always going to attract a large amount of interest.

Certainly the Machiavellian atmosphere as men gathered on every corner of the course to hold whispered discussions about who was doing what and who, ultimately, would get the nod from captain Tony Jacklin added a certain delicious buzz to an already above average event. As the players jostled for position across this tight, tree-lined course — four par threes, three par fives and a total par of 71 — the Press Centre became a hive of mathematical discussion. The possibilities seemed almost infinite but, really, it came down to how Philip Walton of Ireland, Mark Roe of England and Christy O'Connor Junior of Ireland performed.

Sadly, two of them committed Ryder Cup suicide by missing the cut. Walton, drawn to play with Severiano Ballesteros, over the first two days simply never got to grips with the difficulties of partnering the most popular golfer in Europe. As usual, Seve drew the biggest galleries and poor Walton was often left standing over a short putt while German fans thundered off to the next tee. "It was ridiculous at times," said the softly spoken Irishman. "There were cameras clicking all over the place and people constantly moving."

Seve, of course, is used to this sort of thing but the Spaniard was still sensitive enough to feel sorry for Walton and his plight as he played the most important 36 holes of his career. At one stage he even emerged from his own cocoon of concentration to place an arm around Walton's shoulder and tell the younger man to relax a little and just try to play his own game. "It was a nice gesture from a nice man but it failed to do the trick. I suppose the truth is that I chose the worst possible week of the year to play some of my worst golf," admitted Walton.

While he packed his bags to leave and to wonder if his record until this German Open was sufficient for Jacklin to pick him, Roe was suffering his own attack of Ryderitis, the disease that strikes normally confident golfers and reduces them to quivering wrecks. He not only blew his chances of the team to play America but lost another battle, this time for a spot in the English Dunhill Cup team. Roe had begun the German Open just a few hundred pound behind Denis Durnian but while Durnian at last made a cut, Roe messed up everything. After patiently building up a platform from which he could have sealed his best ever season with appearances at both The Belfry and St Andrews in the autumn, poor Mark fell off the gravy train with a thud. Durnian, meanwhile, struggled on to finish on 285, one over par, and in next to last position. After a succession of missed cuts it was a gutsy performance from a nice guy and one that provided at least a crumb of consolation in that Dunhill Cup place.

Meanwhile, away from the sub-plot, the German Open was throwing up some quite remarkable scoring. The Frankfurter Club is the sort of course that encourages birdie chances if a player is near the top of his form. If not, the trees that line the course and the rough that embroiders them can prove wounding. This season, however, no-one was hitting the ball with greater confidence off the tee than Mark James. He arrived in Frankfurt with his Ryder Cup spot secure following victories in the Desert Classic in Dubai, the AGF in France and the NM English Open at The Belfry. The way he opened up in Frankfurt suggested the Leeds-based golfer was about to take his fourth title of 1989.

Certainly his three opening rounds of 65-66-65 suggested either a man at the very peak of his game or a pact with some sporting devil. It was stirring stuff, even if James continued to trudge the

Parry and James limber up in the play-off

fairways with all the apparent joy of a man being dragged round a supermarket on Cup Final afternoon. He was not, however, alone in his brilliance. America's Mike Harwood outshone even James after two rounds with a brace of 65's while Mike Allen continued the rich vein of golf he unearthed to win the Bell's Scottish Open with a descending three round score that read 68-66-64.

In the end it was someone else who took the title. Craig Parry, a 23-year-old Australian who rejoices in the nickname Popeye because of his bulging forearms, spun out of the pack with a dramatic final day 64 to tie with James for first place with a total of 266, 18 under par. James, looking even more morose than usual, lost his chance when he three-putted the second play-off green. It was essentially a neat enough piece of golfing justice for he had whipped the NM English Open title away from Parry when the Aussie had to sit in The Belfry clubhouse and watch James birdie two of the last four holes to win.

Yet while Parry is clearly a man to watch in the future, the hero of the week was a golfer almost 20 years older — Jose Maria Canizares. The Spaniard believed he had to play his way into the top nine automatic places to qualify for the Ryder Cup. A second round 72 seemed to shred his chances but Jose thought otherwise and swept back into contention with a stunning 62 on a damp Saturday afternoon. It meant that when he stood on the final tee on the final day he needed a birdie three to move ahead of Bernhard Langer and clinch that Cup spot.

Easily said, not so easily done. Jose, however, did it in style, cracking an eight-iron approach to 12 feet and holing the putt. 'It was the biggest pressure hole of my career. I am proud to have done what I set out to achieve,' he said. Ironically, Tony Jacklin later confided that Canizares would have been in the side anyway. When told this piece of news, the Spaniard grinned and said: 'I wish Tony had told me that before I played that hole'.

Canizares birdies the 18th to clinch his Ryder Cup place

At the conclusion of the German Open, European Ryder Cup Captain Tony Jacklin announced his team to play the Americans at The Belfry in September. Following a telephone conversation with Sandy Lyle who was competing in America, Jacklin stated that Lyle had asked not to be considered for selection as his indifferent form could not justify a place. Therefore, the three remaining places in the team went to Bernhard Langer, Howard Clark and Christy O'Connor Junior who joined the nine players who qualified automatically.

The full European team:
Ronan Rafferty
Mark James
Jose Maria Olazabal
Nick Faldo
Ian Woosnam
Gordon Brand Junior
Severiano Ballesteros
Sam Torrance
Jose Maria Canizares
Bernhard Langer
Christy O'Connor Junior
Howard Clark

Michael Allen drives from the 17th tee

Defending champion Ballesteros takes the bulk of the crowd with him

COURSE: FRANKFURTER GOLF CLUB, FRANKFURT **YARDAGE: 6,686** **PAR: 71**

POS	NAME	CTRY	1	2	3	4	TOTAL	PRIZE MONEY
1	Craig PARRY	Aus	66	70	66	64	266	£54222
2	Mark JAMES	Eng	65	66	65	70	266	£36126
3	Michael ALLEN	USA	68	66	64	69	267	£20374
4	Mike HARWOOD	Aus	65	65	68	70	268	£16273
5	Jose Maria CANIZARES	Sp	66	72	62	69	269	£10772
	Jerry HAAS	USA	66	69	64	70	269	£10772
	Gordon BRAND Jnr	Scot	71	66	67	65	269	£10772
	Bernhard LANGER	W.Ger	68	69	67	65	269	£10772
9	Rick HARTMANN	USA	67	70	64	69	270	£6596
	Brett OGLE	Aus	66	67	68	69	270	£6596
	Jose RIVERO	Sp	69	68	66	67	270	£6596
	Sven STRUEVER (Am)	W.Ger	73	62	66	69	270	–
12	Bill MALLEY	USA	65	68	69	69	271	£5419
	Ken BROWN	Scot	66	70	65	70	271	£5419
14	Peter SENIOR	Aus	67	70	64	71	272	£4784
	David FEHERTY	N.Ire	68	70	67	67	272	£4784
	Derrick COOPER	Eng	71	65	69	67	272	£4784
17	Eduardo ROMERO	Arg	67	68	69	69	273	£4133
	Luis CARBONETTI	Arg	65	68	68	72	273	£4133
	Carl MASON	Eng	68	69	66	70	273	£4133
	Howard CLARK	Eng	69	73	67	64	273	£4133
21	Richard BOXALL	Eng	67	71	66	70	274	£3563
	Barry LANE	Eng	71	71	64	68	274	£3563
	Mark DAVIS	Eng	68	71	65	70	274	£3563
	Mark McNULTY	Zim	68	71	65	70	274	£3563
	Colin MONTGOMERIE	Scot	74	65	68	67	274	£3563
	Mats LANNER	Swe	68	68	71	67	274	£3563
27	Magnus PERSSON	Swe	72	66	69	68	275	£2978
	Christy O'CONNOR Jnr	Ire	70	70	68	67	275	£2978
	Miguel Angel JIMENEZ	Sp	72	69	69	65	275	£2978
	Armando SAAVEDRA	Arg	69	67	71	68	275	£2978
	John BLAND	SA	69	70	68	68	275	£2978
	Stephen BENNETT	Eng	66	74	64	71	275	£2978
33	Malcolm MACKENZIE	Eng	69	73	66	68	276	£2538
	Marc Antoine FARRY	Fr	67	73	68	68	276	£2538
	Ross DRUMMOND	Scot	68	69	69	70	276	£2538
	Hugh BAIOCCHI	SA	71	67	66	72	276	£2538
	Jean VAN DE VELDE	Fr	67	71	68	70	276	£2538
38	Torsten GIEDEON	W.Ger	70	69	67	71	277	£2245
	Severiano BALLESTEROS	Sp	70	69	66	72	277	£2245
	Roger CHAPMAN	Eng	67	72	69	69	277	£2245
	Martin POXON	Eng	68	71	66	72	277	£2245
42	Mikael KRANTZ	Swe	67	69	71	71	278	£2017
	Gavin LEVENSON	SA	70	71	69	68	278	£2017
	Frank NOBILO	NZ	69	73	65	71	278	£2017
45	David RAY	Eng	70	70	70	69	279	£1724
	Paul CURRY	Eng	70	65	72	72	279	£1724
	Andrew MURRAY	Eng	67	67	74	71	279	£1724
	Wayne RILEY	Aus	73	69	67	70	279	£1724
	Rodger DAVIS	Aus	69	72	69	69	279	£1724
	Sandy STEPHEN	Scot	70	72	69	68	279	£1724
51	Peter MITCHELL	Eng	70	69	73	68	280	£1269
	Vicente FERNANDEZ	Arg	67	70	70	73	280	£1269
	Philip HARRISON	Eng	69	73	68	70	280	£1269
	Keith WATERS	Eng	72	68	72	68	280	£1269
	Gordon J BRAND	Eng	72	69	68	71	280	£1269
	Neil HANSEN	Eng	72	70	68	70	280	£1269
	John SLAUGHTER	USA	70	69	73	68	280	£1269
	Emilio RODRIGUEZ	Sp	71	71	68	70	280	£1269
59	Anders SORENSEN	Den	70	69	71	71	281	£992
	Ossie MOORE	Aus	70	69	72	70	281	£992
61	David A RUSSELL	Eng	74	67	74	67	282	£943
62	Glenn RALPH	Eng	72	69	70	72	283	£754
	John JACOBS	USA	72	67	74	70	283	£754
	Don KLENK	USA	71	68	74	70	283	£754
	Marc PENDARIES	Fr	74	68	72	69	283	£754
	Ross McFARLANE	Eng	70	69	70	74	283	£754
67	David GILFORD	Eng	73	69	68	74	284	£322
	Paul MAYO	Wal	73	66	74	71	284	£322
	Carsten SCHAPMANN (Am)	W.Ger	72	67	73	72	284	–
69	Carlo KNAUSS	W.Ger	71	71	72	71	285	£318
	Denis DURNIAN	Eng	72	69	71	73	285	£318
71	Mark MOULAND	Wal	71	70	71	74	286	£315

SEVE'S
Swiss role of honour

Severiano Ballesteros arrived in Crans-sur-Sierre, 5000 feet above the Rhône Valley in Switzerland more determined than ever to win the Ebel European Masters title. The jackpot first prize of over £69,000, the second richest event in Europe, was incidental to the golfing millionaire. It was the title he was after—the title he had let slip through his fingers a year earlier when Chris Moody had stepped dramatically out of the pack to win.

Seve had been favourite in 1988 to birdie two or three, maybe even all of the last five holes on the final day to win and had failed to do so. He had promised himself that he would play those closing holes so well they would win him the title in 1989. He had won the event in '77 and again in '78 at the start of a remarkable career that has been a significant factor in the massive growth of the Volvo Tour. Ballesteros' decision not to play as regularly in America as Nick Faldo, Sandy Lyle or Bernhard Langer has been a bonus. Seve has won more events world-wide than Lyle, Faldo and Langer put together . . . and he wanted the 1989 Ebel European Masters to provide him with victory No. 59.

There was another reason why Ballesteros was keener than usual to take the top honours on a course which for six months of the year provides nursery slopes for ski beginners. Since 1983 when he was drafted into the Ryder Cup side by Tony Jacklin, Ballesteros has been an inspiration to the team. He knew that to play the same vital role again at The Belfry he needed to be at his best. He needed a good performance in the weeks immediately preceding the match to help boost his and the team's morale after the shock request Sandy Lyle had made to team captain Tony Jacklin not to be considered.

MEMORIES OF A YEAR AGO, WHEN HE HAD LET THE TITLE SLIP OVER THE CLOSING HOLES, SPURRED BALLESTEROS TO HIS 59TH, AND IN THIS CASE, VERY WELCOME, VICTORY

Ballesteros had not won since he swept aside Denis Durnian in the exciting Epson Grand Prix at Chepstow in May. He had been strangely out of tune with his game and he sensed that even the general public were beginning to worry about his form. In the weeks before Crans, Ballesteros had been soliciting help from those colleagues on Tour to whom he turns when he feels his game is less than sharp.

It had been noticeable that Seve, who has no recognised coach, had been spending more time on the practice range taking advice, listening to this prognosis and that. He had even had a chat with Nick Faldo's guru David Leadbetter and, at Frankfurt in the German Open a week earlier, he had discussed his swing with the Volvo Tour's busiest and best-known coach —Bob Torrance. Gradually he was isolating the problem. Everyone had helped but in the hours before the start of the Ebel European Masters, Seve took to looking at his own instruction book and the penny dropped. It was so simple really, but then it always is. He had been closing the club at the top of the back swing producing a series of pulled and pushed shots which he corrected by opening his stance slightly. With a few minor adjustments Seve was ready to take on the world again at the highest venue on the Volvo Tour where the air is so much thinner that it is possible to hit the ball ten per cent further than normal.

Scores are always low at Crans if the weather is good. Baldo Dassu, the former Tour player now retired from top-class action once shot 60 at the mountain course across the road from the one tournament promoter Gaston Barras is having Jack Nicklaus design and build. Jose Maria Canizares once shot 27 on the back nine—11 birdies in a row, five at the finish of the second round and six more at the start of the third in 1978—and he still lost out to Ballesteros! Gaston Barras, whose drive and enthusiasm has made the Ebel-sponsored event one of the most successful at one of the most unlikely of venues, had been delighted to have wooed Ballesteros to Crans. His presence made up for the fact that Nick Faldo, the US Master golfer had decided to give the event a miss and had been released to play in an invitational event in Paris. Sandy Lyle, struggling with his game had come, but

Swiss chocolate box setting for Severiano Ballesteros

eight of the 1989 Ryder Cup men had not been able to schedule Crans on their busy programmes.

Cup men Jose Maria Olazabal, Canizares and Bernhard Langer, who had been showing a return to form after a dismal Open at Troon, were in attendance however, along with Seve. The event was minus its traditional top American challenge although former US Amateur champion Eric Meeks made the trip only to miss the cut in his first international event as a professional. Britain's former top amateur Russell Claydon, who had played a part in the historic triumph over America in the Walker Cup at Peachtree in Atlanta two weeks earlier, was in the field too. It was his second event since leaving the amateur ranks and he made the cut with nothing to spare.

Severiano Ballesteros was the star, however, and a seven-under-par 65 on the first day tied him for the lead with Langer, former Ryder Cup golfer Ken Brown, Grimsby's bespectacled Stephen Bennett, and Mats Lanner, who felt, no doubt that he was quite capable of winning as his countryman Anders Forsbrand had done two years earlier. At half-way Seve had lost his lead to fellow Spaniard Jose Rivero, who produced the form that had eluded him most of the season and cost him his Ryder Cup place. Rivero's half-way total of 14-under-par 130 meant he led by two from the Frenchman, Emmanuel Dussart; Barry Lane, who had been expected to

Second round start lost in the mists of time

make the Ryder Cup side; the consistent Bennett; and Ballesteros.

At 5000 feet the weather can, at times, be a problem. Low cloud can blanket the course for hours until a wind picks up to blow it even higher up the mountain towards the Pleine Mort glacier. On the third day it was thought no play would be possible as fog reduced visibility to 40 yards. It was eerily still. The eight o'clock start was put back to nine, to 10am, to 11.35 and finally John Paramor, the most experienced of the PGA European Tour officials decided on a 1pm deadline. If it was not possible to start by then a smaller number of the survivors of the half-way cut—a group which did not include defending champion Moody—would play two rounds on the Sunday—weather permitting. By a miracle, at 12.45 the flags began to flutter, a breeze sprung up and the third round started five hours late.

Hanging lie?

Derrick Cooper and David Jones look thoroughly fogged off

In the evening gloom it was Rivero who still held centre stage after a 67 for 19-under-par 197 but he had just a single shot lead from Bennett, who was having his tournament of the year. Seve and Barry Lane were two behind on 199, Ballesteros having birdied three of the last four holes to pick up two shots on Rivero who had three-putted the last. Seve was now ready for a last day charge.

An outward 31 on the final day brought Craig Parry sweeping into contention as Rivero, with an eight on his card at the ninth, took ten more shots than the Australian for the first nine. Lane, looking for inspiration, could find none, but Bennett maintained his bid to do what Moody had done a year earlier. With five to play, Ballesteros and Parry were tied on 20 under par, one clear of Bennett and the 21-year-old Swiss pro Paolo Quirici, the week's surprise packet. He had shot 60 round the course earlier in the

Sixth place finish for Barry Lane

year and wanted a finish in the top half-dozen to earn his Tour card for 1990. The diabetic from Lugano in the Italian-speaking area of Switzerland had lost a play-off for 50th place at the 1988 school but when he holed from 60 yards at the 16th for an eagle two and 19-under he knew he had done enough to avoid a second school visit. With rounds of 72, 67, 66 and a closing 65 he finished joint fourth with the recovering Rivero on 270. Bennett was unable to make birdies on the closing run but ended up doubling his season's earnings by finishing third on 269.

The title would go then to Ballesteros or Parry—whoever played the closing holes better. The Australian, built like Ian Woosnam and with the same drive and determination, birdied the long 14th and was momentarily ahead but he took four from the edge at the 15th and they were locked together again at 20-under. It was time for the Ballesteros push. While Parry could only par his way in, Ballesteros, on the holes that had proved so costly a year earlier, birdied the 16th and 17th. Par at the last gave him victory for the third time by two shots on a 22-under-par 266. He had done the job the way he wanted to do it. The Severiano smile was broader than usual . . . and all his Ryder Cup team colleagues were delighted too. Seve was back to his best.

Parry's thrust fell short

High Alpine finish

Third round leader Jose Rivero

Bennett pops the cork for Ballesteros

COURSE: CRANS-SUR-SIERRE, SWITZERLAND YARDAGE: 6,811 PAR: 72

POS	NAME	CTRY	1	2	3	4	TOTAL	PRIZE MONEY
1	Severiano BALLESTEROS	Sp	65	68	66	67	266	£69024
2	Craig PARRY	Aus	66	69	66	67	268	£45988
3	Stephen BENNETT	Eng	65	67	66	71	269	£25935
4	Jose RIVERO	Sp	66	64	67	73	270	£19141
	Paolo QUIRICI	Swi	72	67	66	65	270	£19141
6	Barry LANE	Eng	67	65	67	72	271	£14500
7	Colin MONTGOMERIE	Scot	68	66	67	71	272	£12429
8	Gavin LEVENSON	SA	68	66	71	68	273	£9308
	Mats LANNER	Swe	65	72	65	71	273	£9308
	Jose Maria OLAZABAL	Sp	69	70	69	65	273	£9308
11	Ossie MOORE	Aus	66	70	68	73	277	£6769
	Derrick COOPER	Eng	67	68	74	68	277	£6769
	Manuel GARCIA	Sp	68	69	70	70	277	£6769
	Eduardo ROMERO	Arg	71	66	69	71	277	£6769
	Jose Maria CANIZARES	Sp	69	70	71	67	277	£6769
16	David JONES	N. Ire	67	68	71	72	278	£5377
	Richard BOXALL	Eng	70	70	67	71	278	£5377
	Miguel Angel JIMENEZ	Sp	69	67	71	71	278	£5377
	John BLAND	SA	69	68	70	71	278	£5377
	Jerry HAAS	USA	66	68	72	72	278	£5377
21	Mariano APARICIO	Sp	73	66	72	68	279	£4474
	Brian MARCHBANK	Scot	68	72	70	69	279	£4474
	Massimo MANNELLI	It	67	68	75	69	279	£4474
	Alberto BINAGHI	It	68	72	72	67	279	£4474
	Magnus PERSSON	Swe	68	70	71	70	279	£4474
	Malcolm MACKENZIE	Eng	68	70	72	69	279	£4474
	Keith WATERS	Eng	69	72	67	71	279	£4474
28	Sandy LYLE	Scot	70	69	72	69	280	£3790
	Carl MASON	Eng	68	73	70	69	280	£3790
	Peter McWHINNEY	Aus	73	64	74	69	280	£3790
	Mark McNULTY	Zim	70	71	67	72	280	£3790
32	Roger CHAPMAN	Eng	72	69	71	69	281	£3148
	Paul CARRIGILL	Eng	70	72	70	69	281	£3148
	Leif HEDERSTRÖM	Swe	68	73	72	68	281	£3148
	Paul CURRY	Eng	68	73	71	69	281	£3148
	David A RUSSELL	Eng	69	68	72	72	281	£3148
	Jeff HAWKES	SA	70	69	68	74	281	£3148
	Ken BROWN	Scot	65	72	75	69	281	£3148
	Tony CHARNLEY	Eng	73	69	68	71	281	£3148
	Mike HARWOOD	Aus	66	74	71	70	281	£3148
41	Ron COMMANS	USA	71	70	73	68	282	£2568
	Bernhard LANGER	W. Ger	65	75	73	69	282	£2568
	Lyndsay STEPHEN	Aus	67	70	75	70	282	£2568
	Philip WALTON	Ire	70	71	70	71	282	£2568
	Michael ALLEN	USA	72	68	73	69	282	£2568
46	Ronald STELTEN	USA	67	69	71	76	283	£2237
	Bob E SMITH	USA	70	72	71	70	283	£2237
	Juan ANGLADA	Sp	69	70	72	72	283	£2237
49	Aaron MEEKS	USA	69	69	74	72	284	£1822
	Frank NOBILO	NZ	68	72	71	73	284	£1822
	Gordon J BRAND	Eng	67	72	75	70	284	£1822
	Mikael KRANTZ	Swe	68	71	73	72	284	£1822
	Bill LONGMUIR	Scot	66	74	73	71	284	£1822
	Manuel MORENO	Sp	68	71	73	72	284	£1822
	Michael KING	Eng	68	69	78	69	284	£1822
56	Johan TUMBA	Swe	72	67	74	72	285	£1325
	Vicente FERNANDEZ	Arg	73	69	73	70	285	£1325
	Johan RYSTROM	Swe	71	69	75	70	285	£1325
	Emmanuel DUSSART	Fr	66	67	76	76	285	£1325
	Bernard GALLACHER	Scot	70	72	74	69	285	£1325
	Des SMYTH	Ire	71	71	71	72	285	£1325
62	Steen TINNING	Den	69	72	72	73	286	£1097
	Paul HOAD	Eng	66	74	71	75	286	£1097
	Jean VAN DE VELDE	Fr	71	69	76	70	286	£1097
	Brian EVANS	Eng	70	72	71	73	286	£1097
66	David WHELAN	Eng	68	68	77	74	287	£412
	Hugh BAIOCCHI	SA	74	68	74	71	287	£412
	Jesper PARNEVIK	Swe	70	71	78	68	287	£412
69	Marc PENDARIES	Fr	72	70	72	74	288	£406
	Vijay SINGH	Fij	69	71	72	76	288	£406
	Mark MOULAND	Wal	72	69	72	75	288	£406
72	Wayne STEPHENS	Eng	73	68	75	74	290	£402
73	Glenn RALPH	Eng	68	69	73	81	291	£400
74	Mike CLAYTON	Aus	70	72	77	75	294	£398

PANASONIC EUROPEAN OPEN

MURRAY *mints it in Surrey*

Poignant indeed was the sight of a man striving to attain his first victory before his time ran out. Not just any man, but the 33-year-old professional from Manchester, Andrew Murray, 17 years in golf, 11 years on the Tour, full of heart, humour and honesty.

You crossed your fingers and hoped that this courageous man might achieve his dream in sight of his wife Deborah, five months pregnant with their second child, and their first, 17-month old Benjamin, who one day will know that he, too, witnessed the likely pinnacle of his father's career.

As Andrew Murray and New Zealand's Frank Nobilo claimed first and second place in the European Open at Walton Heath, it flicked across the mind that it might be more appropriate if BUPA were the sponsors rather than Panasonic. Not that either professional wanted to claim any sympathy on medical grounds, but it just so happened that both men recently had been faced with the frailty of the human body. Both knew that health was more important than getting a little white ball into a hole, although that was their objective for the week.

Nobilo had undergone a major operation in February, from which it took him several months to recover. Murray was rendered speechless in July by the result of some X-rays, which showed that his inherited arthritic condition of spondylitis had degenerated further than he knew. Specialist advice was to think about finding another job.

'Why me?' was a reaction that he soon conquered with positive thinking as he realised that if he was going to retire from tournament golf with a bang rather than a whimper, he should make

WITH HIS CAREER THREATENED BY A DEGENERATIVE ARTHRITIC CONDITION, ANDREW MURRAY RECORDED AN EMOTIONAL VICTORY FOR THE BIGGEST PRIZE OF HIS LIFE

his mark pretty rapidly. 'I wanted to be remembered as a winner,' he said, but he will remain in the mind for much more than that.

Ian Woosnam was the defending champion, Sandy Lyle was in the field, Russell Claydon, fresh from Walker Cup euphoria, had gone straight into the professional world where, in two tournaments, he had missed the cut and finished last.

Two days of heat and sunshine were followed by a colder front and some rain; Walton Heath was short, fast running, with some of those tricky bounces which cause trouble. Almost predictably, Sandy Lyle came in with an opening 69 to be up among the leaders: 'I felt happier, which is the main thing. It's been like pulling teeth,' said this likeable man. 'It could be getting the Ryder Cup out of my mind and not having any thoughts of an 85.' You felt sorry that Lyle should suffer. Undoubtedly he would come through, but it seemed unlikely to happen yet.

Masahiro Kuramoto, a fine Japanese player, came in with a 68 which included a double bogey seven when he remained in a bunker at the second. A graduate in Economics, he explained in charming English that he won 26 tournaments in Japan and billions of yen—over half a million dollars—in 1988 alone.

Murray's leading 66 was noted at 6.45pm when there were seven groups still to finish. Murray three-putted thrice and mused, almost to himself: 'Ironic, really, that I should shoot 66 and be half-thinking about another job.'

On the second day, Murray began with five birdies in six holes on the way to a 68 and his ten-under-par 134 gave him the limelight four strokes ahead of the field: 'I may appear calm and serene on the outside,' he told us, 'but like a duck, I'm paddling like hell underneath.' The next morning a highly nervous Andrew Murray met his wife and child at Gatwick Airport: 'I was jumping around so much that my car, complete with golf clubs, was nearly towed away,' he said.

Paired with Claydon in the third round it was a happy and contrasting duo, with solidly-built Claydon chatting aimiably throughout to the more jumpy and frail-looking Murray. 'You couldn't play with anyone nicer,' said Murray appreciatively. 'I'm a nervous character, I'm not like Jack Nicklaus. He's won a few million quid, I've won £120,000.

Maybe if I win four European Opens I'll be a bit better.' Murray's agitation caused him to drop shots at the last three holes, but earlier birdies gave him a 71, an 11-under-par total, three ahead of Nobilo.

Deborah Murray, with a wriggling Benjamin in her arms, said: 'I'm quietly confident about tomorrow.' And as tomorrow came, Murray slept well until 6.30am, while his wife tossed and turned and said her prayers.

The biggest challenge of Murray's career developed into a battle with Nobilo. A tense Murray reminded himself at the 16th that they were both nervous and it was he who possessed the one stroke lead. Of his magnificent six iron to the final green, Murray commented: 'I'll remember it forever.' With hands which could not feel the putter, a nervous first stab left him a testing return putt for victory. The watching world held its breath. A brave putt followed and the emotions spilled over. The warmth felt for Murray was exceptional, but so was the man and the manner of his victory. He articulated his elation: 'This is how Faldo feels every week. I'll savour this moment as long as I live. Leading from wire to wire, as the Americans say, gives it credibility, and in Britain, and with television.

'Winning in that style is worth more than the £58,000. It's the recognition of my peers that really counts. It's fantastic how much support I've received all week from everyone, including the players. Sam Torrance gave me a big hug and that means a lot.'

Murray's final 72 and 11-under-par total was one ahead of Nobilo, with Sam Torrance two further back, Woosnam on seven under with Craig Parry, and Russell Claydon making a tidy £11,375 on five under, helping him towards avoiding the Tour's Qualifying School in December.

Russell Claydon recovers on the 14th, right, while Sam Torrance, below, grimaces at a missed putt

View from the TV tower behind the 17th

Right, happy moment for winner and caddie. Left, runner-up Frank Nobilo

Above and left, Murray's second shot to the final green

Mark James and Nick Faldo are both bracken-bound

Exultation as Murray's final putt drops followed by emotional embrace with his family

COURSE: WALTON HEATH GOLF CLUB **YARDAGE: 7,108** **PAR: 72**

POS	NAME	CTRY	1	2	3	4	TOTAL	PRIZE MONEY
1	Andrew MURRAY	Eng	66	68	71	72	277	£58330
2	Frank NOBILO	NZ	70	69	69	70	278	£38860
3	Sam TORRANCE	Scot	70	71	69	70	280	£21910
4	Craig PARRY	Aus	73	72	70	66	281	£16165
	Ian WOOSNAM	Wal	71	68	70	72	281	£16165
6	Russell CLAYDON	Eng	70	68	71	74	283	£11375
	Ross DRUMMOND	Scot	70	69	71	73	283	£11375
8	Sandy LYLE	Scot	69	74	71	70	284	£7863
	Rodger DAVIS	Aus	69	73	72	70	284	£7863
	David FEHERTY	N.Ire	72	71	71	70	284	£7863
11	Mark JAMES	Eng	70	73	75	67	285	£6230
	Scott HOCH	USA	69	69	77	70	285	£6230
13	Peter FOWLER	Aus	67	72	79	68	286	£4947
	Martin POXON	Eng	70	71	72	73	286	£4947
	Michael ALLEN	USA	74	69	76	67	286	£4947
	Vijay SINGH	Fij	74	70	73	69	286	£4947
	Derrick COOPER	Eng	72	69	70	75	286	£4947
	John BLAND	SA	73	73	71	69	286	£4947
	Peter SENIOR	Aus	70	68	71	77	286	£4947
20	Eduardo ROMERO	Arg	70	73	74	71	288	£3990
	Roger CHAPMAN	Eng	71	67	78	72	288	£3990
	Nick FALDO	Eng	72	73	73	70	288	£3990
	Tony JOHNSTONE	Zim	71	76	71	70	288	£3990
	Rick HARTMANN	USA	70	70	76	72	288	£3990
25	Colin MONTGOMERIE	Scot	71	70	76	72	289	£3622
	Howard CLARK	Eng	70	72	77	70	289	£3622
27	Jesper PARNEVIK	Swe	73	74	72	71	290	£3155
	Peter TERAVAINEN	USA	72	75	76	67	290	£3155
	Ronan RAFFERTY	N.Ire	74	72	74	70	290	£3155
	Hugh BAIOCCHI	SA	73	67	75	75	290	£3155
	Paul KENT	Eng	74	69	74	73	290	£3155
	Des SMYTH	Ire	73	68	76	73	290	£3155
	Joe HIGGINS	Eng	71	75	77	67	290	£3155
34	Masahiro KURAMOTO	Jap	68	75	72	76	291	£2765
	Ken BROWN	Scot	72	73	76	70	291	£2765
36	Jean VAN DE VELDE	Fr	70	71	80	71	292	£2450
	Steen TINNING	Den	71	71	79	71	292	£2450
	Stephen McALLISTER	Scot	69	72	73	78	292	£2450
	Ron COMMANS	USA	71	73	74	74	292	£2450
	Marc PENDARIES	Fr	71	74	75	72	292	£2450
	David LLEWELLYN	Wal	71	72	75	74	292	£2450
	Gordon BRAND Jnr	Scot	69	74	77	72	292	£2450
43	Wayne RILEY	Aus	72	75	77	69	293	£2065
	Stephen BENNETT	Eng	71	71	76	75	293	£2065
	Tony CHARNLEY	Eng	75	68	77	73	293	£2065
	Gordon J BRAND	Eng	73	73	71	76	293	£2065
47	Jamie HOWELL	USA	72	74	77	71	294	£1750
	Richard BOXALL	Eng	75	72	73	74	294	£1750
	Luis CARBONETTI	Arg	74	73	77	70	294	£1750
	John SLAUGHTER	USA	72	72	80	70	294	£1750
	Denis DURNIAN	Eng	75	70	72	77	294	£1750
52	Jimmy HEGGARTY	N. Ire	72	75	72	76	295	£1299
	David JONES	N. Ire	71	73	78	73	295	£1299
	Andrew STUBBS	Eng	76	69	73	77	295	£1299
	Mats HALLBERG	Swe	73	74	78	70	295	£1299
	Paul HOAD	Eng	72	73	77	73	295	£1299
	Eamonn DARCY	Ire	75	70	79	71	295	£1299
	Mike SMITH	USA	68	74	78	75	295	£1299
	Neil COLES	Eng	72	72	77	74	295	£1299
60	Paul MAYO	Wal	73	73	77	73	296	£962
	David A RUSSELL	Eng	74	72	79	71	296	£962
	Wayne STEPHENS	Eng	72	74	75	75	296	£962
	Grant TURNER	Eng	70	73	80	73	296	£962
	Anders SORENSEN	Den	71	74	76	75	296	£962
	Chris MOODY	Eng	73	70	77	76	296	£962
66	Jerry HAAS	USA	73	72	78	74	297	£350
67	Paul CURRY	Eng	71	76	73	78	298	£348
68	Kevin DICKENS	Eng	77	70	79	73	299	£346
69	Johan TUMBA	Swe	72	74	75	80	301	£344
70	Bradley HUGHES	Aus	72	75	76	79	302	£342
71	Bryan NORTON	USA	70	75	81	77	303	£339
	Glenn RALPH	Eng	74	73	79	77	303	£339
73	Manuel MORENO	Sp	71	76	78	79	304	£336

MANUFACTURERS HANOVER
TROPHÉE

ROMERO *is the dark horse*

WHILE ALL EYES WERE ON THE ASSEMBLY OF WORLD STARS GATHERED IN PARIS, IT WAS THE UNFANCIED EDUARDO ROMERO FROM ARGENTINA WHO SWEPT IN TO TAKE THE TITLE

Even with a dozen attempts you wouldn't have picked the winner of the Trophée Lancôme. The obvious choices were any one of Europe's eleven Ryder Cup players or maybe Greg Norman, who had won two tournaments in the preceding three weeks.

If none of those appealed, then there was Curtis Strange, though as Seve Ballesteros would pointedly remark in a bit of pre-Ryder Cup psychological warfare a few days later: 'Curtis has never won a tournament in Europe.' Even Andrew Murray could be considered a contender. The way he had led from fantastic start to nervous finish at Walton Heath the previous week meant that he had left behind the ranks of journeymen pros.

The chances are that you'd never have picked Eduardo Romero, who had had only two top-ten finishes in his previous 20 tournaments. The Argentinian might look the spitting image of Rodger Davis but so far he hadn't played like him. No one gave Romero a glance, particularly not when Andrew Murray holed his second shot for an eagle on the ninth in his opening round. He thought to himself: 'This is all right.' We thought to ourselves: 'Here we go again,' and the Parisians clapped and said *'C'est magnifique.'* Murray went on to record a 64, thereby setting a record for the new course, which is a composite of seven holes from the Blue and eleven holes from the Red.

It's interesting to note the effect on a player who had made a quantum leap forward. Chris Moody improved steadily last year after stealing the Ebel European Masters-Swiss Open from half a dozen players. He credited his victory to working with David Leadbetter and took some pleasure in repeating Leadbetter's remark, on hearing that Moody had won in Switzerland: "Even I didn't know I was that good."

It wasn't only Murray's bank balance that received a boost when he won at Walton Heath. His confidence and self-esteem soared, too. He was flattered by the compliments paid to him by his peers. Always a nervous fellow with a ready line in self-deprecation, he now said: "Suddenly I feel like I belong." And knowing that, he began playing as though he belonged, too. He led the field by two shots after his 64. Even his second round of 78 was part of the learning process. It brought him back to earth and then he showed his courage with rounds of 68 and 65 to finish equal ninth, ahead of Greg Norman, Seve Ballesteros and Curtis Strange, three of the very men of whom he had once been in total awe.

Peter Fowler took over the lead from Murray after a second round 64. A tall, gawky Australian, Fowler had a secret weapon—his mother-in-law. Since the birth of her daughter's second child in April, mother-in-law had been trailing around the golf tournaments of Europe helping to change nappies and sharing a room with her new grandchild so her son-in-law could get some sleep. While Fowler played golf, she was left holding the baby. It worked well.

There was so much happening on top of everything else—Peter Senior was disqualified for taking an illegal drop—that little attention was paid to Romero who followed his opening 69 with a 65. Instead we concentrated on the familiar faces, the promising Mark Davis, who had a 66, Frank Nobilo, narrowly beaten the previous week, who had a 65, on Greg Norman's 74, on Strange's 70. And on Bernhard Langer, who had another 68.

Most golfers play well only when they're feeling well. Langer plays well when he's well *and* when he's ill. A couple of nights earlier while suffering from a sinus infection he slept beneath five blankets, while wearing a sweater and trousers. He shivered for most of the night and thought about pulling out of the tournament. Just as well he didn't. He played superbly, a second 68 helping him get rid of his sinus problems.

By the third round Romero was demanding our attention. A 66 took him to 10 under par, two shots behind

Club examination by Strange and Feherty, below

Bunker trouble for Romero, above

Fowler and ahead of Langer and Jose Maria Olazabal. These two were leading their Ryder Cup team-mates into form. Ballesteros was the only player over par.

Sandy Lyle and Nick Faldo had a spat when Lyle twice distracted Faldo as he was about to play. Lyle apologised but the incident underlined the pressure they were under—Lyle to regain some kind of form and Faldo to be at his best for the Ryder Cup.

Sunday was a lovely warm day, and *le tout Paris* was there dressed as only Parisians can. They probably thought that if Fowler faltered they would see a victory by Olazabal or Langer. And that's how it looked for 15 holes. On the 16th, Romero, a long hitter, sank a 50-yard wedge shot for an eagle three to take the lead. Two pars, once getting up and down from a bunker, gave him a 66 and a one-stroke victory, the first for ten years by a player from Argentina on the European Tour. He looked more than ever like a former film star from a South American movie as he smiled in the setting sun. He looked a very happy man. And why shouldn't he? He had just won nearly £70,000, which is more money than he won in the whole of last season as well as being a lot of pesos in Argentina.

Hats off to the winner

It's the real swing from Faldo, right

'Allo, 'allo, qu'est ce qui se passe ici?

Fowler père et enfant sur le putting green

Double line up for Romero and caddie

Technical hitch for Curtis Strange

Tunnel vision from Bernhard Langer

Olazabal catches the post

Victory salute from Romero

COURSE: ST NOM LA BRETECHE, VERSAILLES YARDAGE: 6,756 PAR: 70

POS	NAME	CTRY	1	2	3	4	TOTAL	PRIZE MONEY
1	Eduardo ROMERO	Arg	69	65	66	66	266	£68330
2	Bernhard LANGER	W.Ger	68	68	66	65	267	£35585
	Jose Maria OLAZABAL	Sp	67	70	65	65	267	£35585
4	Peter FOWLER	Aus	66	64	68	70	268	£20600
5	David FEHERTY	N.Ire	68	69	67	65	269	£17400
6	Vijay SINGH	Fij	70	71	66	67	274	£12320
	Howard CLARK	Eng	69	74	67	64	274	£12320
	Craig PARRY	Aus	68	69	68	69	274	£12320
9	Sam TORRANCE	Scot	72	68	69	66	275	£8306
	Andrew MURRAY	Eng	64	78	68	65	275	£8306
	Mats LANNER	Swe	72	74	62	67	275	£8306
12	Brett OGLE	Aus	71	72	67	66	276	£6467
	Ronan RAFFERTY	N.Ire	67	74	66	69	276	£6467
	Frank NOBILO	NZ	72	65	72	67	276	£6467
	Rodger DAVIS	Aus	70	68	71	67	276	£6467
16	Barry LANE	Eng	72	69	68	68	277	£5340
	Des SMYTH	Ire	70	74	67	66	277	£5340
	Greg NORMAN	Aus	66	74	69	68	277	£5340
	Curtis STRANGE	USA	67	70	72	68	277	£5340
20	Vicente FERNANDEZ	Arg	73	67	71	67	278	£4550
	Severiano BALLESTEROS	Sp	70	68	71	69	278	£4550
	Tony JOHNSTONE	Zim	71	69	71	67	278	£4550
	Christy O'CONNOR Jnr	Ire	70	69	69	70	278	£4550
	David WILLIAMS	Eng	70	68	73	67	278	£4550
	Jose RIVERO	Sp	75	68	69	66	278	£4550
26	Mark DAVIS	Eng	72	66	68	73	279	£4010
	Masahiro KURAMOTO	Jap	73	69	72	65	279	£4010
	Colin MONTGOMERIE	Scot	66	69	74	70	279	£4010
29	Nick FALDO	Eng	71	70	69	70	280	£3590
	Roger CHAPMAN	Eng	66	72	72	70	280	£3590
	John BLAND	SA	71	73	68	68	280	£3590
	Jean VAN DE VELDE	Fr	67	73	72	68	280	£3590
33	Gordon J BRAND	Eng	70	72	71	68	281	£3170
	Philip WALTON	Ire	72	66	72	71	281	£3170
	Eamonn DARCY	Ire	72	72	70	67	281	£3170
	Mark ROE	Eng	69	73	69	70	281	£3170
	Michael KING	Eng	72	69	70	70	281	£3170
38	Malcolm MACKENZIE	Eng	73	75	68	66	282	£2930
39	Mark McNULTY	Zim	70	74	69	70	283	£2770
	Mark JAMES	Eng	73	71	69	70	283	£2770
	Jesper PARNEVIK	Swe	72	70	72	69	283	£2770
42	Jeff HAWKES	SA	75	75	66	68	284	£2490
	Magnus PERSSON	Swe	71	72	72	69	284	£2490
	Jose Maria CANIZARES	Sp	71	73	70	70	284	£2490
	Stephen BENNETT	Eng	70	72	71	71	284	£2490
46	Mark MOULAND	Wal	70	74	73	68	285	£2250
	Richard BOXALL	Eng	74	72	72	67	285	£2250
48	Carl MASON	Eng	67	71	76	72	286	£2050
	Marc FARRY	Fr	75	73	70	68	286	£2050
	Emmanuel DUSSART	Fr	74	73	74	65	286	£2050
51	Sandy LYLE	Scot	72	69	72	74	287	£1850
	Hugh BAIOCCHI	SA	74	74	69	70	287	£1850
53	Ove SELLBERG	Swe	76	73	73	67	289	£1690
	Philip PARKIN	Wal	73	74	71	71	289	£1690
55	Michael ALLEN	USA	77	74	69	71	291	£1450
	Ken BROWN	Scot	73	73	74	71	291	£1450
	David GILFORD	Eng	73	74	73	71	291	£1450
	Grant TURNER	Eng	73	72	76	70	291	£1450
59	Tony CHARNLEY	Eng	75	73	77	67	292	£1280
60	Gordon BRAND Jnr	Scot	71	78	67	77	293	£1240
61	Denis DURNIAN	Eng	75	77	69	74	295	£1200
62	Jerry HAAS	USA	74	76	74	72	296	£1160
63	Derrick COOPER	Eng	76	77	75	72	300	£1120
64	Luis CARBONETTI	Arg	75	78	75	73	301	£1080
65	Paul WAY	Eng	74	79	71	80	304	£1040
66	Peter SENIOR	Aus	70	DISQUALIFIED				£1000

EUROPEANS
maintain the momentum

In the cool of a sunlit September evening, Tony Jacklin stood clutching the Ryder Cup tightly to his chest and the smile on his face signalled that the European beat goes on. The Johnnie Walker Ryder Cup matches had ended in a tie after a pulsating, emotional finish that left both players and spectators drained, but the important thing was that the European team retained the trophy and the momentum of the previous two victories had not been halted.

It was, perhaps, equally important that the American team did not lose in order to prevent rampant nationalism swamping the contest and undermining one of the last bastions of genuine international sporting endeavour. In the build up to the battle at The Belfry a great many brave, and sometimes foolish, words had been winging their way across the Atlantic regarding what the Americans were going to do to the Europeans. Having been despatched from a White House reception with the Presidential exhortation 'Don't come back without the Cup' ringing in their ears, Ray Floyd and his men certainly had the motivation.

There comes a time when the tub-thumping and the jingoism has to stop and the clubs are unsheathed in earnest. On the Thursday afternoon Jacklin and Floyd announced their pairings for the following morning foursomes with Jacklin, by way of a final riposte, declaring that the Cup wasn't going anywhere that week.

Jacklin had led with strength, putting Nick Faldo and Ian Woosnam out first, a move that Floyd had anticipated and responded to with his pairing of Tom Kite and Curtis Strange. The second match found Mark James and Howard

BILLED AS THE 'MATCH OF THE CENTURY' THE 28TH CONTEST FOR THE RYDER CUP HAD EVERYTHING, EXCEPT A WINNER

Clark against Larry Wadkins and Payne Stewart while Jacklin had slipped his second 'banker' team of Seve Ballesteros and Jose Maria Olazabal in the third match where they faced Tom Watson and Chip Beck. Floyd had thought that the Spaniards would be in the bottom game which is where he had tucked his tough men, Ken Green and Mark Calcavecchia, who were playing Ronan Rafferty and Bernhard Langer.

On a dull day it was, peculiarly, Woosnam who struck the opening shot since it is traditional to allow the visitors the first blow. But it was also the home side that drew first blood, moving to two up after three holes. That happy position changed very quickly as two birdies from the Americans and a complete hash of the 10th by the home team swung the match the other way. A birdie putt at the 14th from Woosnam and another rallying birdie at the long 15th levelled matters and that is how they remained until they reached the 18th tee.

The first act of the drama which was to unfold on this dramatic hole in the ensuing days then took place. Playing into a strong wind, it was all the American duo could do to clear the water with both drive and second shot. Meanwhile, Woosnam had dumped the European second shot in the right hand bunker leaving Faldo with one from that awkward distance of around 30 yards. From the edge of the water, Strange played a fine pitch to around 12 feet and Faldo responded with one to eight feet. The Americans then holed and with the burden squarely on his shoulders, Woosnam followed suit for the half.

In the second match, Wadkins and Stewart produced the best golf of the morning, being round in 68, but only winning on the final green against Clark and James. The latter even had a good chance of squaring the match at the 18th when the Americans had to lay up short of the water but, faced with a long chip from the fringe, James was unable to put the ball close enough for Clark to hole.

Ballesteros and Olazabal against Beck and Watson was really a point squandered as the Spaniards moved to three up when Olazabal drove to within 12 feet of the hole across the water at the 10th. The Americans fought back and, with two birdies and an errant Ballesteros drive on the 13th, had levelled the score after 14 holes. Europe went one up when Beck charged a long putt on the 15th but the home side three-putted the 16th and

the match stayed square to the end.

The Rafferty/Langer combination never got going against Calcavecchia and Green with the Americans sitting back while their opponents self-destructed. Out in 41, Rafferty and Langer were fortunate to be only three down and their hopes of any rescue act disappeared when they halved the long 15th in seven.

The European mood at lunch was therefore as gloomy as the weather. Nursing a 3-1 deficit was not part of the

The opening ceremony, left

Faldo and Woosnam in the pink again

Watery grave for Clark at the 10th

game plan. Jacklin did not panic however, dropping the Rafferty/Langer pairing in favour of Sam Torrance and Gordon Brand Junior but otherwise sticking with his pairings. On the other hand, Floyd stuck with his promise to give every player an outing on the first two days. In came Paul Azinger to join Strange in the top match against Torrance and Brand, Wadkins partnered Fred Couples against Clark and James, Mark McCumber joined Calcavecchia against Faldo and Woosnam and in the final game it was Watson and Mark O'Meara against Ballesteros and Olazabal.

Two years ago at Muirfield Village the Europeans had whitewashed the Americans in the first day four-balls and by golly, they did it again. The inspiration came from Ballesteros and Olazabal as they simply ripped into Watson and O'Meara. They won the first five holes and although the Americans got it back to three, an inspired burst of 2-3-2-3 from the 10th by Ballesteros put the issue beyond doubt. Spurred on by these events from the back of the field, the other three European pairings responded in like fashion. Clark and James always had the edge over Couples and Wadkins while Woosnam and Faldo, although taken to the 18th by Calcavecchia and McCumber, had too much firepower as both the Americans found the water with their second shots to the 18th — Calcavecchia's second actually skipped across the surface to land on the 'beach' at the water's edge.

In the top game, Torrance and Brand were two up with two to play but then Strange holed a monster putt for an eagle at the 17th. Neither Azinger nor Strange could make the second shot carry on the 18th and wisely laid up. Torrance unleashed a massive drive but even he needed a two iron for his second, which he flew over the back of the green. Brand hit a wood which bounced off a hospitality marquee into the right-hand bunker leaving him a shot of some 40 yards. Torrance played a heavy-handed pitch and with the Americans looking good for a four, it all depended on Brand. He struck a truly magnificent shot, picking the ball from the sand with a pitching wedge and leaving it eight feet beyond the pin. The putt went bravely down and the clean sweep was complete.

The Americans were stunned. To lose one set of four-balls may be regarded as slightly freakish, to lose two is nothing short of disastrous. The Europeans had turned a two point deficit into a two point lead and, more importantly, had struck a huge psychological blow.

Would there be an American backlash on the second day and could the Europeans withstand it? The question was successfully answered with honours even after the morning foursomes. The old firms of Faldo/Woosnam and Ballesteros/Olazabal again did the business against Wadkins/Stewart and Kite/Strange respectively. Brand and Torrance ran into a torrid display from Beck and Azinger who were six under par when the match ended on the 15th and the new all-Irish combination of O'Connor and Rafferty, despite having the most vociferous support, never gelled and lost to Green and Calcavecchia.

For the afternoon four-balls, Floyd changed his tactics regarding giving everybody a run out on the day and stuck with Beck and Azinger and Green and Calcavecchia. In the top game where Beck and Azinger faced Woos-

Olazabal drives the 10th on the first day

Fiesta time for Ballesteros and Olazabal on the 18th

First day scoreboard

Up periscopes

Vital putt from Ballesteros to win second day foursomes

Olazabal shadowed the Americans all the way

nam and Faldo it looked a wise move. The Americans simply carried on where they left off in the morning and between the four players there were 20 birdies in the 17 holes needed before the Americans won.

In the second game, Ballesteros and Olazabal cruised through comfortably against Green and Calcavecchia but the third game, Langer and Canizares against Kite and McCumber, found McCumber in towering form and that was another point to the Americans.

Now only one point separated the sides as the huge crowd flocked to catch the final match. Never more than a hole in it, the American duo of Stewart and Strange were one up on the 16th tee over Clark and James. Then Clark conjured up a birdie on the 16th and on the next hole, James hit two majestic shots to the green. Strange and Stewart, both lying in the middle of the fairway from their drives, must have thought James' ball was a great deal closer than it was. They both wilted under the pressure, carving their second shots high, wide and into some inhospitable shrubs and small trees. Neither could do any better than five and with James getting down in two more rather nervy shots, the Europeans went one up. Two cast iron, rock solid pars on the final hole meant that the home side had snatched a victory from a possible defeat and the margin remained at two points. "To turn that game round was incredible," enthused Jacklin. "I'm ecstatic. It just shows you what human beings are capable of under pressure."

The two captains submitted their final selections for the singles with the same tactic of putting strength at the top and the bottom. But golf being the perverse game it is, it didn't work out that way.

Europe needed five points from the singles to retain the Cup, five and a half to win outright. For the greater part of the last afternoon that appeared a remote target as the Americans swarmed all over the opposition. At one stage they were up in nine matches, down in one and square in two. Ballesteros had his hands full against Azinger in the top match, Clark was being destroyed by an inspired Kite in the fifth, Beck had Langer under control in the second, but in the remainder there was only one hole in it apart from James who certainly had the measure of O'Meara.

Gradually the impetus swung back towards the Europeans. The Americans seemed unable to kill their opponents off even though they had them down; and then there was the 18th.

This hole, along with the 10th, provides the perfect setting for a dramatic finish. Over the water from the tee, turn almost 90 degrees left for the second and over the water again to a three-tiered green that is 50 yards long.

First to arrive there on that gripping final afternoon was Azinger, one up on Ballesteros. The American drove into the water. Ballesteros was well clear but had run out of fairway the other side and had a fluffy lie in the rough. Azinger dropped another ball on the tee side of the hazard and hit an amazing shot with a wood across the lake into a bunker on the left of the green. Up stepped Ballesteros and with perhaps his worst swing since the 15th in the 1986 US Masters, dumped the ball in the water. The silence was deafening. Elation became deflation as Ballesteros pitched up to the green 20 feet past the flag. Surely even he couldn't conjure a five after all that? But he could, rolling in the downhill putt to leave Azinger a putt of five feet to win the match. He holed it and the teams were tied, Kite having beaten Clark by 8 & 7.

Beck beat Langer without arriving at the 18th so the next pair up were Stewart and Olazabal. The young star of the European team had squared the match at the 15th and that is how it remained on the 18th tee. Olazabal drove safely into the middle of the fairway. The American drove into the water. Three splash shots followed from Stewart and the match was over

Right behind them came the match

The photographic corps lines up

Dusk falls on the 18th as Clark and James win crucial point in second day fourballs

View from the crowd

between Calcavecchia and Rafferty. The Irishman had hung on and the match was square on the 18th tee. The American drove into the water Rafferty drove safely and when Calcavecchia's next shot also found the water he conceded the hole without even requiring Rafferty to hit his second.

Meanwhile James had won on the 16th green and that was three of the five points in the bag. Where would the other two come from?

They came from the most unexpected quarter. O'Connor facing Couples was sometimes 50 yards behind off the tee but despite going two down he hung on manfully and squared the match with a fine putt on the 16th. He nearly squandered the 17th but Couples failed to take advantage with a nervy putt and so once again to the 18th all square. O'Connor drove safely and then Couples struck a massive shot into the prime position. Jacklin rushed to O'Connor's side: 'Put it on the green,' he said, 'and I guarantee you something will happen.' In the cauldron of that finishing hole, Jacklin knew that the Americans were feeling it as much as the Europeans. O'Connor told himself to 'make a good turn' with his two iron from 230 yards and, wonder of wonders, the ball flew unerringly at the flag, settling down six feet below the hole. Couples was shattered and Jacklin was right. Something happened to Couples' nine iron second shot in that it never looked remotely like hitting the putting surface. Three more shots from the American and O'Connor was saluting the crowd before breaking down in a welter of emotion.

European tension as match reaches its climax

Stewart gets that sinking feeling on the 18th

Right behind came Canizares who had played beautifully all afternoon. Three birdies on the inward half put the Spaniard level with Green on the last hole. Both players hit the green in two; Canizares with a six iron to 60 feet above the hole, Green well below. Canizares sent a lovely putt down the slope to within four feet of the hole, Green ran his five feet above the hole and the one back never looked like going in. As the crowd held its breath, Canizares slid in his sidehill effort and the magical 14 points had been reached.

Only one half was required from the remaining four matches on the course. It wouldn't come from Torrance who never got to grips with Watson but surely either Brand, Faldo or Woosnam would nick something? It was not to be. Brand couldn't make a four on the 18th against McCumber, Faldo drove into the water on the 18th against Wadkins and Woosnam was subjected to four consecutive birdies from Strange from the 15th.

Hallelujah chorus for O'Connor after his triumphant last hole victory

It was therefore a slightly subdued atmosphere at the end. Deprived of the certainty of victory or defeat, the

COUPLES
USA

INDIVIDUAL RECORDS

EUROPE

	P	W	H	L
Olazabal	5	4	1	0
Ballesteros	5	3	1	1
James	4	3	0	1
Faldo	5	2	1	2
Woosnam	5	2	1	2
Clark	4	2	0	2
Rafferty	3	1	0	2
Torrance	3	1	0	2
Brand	3	1	0	2
O'Connor	2	1	0	1
Canizares	2	1	0	1
Langer	3	0	0	3

UNITED STATES

	P	W	H	L
Beck	4	3	1	0
Azinger	4	3	0	1
Kite	4	2	1	1
Calcavecchia	5	2	0	3
Wadkins	4	2	0	2
Strange	5	1	1	3
Stewart	4	1	0	3
Watson	3	1	1	1
Green	4	2	0	2
McCumber	3	2	0	1
Couples	2	0	0	2
O'Meara	2	0	0	2

Canizares celebrates the retention of the Cup

emotions on both sides were mixed. The Americans were stunned that they couldn't finish the job, the Europeans were relieved to have escaped, then disappointed not to have clinched it.

The Jacklin era was over but the terms of his captaincy will remain for his successor, along with that elegant gold trophy which didn't go anywhere after possibly the three most exciting days of the golfing year.

Crowds were up in arms with joy

Woosnam concedes his match with Curtis Strange

Final day hero O'Connor receives the plaudits

Happy Europeans in their moment of triumph

Celebratory samba from Olazabal

COURSE: THE BELFRY **YARDAGE: 7,176** **PAR: 72**

FIRST DAY FOURSOMES

USA	RESULT	EUROPE	SCORE	USA	EUROPE
T. KITE C. STRANGE	Halved with	N. FALDO I. WOOSNAM		½	½
L. WADKINS P. STEWART	Beat	H. CLARK M. JAMES	1 Hole	1	0
T. WATSON C. BECK	Halved with	S. BALLESTEROS J. M. OLAZABAL		½	½
M. CALCAVECCHIA K. GREEN	Beat	B. LANGER R. RAFFERTY	2 & 1	1	0
				3	1

FOURBALLS

USA	RESULT	EUROPE	SCORE	USA	EUROPE
C. STRANGE P. AZINGER	Lost to	S. TORRANCE G. BRAND Jnr.	1 Hole	0	1
F. COUPLES L. WADKINS	Lost to	H. CLARK M. JAMES	3 & 2	0	1
M. CALCAVECCHIA M. McCUMBER	Lost to	N. FALDO I. WOOSNAM	2 Holes	0	1
T. WATSON M. O'MEARA	Lost to	S. BALLESTEROS J. M. OLAZABAL	6 & 5	0	1
				0	4

SECOND DAY FOURSOMES

USA	RESULT	EUROPE	SCORE	USA	EUROPE
L. WADKINS P. STEWART	Lost to	I. WOOSNAM N. FALDO	3 & 2	0	1
C. BECK P. AZINGER	Beat	G. BRAND Jnr. S. TORRANCE	4 & 3	1	0
M. CALCAVECCHIA K. GREEN	Beat	C. O'CONNOR Jnr. R. RAFFERTY	3 & 2	1	0
T. KITE C. STRANGE	Lost to	S. BALLESTEROS J. M. OLAZABAL	1 Hole	0	1
				2	2

FOURBALLS

USA	RESULT	EUROPE	SCORE	USA	EUROPE
C. BECK P. AZINGER	Beat	N. FALDO I. WOOSNAM	2 & 1	1	0
T. KITE M. McCUMBER	Beat	B. LANGER J. M. CANIZARES	2 & 1	1	0
P. STEWART C. STRANGE	Lost to	H. CLARK M. JAMES	1 Hole	0	1
M. CALCAVECCHIA K. GREEN	Lost to	S. BALLESTEROS J. M. OLAZABAL	4 & 2	0	1
				2	2

THIRD DAY SINGLES

USA	RESULT	EUROPE	SCORE	USA	EUROPE
P. AZINGER	Beat	S. BALLESTEROS	1 Hole	1	0
C. BECK	Beat	B. LANGER	3 & 2	1	0
P. STEWART	Lost to	J. M. OLAZABAL	1 Hole	0	1
M. CALCAVECCHIA	Lost to	R. RAFFERTY	1 Hole	0	1
T. KITE	Beat	H. CLARK	8 & 7	1	0
M. O'MEARA	Lost to	M. JAMES	3 & 2	0	1
F. COUPLES	Lost to	C. O'CONNOR Jnr.	1 Hole	0	1
K. GREEN	Lost to	J. M. CANIZARES	1 Hole	0	1
M. McCUMBER	Beat	G. BRAND Jnr.	1 Hole	1	0
T. WATSON	Beat	S. TORRANCE	3 & 1	1	0
L. WADKINS	Beat	N. FALDO	1 Hole	1	0
C. STRANGE	Beat	I. WOOSNAM	2 Holes	1	0
				7	5
			RESULT	14	14

OGLE'S
winning look

Since Nick Faldo captured the Peugeot French Open at the start of July there had been 13 Tour events (Volvo British Seniors and Murphy's Cup included) and they had produced eight non-European winners. That tally became nine out of 14 when Australian Brett Ogle put £22,570 into his tucker-bag from the Equity and Law Challenge final at Royal Mid-Surrey.

He did it in style, too. Over the 54 holes the 25-year-old from Sydney gathered an eagle and 23 birdies for a total of 25 points under the unique attacking format. The closest any of his 32 challengers came to him was the 21 of Scotland's Colin Montgomerie, last season's Rookie of the Year.

Both men took advantage of the 5,802-yard composite lay-out — each half with a par of only 34 — to achieve their first-ever rounds of 59. Because of the unconventional scoring system they will not count for record purposes, but as Ogle stated: 'You've still got to get the ball round and you've still got to make the putts.'

He had qualified for the final in 28th place (the number of each player's birdies, eagles and three-point albatrosses being totted up for 28 tournaments up to and including the Panasonic European Open), but if that makes Ogle sound like one of the outsiders it would be misleading. His 253-point total was amassed over 64 rounds and of the top 30 only compatriot Peter Senior (255 points from 59 rounds) played less. Irishman Philip Walton gathered his 371 points — 32 more than second-placed Sam Torrance — from 91 rounds.

Walton, so disappointed to have just missed out on Ryder Cup selection, duly turned up at the Richmond course to pick up his £10,000 bonus, but earned only an extra £965 for 16th place before heading off to St Andrews for his Dunhill Cup debut. The bonuses of £6,000, £3,000 and £1,000 available to Torrance, Gordon Brand Junior and Ronan Rafferty respectively went unclaimed, understandably so with the two-day final sandwiched between the Ryder and Dunhill Cup tussles.

IN TAKING HIS FIRST TITLE ON EUROPEAN SOIL, AUSTRALIA'S BRETT OGLE FOLLOWED ON FROM BARRY LANE AND RONAN RAFFERTY AND LOOKS TO HAVE AN EQUALLY BRIGHT FUTURE

That was good news for those who did play, for the money was put back into the 'pot', making a total prize fund of £79,000, with the winner's share going up from £20,000 to £22,570. It also increased the possibility of a first-time winner on the Tour again — and so it proved. The omens are good for Ogle: inaugural champion Barry Lane went on to his first fully-fledged tournament success in the Bell's Scottish Open and the post-script to Rafferty's 1988 title-winning performance is even more impressive.

The pedigree of the lanky Aussie, one of the biggest hitters around, is not in doubt. He was leading amateur in the 1985 Australian Open and since joining the play-for-pay brigade a year later he has donned the Tahiti, Pacific Harbour and Tasmanian Open crowns. He was also third behind Rodger Davis and Fred Couples in the Bicentennial Classic at Royal Melbourne at the end of 1988, which earned him his biggest cheque of £45,000.

That helped him buy a house in Virginia Water as a base for his first full assault on the Volvo Tour and he was quickly drawing attention to himself by finishing runner-up in the curtailed Credit Lyonnaise Cannes Open. There were six other top ten placings before he went into a mini-slump, which he was helped out of by Burhill professional Lee Johnson.

His 59 came in the opening round of the final and even included a bogey. The ten points gave him an overnight advantage of two over David Gilford. Montgomerie was way down on four, having waited 12 holes for his first birdie, but then charged into second spot with his ten-birdie 59. He and partner Richard Boxall triggered each other into some superb play in the afternoon as well — a contributory factor, Montgomerie pointed out, being that their 36 holes took just five and a half hours.

Ogle knew early in his final round (a

A leap to the top for Brett Ogle

Roger Chapman's son receives a putting lesson from David Feherty

Carl the sand Mason

Eyes left from Montgomerie

COURSE: ROYAL MID SURREY, RICHMOND **YARDAGE: 5,802** **PAR: 68**

POS	NAME	CTRY	BIRDIES	EAGLES	POINTS	PRIZE MONEY
1	Brett OGLE	Aus	23	1	25	£22570
2	Colin MONTGOMERIE	Scot	21		21	£11285
3	David FEHERTY	N.Ire	20		20	£7335
4	Richard BOXALL	Eng	20		20	£4850
5	Peter SENIOR	Aus	15	2	19	£3665
6	Carl MASON	Eng	19		19	£2935
7	Mike HARWOOD	Aus	16	1	18	£2370
8	Tony CHARNLEY	Eng	18		18	£2030
9	Des SMYTH	Ire	15	1	17	£1720
10	Michael ALLEN	USA	15	1	17	£1465
11	Paul CARRIGILL	Eng	17		17	£1240
12	Peter MITCHELL	Eng	17		17	£1125
13	Russell CLAYDON	Eng	17		17	£1055
14	Mark ROE	Eng	14	1	16	£1025
15	Malcolm MACKENZIE	Eng	14	1	16	£995
16	Philip WALTON	Ire	16		16	£965
17	Neil HANSEN	Eng	16		16	£935
18	David WILLIAMS	Eng	16		16	£905
19	David GILFORD	Eng	16		16	£875
20	Eamonn DARCY	Ire	15		15	£845
21	Ross McFARLANE	Eng	13	1	15	£815
22	Brian MARCHBANK	Scot	14		14	£785
23	Stephen BENNETT	Eng	14		14	£755
24	Gordon J BRAND	Eng	14		14	£725
25	Peter TERAVAINEN	USA	12	1	14	£700
26	Barry LANE	Eng	14		14	£675
27	Derrick COOPER	Eng	11	1	13	£660
28	Vijay SINGH	Fij	13		13	£645
29	Mark DAVIS	Eng	11	1	13	£630
30	Neil COLES	Eng	12		12	£620
31	Roger CHAPMAN	Eng	12		12	£610
32	Andrew SHERBORNE	Eng	11		11	£600
33	Ken BROWN	Scot	9		9	£590

round that began with him mistakenly playing Carl Mason's ball out of a bunker at the first) what was required to win. He was equal to the demand, six birdies in seven holes around the turn allowing him the luxury of free-wheeling to the title in the knowledge that, for once, bogeys or worse could not bring him back to the field. He was home in 28, which proved two things. The course was set up for such scoring and this man can play a bit.

Body English from Richard Boxall

Titleist

AMERICA'S *consolation cup*

The shadows of the famous St Andrews skyline were only just beginning to form on the 18th fairway when darkness fell on the golfers from the Land of the Rising Sun. Japan, respected but unfancied at the outset, had battled manfully to reach the final of the Dunhill Cup only to find that their ambitions were ambushed by the Americans.

Mark Calcavecchia, who has the gait of a gunslinger and the short game of an angel, proved just why he is being hailed as one of the game's next great players. On the final day of his first week at the Home of Golf he scored morning and afternoon victories over Hajimi Meshiai, returned a better-ball score of 60 for two rounds and ensured that America gained consolation for the previous week's Ryder Cup disappointment by winning the Dunhill Cup for the first time.

America's win, securing $100,000 each for Calcavecchia, skipper Curtis Strange and Tom Kite, was not a surprise, but it came at the end of a week of shocks. The three-man team and medal-matchplay format designed, among other things, to ensure all the matches go the full 18 holes, has had its detractors but none could grumble at the drama, excitement and high standards which were the hallmark of the 1989 Dunhill Cup.

From the first day to the last, the unexpected became the norm. Nobody could have predicted what was to happen on the Thursday when the 16 survivors from a starting field of 44 went to the first tee. Greg Norman, Australia's captain, would finish the day in a state of shock. His trio, second favourites before a ball was struck over the Old Course, were really feeling

HAVING FAILED IN THEIR MISSION TO CAPTURE THE RYDER CUP, THE AMERICANS MADE SURE THEY RETURNED WITH SOMETHING TO SHOW FOR THEIR EFFORTS IN BRITAIN

down under when 500-1 outsiders France defeated them 2-1. The unknown Marc Pendaries, 137th in the money list, reduced the Great White Shark to a golfing tiddler in recording a two-shot win 71-73. Norman had led by four shots after seven holes and three after nine. The more experienced Emmanuel Dussart accounted for Ian Baker-Finch, 72-73. Wayne Grady's triumph over Gery Watine was too little, too late.

Australia was in good company when the doors opened for that night's sorrow-drowning ritual. Wales, led by Ian Woosnam, were first into the trough after mustering just a half point against Argentina. Woosnam's 72 was three too many against Miguel Fernandez and Philip Parkin's 75 was seven strokes more than Eduardo Romero's 68. Mark Mouland and Vicente Fernandez each went round in 70. Europe's Ryder Cup star Jose Maria Olazabal continued where he'd left off at The Belfry. He beat Sweden's Mats Lanner but Jose Maria Canizares lost by one stroke to Ove Sellberg and Jose Rivero by the same margin to Magnus Persson.

Defending champions Ireland, although only Ronan Rafferty remained from the previous year's threesome, scraped through against the unknown Chinese team from Taipei. Christy O'Connor Junior, another Ryder Cup hero, had to go to the fourth extra hole before his countrymen could lift glasses of Guinness in a triumphant toast. And England also needed extra time to secure their place in the second round when Denis Durnian beat Canada's Richard Zokol at the second extra hole.

There were just as many individual shocks. Park Nam Shin went out with his head held higher than anybody else after birdieing the 18th to beat the Open champion Mark Calcavecchia by one stroke. Sandy Lyle at last seemed to be showing a long overdue return to form with a best-of-the-day 66 in Scotland's 2-1 win over New Zealand. Sadly for Sandy, he was to grab the headlines again the following day but for all the wrong reasons.

The quarter finals included a clash between Scotland and England with the old enemy from south of the border seeking a third successive victory. Even though Howard Clark beat his Ryder Cup colleague Sam Torrance, the scoreboard told a story of impending doom for England. Durnian, after doing nothing wrong the previous day, could

Ireland's hopes were sunk when Christy O'Connor Junior found the Swilcan Burn

Mark James sinks his birdie putt on the first extra hole against Sandy Lyle

The crumpled landscape of the Old Course

do nothing right this time and was overwhelmed 71-78 by Gordon Brand Junior. Lyle was four shots up on Mark James with as many holes to play. When Clark shook hands with Torrance he wished the Scot the best of luck in the next round. Torrance advised him not to be so premature but neither expected what followed. Lyle's summer of sadness returned to haunt him. A ten-foot putt for a birdie on the 18th by James sent the match into sudden-death and it was not a lingering one for Lyle. Another three, this time with a putt from 12 feet, gave James and his team a win against all the odds.

Elsewhere, France suffered a reaction to their first day's heroics for they fell 3-0 to Japan. America were stretched by Argentina but still went through on the same scoreline while Ireland were rarely in trouble against the slipping Swedes. It all meant that the semi-final line-up read: USA versus Ireland and England versus Japan.

England were widely expected to account for Japan but the overseas visitors triumphed 2-1, Ozaki's 70 outscoring Durnian's 72 and Suzuki comfortably beating Clark. Ireland came within a whisker of upsetting America for a second successive week as the match rested on the outcome of the play-off between Kite and O'Connor Junior — Philip Walton having lost to Calcavecchia while Raffety beat US Open champion Strange by one shot. O'Connor put his approach to the first in the Swilcan Burn. Kite needed no further invitation to seal victory and Ireland were left to face England in the third-place play-off the next day, a play-off England won 2-1.

The final was to be Calcavecchia's day. The Americans all but made sure of victory in the morning because after Calcavecchia (67) had beaten Meshiai (68), Kite halved with Ozaki, both going round in 68, and Strange beat Suzuki by three strokes. It was Suzuki's first defeat of the week. Then Calcavecchia had a 66 to give the US victory and make sure he was in the right frame of mind to return to the Old course in 1990 to defend his Open title. The Stars and Stripes fluttered over St Andrews as the sun set on the course, the event and on Japan.

The gallant Japanese runners-up

Shadowy finale as America wins

Ireland's Philip Walton lets fly

Sandy Lyle and Mark James each cast a long shadow

COURSE: OLD COURSE, ST ANDREWS **YARDAGE: 6,933** **PAR: 72**

FIRST ROUND

Argentina beat Wales 2½ – ½		
Eduardo ROMERO (68)	beat	Philip PARKIN (75)
Vicente FERNANDEZ (70)	halved with	Mark MOULAND (70)
Miguel FERNANDEZ (69)	beat	Ian WOOSNAM (72)
USA beat Korea 2 – 1		
Mark CALCAVECCHIA (71)	lost to	Park Nam SHIN (70)
Tom KITE (72)	beat	Choi Yoon SOO (75)
Curtis STRANGE (67)	beat	Choi Sang HO (79)
Sweden beat Spain 2 – 1		
Mats LANNER (70)	lost to	Jose Maria OLAZABAL (67)
Ove SELLBERG (71)	beat	Jose Maria CANIZARES (72)
Magnus PERSSON (71)	beat	Jose RIVERO (72)
Ireland beat China (Taipei) 2 – 1		
Philip WALTON (69)	beat	Lu Chien SOON (76)
Ronan RAFFERTY (73)	lost to	Yu Chin HAN (71)
Christy O'CONNOR Jnr (73)	beat	Hsieh Chin SHENG (73) (4th play-off hole)
Scotland beat New Zealand 2 – 1		
Gordon BRAND Jnr (76)	lost to	Simon OWEN (72)
Sam TORRANCE (67)	beat	Grant WAITE (70)
Sandy LYLE (65)	beat	Frank NOBILO (75)
Japan beat Italy 2 – 1		
Koichi SUZUKI (74)	beat	Massimo MANNELLI (76)
Naomichi OZAKI (68)	beat	Costantino ROCCA (73)
Hajime MESHIAI (73)	lost to	Alberto BINAGHI (72)
France beat Australia 2 – 1		
Emmanuel DUSSART (72)	beat	Ian BAKER-FINCH (73)
Marc PENDARIES (71)	beat	Greg NORMAN (73)
Gery WATINE (70)	lost to	Wayne GRADY (67)
England beat Canada 2 – 1		
Denis DURNIAN (72)	beat	Richard ZOKOL (72) (2nd play-off hole)
Mark JAMES (73)	lost to	Dave BARR (71)
Howard CLARK (71)	beat	Dan HALLDORSON (72)

First Round losers receive US$7,500 each = £4,648

SECOND ROUND

Japan beat France 3 – 0		
Naomichi OZAKI (71)	beat	Emmanuel DUSSART (73)
Koichi SUZUKI (73)	beat	Marc PENDARIES (75)
Hajime MESHIAI (72)	beat	Gery WATINE (74)
USA beat Argentina 3 – 0		
Tom KITE (70)	beat	Vicente FERNANDEZ (72)
Mark CALCAVECCHIA (72)	beat	Miguel FERNANDEZ (77)
Curtis STRANGE (68)	beat	Eduardo ROMERO (70)
Ireland beat Sweden 3 – 0		
Philip WALTON (72)	beat	Mats LANNER (74)
Ronan RAFFERTY (68)	beat	Ove SELLBERG (78)
Christy O'CONNOR Jnr (73)	beat	Magnus PERSSON (76)
England beat Scotland 2 – 1		
Howard CLARK (67)	beat	Sam TORRANCE (69)
Denis DURNIAN (78)	lost to	Gordon BRAND Jnr (71)
Mark JAMES (70)	beat	Sandy LYLE (70) (1st play-off hole)

Second Round losers receive US$15,000 each = £9,296

SEMI-FINALS

USA beat Ireland 2 – 1		
Mark CALCAVECCHIA (69)	beat	Philip WALTON (71)
Tom KITE (71)	beat	Christy O'CONNOR Jnr (1st play-off hole)
Curtis STRANGE (72)	lost to	Ronan RAFFERTY (71)
Japan beat England 2 – 1		
Naomichi OZAKI (70)	beat	Denis DURNIAN (72)
Koichi SUZUKI (66)	beat	Howard CLARK (70)
Hajime MESHIAI (73)	lost to	Mark JAMES (71)

PLAY-OFF FOR THIRD AND FOURTH PLACES

England beat Ireland 2 – 1		
Denis DURNIAN (72)	lost to	Philip WALTON (71)
Howard CLARK (72)	beat	Ronan RAFFERTY (75)
Mark JAMES (69)	beat	Christy O'CONNOR Jnr (76)

Ireland receive US$26,666 each = £16,526
England receive US$36,666 each = £22,724

FINAL

USA beat Japan 3½ – 2½		
Mark CALCAVECCHIA (67)	beat	Hajime MESHIAI (68)
Tom KITE (68)	halved with	Naomichi OZAKI (68)
Curtis STRANGE (72)	beat	Koichi SUZUKI (75)
Mark CALCAVECCHIA (66)	beat	Hajime MESHIAI (68)
Tom KITE (74)	lost to	Koichi SUZUKI (71)
Curtis STRANGE (71)	lost to	Naomichi OZAKI (69)

Japan receive US$50,000 each = £30,988
USA receive US$100,100 each = £61,977

Curtis Strange sits it out

THE GERMAN MASTERS

LANGER *dines out at home*

A good host, social etiquette demands, will always offer the best meat to his guests. Bernhard Langer very nearly got things right at the Solitude club but then with monstrous inelegance left his friends scratching round for scraps by slicing off the choicest fare and putting it on his own plate. Not only did Langer win the tournament which he and his brother, Erwin, co-promoted with Mark McCormack's International Management Group, but he admitted before the event got under way that he had paid himself appearance money to play in the first place. 'This is business, and I pay myself only my usual fee,' he said. This was gravy of the richest quality, and mein host snaffled the lot.

In any case, the paying customers could not complain that they did not get value for money. Those who had braved the bitter cold and rain of a late autumn Sunday afternoon to make the 30-mile trip from Stuttgart found it all worthwhile as Langer won with a total of 276, 12 under par, after beating off a spirited challenge mounted late on the final day by Jose Maria Olazabal and Payne Stewart. For the West German it was his second Volvo Tour victory of the season, following his success in the Peugeot Spanish Open at El Saler in April. It came after an unhappy Ryder Cup when in three matches he had failed to win a point, and it gave further proof that the third battle of his career with the yips, the devil that had been sitting heavily on his shoulders for the better part of 18 months, had been conquered. But he did not do it without setting thousands of Teutonic hearts a-flutter. He almost made a mess of the 72nd hole when he went into a greenside bunker, only to escape with

BERNHARD LANGER ENJOYED RICH FARE IN WINNING HIS OWN CO-PROMOTED EVENT

a stroke of exquisite delicacy and hole a putt of three feet for a par. Even then he could have been caught on the final green by his two nearest rivals, each of whom needed a birdie to take the tournament to extra holes. Olazabal hit a fine third shot to ten feet, Stewart followed him in to about 12. Both putts were holeable, both missed by a whisker. At last the long, long intake of breath could be released.

To take the only title he had not won in his native land — a tournament that he had conceived himself in 1987, resisting the suggestion that it should be called the Bernhard Langer Masters — he had to beat a high-quality field that included the Open champion, Mark Calcavecchia, the US PGA champion, Stewart, and their compatriot, Fred Couples, as well as Nick Faldo, Olazabal and Severiano Ballesteros. Not that Calcavecchia or Ballesteros bothered Langer for too long. Calcavecchia easily missed the cut, Ballesteros did even worse with a pair of 75s. He was not in prime form before the first round, and was even less happy after it when he took three to get out of a bunker at the short eighth — his 17th — then three-putted from seven feet to finish with a four-over-par seven. It was only the second cut he had missed all year. He was not the only one to fall foul of the eighth hole a cunningly constructed little gem cut into the side of a hill with an easy way into the sand and no easy way out of it. Michael Allen, the Bell's Scottish Open champion, took eight at the same hole; he putted into the bunker twice.

Langer's 67 gave him the first-round lead, one shot ahead of Rodger Davis, David Llewellyn, Richard Boxall and Keith Waters. Waters was lucky to be

Furrowed brows from Faldo

Ogle and caddie beat the cold

Olazabal drives into second place

alive, let alone playing golf. He was a passenger in a car being driven through Lincolnshire by fellow professional Stephen Bennett on the Monday before the tournament when they were confronted by a lorry and a car driving side by side towards them. Bennett took to the grass verge and the two drove on, counting lucky stars by the galaxy.

Faldo took over at halfway, adding a 66 to his first-round 69. He led by a shot from Stewart, clad in the maroon and yellow colours of Washington Redskins, which put a few more dollars into his pocket and at the same time offended the eye of all but the terminally colour-blind. Stewart, in fact, just would not go away. He took over the lead with a 70 on the third day as Faldo faded to an outward 40 and a round of 74. He said nothing, but let everybody know what he thought of his performance by traipsing off to the practice ground and hitting balls until dusk fell.

Langer had said all week that if he were still in contention at the start of the final day it would be good for the tournament. He was, and it was. But it was a close-run thing.

Wilson
BOSS
5

Stewart surveys his kingdom, above

Another straight drive from Langer, right

Rain is water off Langer's back, below

Stewart escapes from trees

The German Master and his wife

COURSE: STUTTGARTER GOLF CLUB **YARDAGE: 6,839** **PAR: 72**

POS	NAME	CTRY	1	2	3	4	TOTAL	PRIZE MONEY
1	Bernhard LANGER	W.Ger	67	71	70	68	276	£55302
2	Payne STEWART	USA	69	67	70	71	277	£28813
	Jose Maria OLAZABAL	Sp	73	66	69	69	277	£28813
4	Brett OGLE	Aus	73	68	71	68	280	£15336
	Fred COUPLES	USA	69	72	73	66	280	£15336
6	Derrick COOPER	Eng	70	72	71	68	281	£11618
7	Stephen BENNETT	Eng	72	70	70	70	282	£8564
	Bernard GALLACHER	Scot	73	71	70	68	282	£8564
	Nick FALDO	Eng	69	66	74	73	282	£8564
10	Rodger DAVIS	Aus	68	69	72	74	283	£6639
11	Mike HARWOOD	Aus	72	70	74	68	284	£6107
12	Eduardo ROMERO	Arg	70	72	69	74	285	£5377
	Andrew SHERBORNE	Eng	71	69	74	71	285	£5377
	Barry LANE	Eng	72	69	76	68	285	£5377
15	Eamonn DARCY	Ire	74	72	68	72	286	£4780
	Magnus PERSSON	Swe	70	73	69	74	286	£4780
17	Bill LONGMUIR	Scot	74	66	79	68	287	£4088
	Vijay SINGH	Fiji	74	74	72	67	287	£4088
	Miguel Angel MARTIN	Sp	69	71	74	73	287	£4088
	Richard BOXALL	Eng	68	73	74	72	287	£4088
	Jimmy HEGGARTY	N.Ire	71	70	79	67	287	£4088
	Keith WATERS	Eng	68	71	76	72	287	£4088
23	Brian MARCHBANK	Scot	74	72	71	71	288	£3485
	Mark McNULTY	Zim	73	73	72	70	288	£3485
	Malcolm MACKENZIE	Eng	74	70	72	72	288	£3485
	Bob E SMITH	USA	72	68	74	74	288	£3485
	Chris MOODY	Eng	74	68	73	73	288	£3485
28	Tom PURTZER	USA	73	70	74	72	289	£2943
	David LLEWELLYN	Wal	68	76	69	76	289	£2943
	Anders SORENSEN	Den	76	71	71	71	289	£2943
	Peter SENIOR	Aus	72	76	70	71	289	£2943
	Ove SELLBERG	Swe	73	72	72	72	289	£2943
	Philip WALTON	Ire	73	71	71	74	289	£2943
34	Antonio GARRIDO	Sp	70	73	77	70	290	£2489
	Tony CHARNLEY	Eng	70	70	71	79	290	£2489
	Peter FOWLER	Aus	76	71	72	71	290	£2489
	Paul WAY	Eng	71	69	73	77	290	£2489
	Vicente FERNANDEZ	Arg	73	74	71	72	290	£2489
	Jose RIVERO	Sp	73	75	71	71	290	£2489
40	Denis DURNIAN	Eng	76	70	73	72	291	£2224
	Michael ALLEN	USA	73	72	73	73	291	£2224
42	David A RUSSELL	Eng	72	76	71	73	292	£2024
	David GILFORD	Eng	77	69	75	71	292	£2024
	Mark MOULAND	Wal	72	74	72	74	292	£2024
	Peter BAKER	Eng	76	71	74	71	292	£2024
46	Ron COMMANS	USA	71	74	74	74	293	£1659
	Armando SAAVEDRA	Arg	73	75	71	74	293	£1659
	Stephen McALLISTER	Scot	72	74	74	73	293	£1659
	David RAY	Eng	69	74	76	74	293	£1659
	Ian BAKER-FINCH	Aus	75	73	73	72	293	£1659
	Craig PARRY	Aus	73	73	72	75	293	£1659
	Ruud BOS	Hol	73	74	71	75	293	£1659
53	Ian YOUNG	Scot	72	74	73	75	294	£1361
	Wayne RILEY	Aus	72	76	71	75	294	£1361
55	Mats LANNER	Swe	71	76	75	73	295	£1195
	Anders FORSBRAND	Swe	72	75	76	72	295	£1195
	Jerry ANDERSON	Can	73	70	74	78	295	£1195
58	John MORGAN	Eng	75	69	75	77	296	£995
	Frank NOBILO	NZ	70	77	73	76	296	£995
	Mike SMITH	USA	73	75	74	74	296	£995
	Peter TERAVAINEN	USA	71	69	82	74	296	£995
	Martin POXON	Eng	75	73	71	77	296	£995
	Sven STRUEVER (Am)	W.Ger	72	73	74	77	296	–
63	Emmanuel DUSSART	Fr	72	76	73	77	298	£896
64	Juan ANGLADA	Sp	75	70	75	79	299	£863
65	Russell CLAYDON	Eng	72	76	77	76	301	£829
66	Lyndsay STEPHEN	Aus	75	73	78	76	302	£332
67	Roger CHAPMAN	Eng	72	76	75	81	304	£330
68	Manuel CALERO	Sp	74	72	78	81	305	£328

SUNTORY WORLD MATCH-PLAY CHAMPIONSHIP

FALDO'S *final flourish*

AFTER FINISHING RUNNER-UP THE YEAR BEFORE, NICK FALDO WENT ONE BETTER IN DEFEATING IAN WOOSNAM IN A THRILLING FINAL

Nick Faldo had nothing left to prove after he had brought down the curtain on a spectacular Suntory World Match-play Championship at Wentworth. His leap for joy as his title-winning eagle putt sped into the 36th hole of an enthralling final said it all. That spontaneous expression of elation was first seen at Augusta in April when his 30-foot extra time putt won him the US Masters from Scott Hoch. The Wentworth version not only celebrated his first victory after twice being runner-up, it was also the last act in an epic of escapology on which he can look back with pride.

For Faldo had capped his finest season thus far with a trilogy of triumph. He had beaten a close friend, then the man most golfers regard as the game's most gifted player, and finally the partner who shared his Ryder Cup glory. What is more he had done it in record style by streaking to 30 under par for the 105 holes necessary to become the third British winner in succession.

If the US Masters signalled Faldo's elevation to the ranks of the modern superstars, then his lift-off on the last green of Wentworth 1989 confirmed the 32-year old Englishman as an all-round champion. He is now certainly among the top three of that select group of players at the pinnacle of the game. It was perhaps inevitable that he should get there by demonstrating that one of the keys to successful match-play lies in being a strong medal player.

Faldo dropped only two shots to the card all week, and although he made the occasional misjudgment of his medium irons, the quality of his short game, and particularly his putting, more than compensated. He had rounds of 67 and 66 and was 12 under par when he defeated David Frost with a birdie at the 38th: he shot 65 and 30, then four pars and a birdie to remove Severiano Ballesteros by 6 and 5; and produced 67 and 64 to beat Ian Woosnam by one hole on the suspense-filled last afternoon. So much for the awesome reputation of the so-called Burma Road. Never has the famous West Course been so emphatically put to the sword.

Faldo had exhibited his mastery of his home ground on his first European appearance of 1989 in the Volvo PGA Championship in May. He had beaten the best that Europe could offer with some aplomb, but his October encore owed as much to his mental resolve as his undoubted skill with his clubs. Open champion Johnny Miller used to talk about "computerising" golf, using the traffic light system to categorise shots to be played as red, amber, or green. Faldo is a target man. He rates golf shots on a scale of one to ten, the higher figure being the best he can possibly hit.

'I ask myself what is the best I can do,' he explained, 'and if the answer is three feet from the flag, then that is my target. I then stand up and try to hit a ten every time. When I see nothing but the green and the pin, and I mean nothing else, then that is the reason my scoring is so good.

'Mentally it targets you well, and I was really well targeted for the whole of the week. Whenever I play badly it is because I look up and see bunkers and trees. Now maybe I will try the method in stroke-play some time!'

The other factor which turned Faldo from stroke-play's Mr Par Excellence into match-play champion of the world was a putting technique which he was employing for the first time in serious competition. It is said that all artists are recognisable by their brush strokes. If so, Faldo could prove just as much a trend-setter as Sam Torrance in 1989—even if Picasso might not have recognised his canvas. Faldo's "brush" strokes stemmed from his need to curb a tendency to decelerate his putter head at impact. Long time coach David Leadbetter had suggested back in the spring that the Englishman should try hitting his putts on the upswing, striking the ball halfway up. The action, as though brushing dust into a pan, would impart top spin, and the ball would "dive" into the hole. Faldo gave his putter the brush-up, and the method worked to perfection as he putted

Ballesteros off the course in the semi-final. Once Nick realised all he had to do was concentrate on maintaining the tempo of his stroke, the Suntory galleries saw the records start to tumble to Faldo's flair.

In the first round attention was focussed on the seven newcomers to this special event, celebrating its 26th year. Europe's top two, Jose Maria Olazabal and Ronan Rafferty, did not disappoint their supporters. Olazabal accounted for Scott Hoch, who had been runner up to Faldo for the US Masters, while the Irishman produced two eagles and 12 birdies to beat Mike Reid. The Spaniard had appeared at Wentworth three years earlier and is well accustomed to the big occasion. If Rafferty was apprehensive on his debut, there was little outward indication as he produced two eagles and 12 birdies to win 3 and 2.

Chip Beck, top scorer for the United States in the Ryder Cup matches and South African David Frost were the other first day winners. Beck overwhelmed Japan's Aki Omachi and Frost, the World Series champion, was always comfortable against Ian Baker-Finch, although the Australian counter-attacked strongly in the afternoon, getting out in 31.

The stage was then set for the entry of the seeded elite, the same European quartet who were so rated the previous

Rafferty ambushed on the 13th

year. As defending champion, Sandy Lyle took highest honours, followed by Faldo, Ballesteros, who was trying to emulate Gary Player's record of five victories, and Ian Woosnam, the 1987 champion.

Rafferty had achieved the distinction of beating Open Champion Mark Calcavecchia, US Open champion Curtis Strange and now Reid in successive matches. Now he faced Lyle, who ambled out of his garden gate on the adjacent East Course with the intention of playing a few warm up holes and was stung on the ear by a bee. Lyle shrugged off the irritation to immediately take the lead and went round in 66, but he could not shrug off Rafferty, even when he turned for home two ahead.

The Irishman won both the 28th, where he chipped in from 20 yards for his birdie two, and the 29th where the defending champion missed the green with an 80 yards wedge shot. Rafferty went ahead for the first time with another two at the 32nd, then was handed a semi-final place when Lyle hooked into the woods at the 34th, and had an air shot when he tried to play out left-handed with a reversed nine-iron. Sandy kept the match alive with a winning birdie at the next but surrendered his title when he failed to beat his rival's four at the last. 'It has been Ronan's year,' he said. 'He has grown with the job and gained maturity.'

Beck, who graduated in journalism at the University of Georgia, produced the most graphic quote of the year, after being steamrollered 9 and 8 by Ballesteros in their second round match. 'Every good man is tested in the crucible of humiliation and that is where I have been,' said the American who sank a six-yard birdie putt at the 26th to save himself from a devastating record 11 and 10 defeat.

Ballesteros, competing for the 14th successive year, had been five up at lunch after a 66. He raced away by winning four of the first five afternoon holes, and was able to put his feet up in time for afternoon tea. The Spaniard had arrived at Wentworth feeling excessively weary after a season which he admitted he had not planned correctly. He was almost alone among the leading players in not taking rest periods of at least a fortnight. By the time he had unwound it was time to start practising again for the next engagement. He would pursue a different schedule in 1990.

Woosnam made a typically explosive start to his title chase, birdieing three of the first four holes against Olazabal who responded with four birdies in the last five to lead by one after the first round. But the Spaniard's putting let him down in the afternoon as he missed three chances under eight feet for wins in the first four holes. The Welshman went out in 33 to turn two ahead and when he started back with a hat trick of birdies there was no way back for Jose Maria.

Meanwhile Faldo was engaged in a war of attrition with Frost, a fellow pupil of David Leadbetter, the Florida-based

Silver linings for Faldo and Woosnam on the sixth

Ballesteros almost walked on water in defeating Beck

coach who has played such a major part in the Englishman's success. Frost shot 66 to Faldo's 67, then the scores were reversed in the second round. Each had claimed 12 birdies, the South African also having an eagle when he holed from 50 feet at the fourth in the afternoon on the way to a three hole lead with 11 to play. The 25th and decisive birdie was claimed by Faldo at the 38th with a seven iron tee shot which deposited his ball 24 inches from the hole.

A semi-final line-up of Rafferty/Woosnam and Ballesteros/Faldo was a true reflection of current form, with the destiny of the European record first prize of £100,000 anybody's guess. When Rafferty eagled the fourth for the third time to take the lead for the second time, an upset looked possible. But Woosnam was round in 66 to 68 to edge two ahead at halfway, and was never caught.

The crucial hole was the 12th where the Welshman plugged his four iron second shot in a greenside bunker. Rafferty's three iron to a generous target was hooked into trees and the birdie four he looked sure to get to level escaped him. Woosnam holed from eight feet for his par five to stay ahead, and went through by 2 and 1.

Woosnam drives from the 15th tee while, below, colourful umbrellas intervene on the 16th

When Ballesteros missed a four foot putt for par on the first green to immediately go one down to Faldo he must have realised he would be in for a frustrating day with his putter. The two three-footers which he failed to hole at the 10th and 11th for wins had him shaking his head sadly. Against a golfer of Faldo's class that was suicide. The Englishman's immaculate golf took him four clear at lunch and then an outward five birdies sealed the Spaniard's fate. 'I saved my best to beat the best,' exclaimed Nick.

'I gave away too much ground by missing every possible putt,' said Seve, 'whereas Nick's putting was tremendous.'

The final brought together the Ryder Cup partners, with honours even, each having recorded a one hole victory in their two previous meetings. For Woosnam the final was the opportunity of a second title in three years; for Faldo the realisation that he could maintain his uncanny record of following in the footsteps of Lyle who had won the US Masters and the Matchplay the previous season.

Another fast start sped the Welshman into a three hole lead after 14 holes, before he selected a one iron off the 15th tee and pulled it into the woods. A left-handed swish with an eight iron plunged him into further trouble, and Faldo followed with a birdie and eagle to square. By the afternoon turn Woosnam was back in a three hole lead and playing with a freedom that suggested the title was his. Like everyone else he had not reckoned with the quality of Faldo's brush strokes on the greens and the depth of his determination.

It was Faldo's reduction of the last three holes to a mere 11 strokes that raised the excitement to a crescendo. He squared at the 16th by wedging to a yard, then after badly missing the green with his long iron to the 17th, nursed his pitch from ten yards below the green only six feet from the flag. Woosnam, who had hit a phenomenal second from under a bush to within ten feet of the hole, pushed the eagle putt wide to leave the pair level on the 36th tee. The one iron shot that Faldo then struck like an arrow from 230 yards to finish 20 feet behind the flag deserves to rank among the great title-winning strokes. Faldo, home in a record 30 and eight under par for the afternoon, had saved his very best for the very last. 'It's been a long wait to get there,' he exclaimed. 'This tournament has a fantastic tradition and a place all of its own. Some great players have their names on the trophy.'

Few would argue that Faldo is worthy of inclusion in that category. He certainly laid claim to a special place among champions after receiving the trophy. England's finest current golfer announced he was donating his £100,00C first prize to children's charities. It was the sporting gesture of the season.

Suntory duel — Faldo and Woosnam start the final

COURSE: WENTWORTH CLUB (West Course) **YARDAGE: 6,945** **PAR: 72**

FIRST ROUND

WINNER	CTRY	LOSER	CTRY	SCORE	
Ronan RAFFERTY	N.Ire	Mike REID	USA	3 & 2	First round
Jose Maria OLAZABAL	Sp	Scott HOCH	USA	4 & 2	losers
Chip BECK	USA	Aki OMACHI	Jap	8 & 6	received
David FROST	SA	Ian BAKER-FINCH	Aus	4 & 3	£12,500

SECOND ROUND

Ronan RAFFERTY	N.Ire	Sandy LYLE	Scot	1 hole	Second round
Ian WOOSNAM	Wal	Jose Maria OLAZABAL	Sp	3 & 2	losers
Severiano BALLESTEROS	Sp	Chip BECK	USA	9 & 8	received
Nick FALDO	Eng	David FROST	SA	at 38th	£17,500

SEMI-FINALS

Ian WOOSNAM	Wal	Ronan RAFFERTY	N.Ire	2 & 1
Nick FALDO	Eng	Severiano BALLESTEROS	Sp	6 & 5

PLAY-OFF FOR 3rd and 4th PLACES

Severiano BALLESTEROS £30,000	Sp	Ronan RAFFERTY £20,000	N.Ire	5 & 3

FINAL (October 15)

Nick FALDO £100,000	Eng	Ian WOOSNAM £60,000	Wal	1 hole

Left, eyrie view of winning eagle putt leaves Faldo, above, gobsmacked

FEHERTY
the reluctant champion

David Feherty revealed some of the pressures of a professional golfer's life when he won the BMW International Open in Munich. 'Anyone who enjoys what I had to go through out there today must be a pervert,' he said after scoring a 19-under-par aggregate of 269 and a five stroke winning margin over Fred Couples.

Everyone smiled at another of this popular and intelligent Irishman's quips. But he went on: 'I'm serious. I don't like this game at all. I don't like all the travelling, although I enjoy being there, and I never play golf socially. I would rather play tennis or bowls. No, I only enjoy this game when it's over—when I can look back.' He had a lot of high quality golf to look back on as he left Munich with his first title in three years and a cheque for £45,820.

Arriving in the capital of Bavaria too late to get to the course for a full practice round, Feherty certainly lacked confidence after missing the cut in Stuttgart the previous week. So he went out "blind" on the newly-opened course on a bitterly cold, damp day—and shot an incredible ten-under-par 62 containing 11 birdies. It was the best round of his career. It did not, however, constitute a course record because three weeks of rain had necessitated moving some tees forward and allowing the picking and placing of the ball on the muddy fairways.

But it impressed Davis Love III. He could not believe that his own superb 65 on his first visit to Germany had left him three strokes off the lead. 'I played well,' said Love, 'but his golf must have been magic.' Love then took a swipe at some of his compatriots and their cossetted life on the US Tour. 'We

DAVID FEHERTY LED ALL THE WAY IN MUNICH AND THEN INSISTED THAT HIS VICTORY WAS NOT ALTOGETHER AN ENJOYABLE EXPERIENCE

Americans are spoilt,' said Love. 'If the weather was as bad at home as it was on the first day, we would probably have delayed the tournament. But playing in the cold, wet and wind teaches you more shots and how to play in adversity.'

Conditions improved for the second round and while Love dashed his title hopes with a one-over-par 73, Feherty continued in the same sparkling vein. The Ulsterman was round in 66 for a 16-under-par halfway total of 128. Only Sandy Lyle had bettered that when he was 17 under par at the same stage in the 1983 Ebel Swiss Open. But Lyle did not win, losing a play-off to Nick Faldo, and therefore Feherty's six stroke lead over Kent's Peter Mitchell was not a comfortable cushion.

Bernhard Langer, winner the previous week, headed a list of distinguished names who missed the cut. Mark Calcavecchia, who also missed out in the German Masters, Gary Koch, who opened with a 66 and followed with an 80, Sam Torrance and Ken Brown were also all on their way as the axe fell at 143.

Feherty's discomfort continued as his third round 68 increased his lead to eight shots with his nearest challenger being Fred Couples as Mitchell had collapsed to a 78. Feherty eagled the final hole to put himself in the position of being the one player who could lose the tournament since with such a lead it was unlikely anyone else was going to win it from behind. As Couples succinctly put it: 'It's entirely in David's hands now.'

Feherty's tension was there for all to see on the final afternoon. He took three putts at the second and when he walked onto the sixth green his lips tightened when he saw that Philip Walton had picked up two birdies and was within six shots. A birdie putt at the seventh helped Feherty relax and, although he denied it later, he must have realised he was beyond reach and it only remained to see who was going to be second.

Walton was favourite as he came to the last one ahead of Couples. But the Irishman faltered, took four from 85 yards and then watched helplessly a few minutes later as Couples birdied to clinch the £30,540 second prize. Eamonn Darcy had a run of five successive birdies from the sixth to move from 12th to fourth place, and Mark Mouland and Mike Harwood, placed joint fifth, were equally delighted with their week's work. So, too, were

Mike Harwood

Ove Sellberg

Mark Calcavecchia

Walton wilted on the final hole

American line-ups, Tom Purtzer, above, and Fred Couples, right

Gordon J. Brand and Tom Purtzer, seventh on 278 and Russell Claydon. He had three 70s and a 72 to earn £3,680.

And Feherty? He was still questioning his reasons for playing the game. 'Sometimes golf makes you despise yourself, and then something like this happens and it gives you back some esteem. But I really stopped enjoying the game when I began working hard at it three or four years ago. Now I wouldn't even watch it for pleasure.'

That's a pity. But at least Feherty left Munich with the consolation of a handsome cheque and the knowledge that he had given spectators a lot of pleasure with his skill and demeanour on the course.

Novel green protection

Salute from the winner

COURSE: GOLFPLATZ MUNCHEN, NORD-EICHENRIED **YARDAGE: 6,910** **PAR: 72**

POS	NAME	CTRY	1	2	3	4	TOTAL	PRIZE MONEY
1	David FEHERTY	N.Ire	62	66	68	73	269	£45820
2	Fred COUPLES	USA	68	69	67	70	274	£30540
3	Philip WALTON	Ire	67	70	68	70	275	£17210
4	Eamonn DARCY	Ire	70	69	70	67	276	£13750
5	Mark MOULAND	Wal	70	70	68	69	277	£10645
	Mike HARWOOD	Aus	70	71	66	70	277	£10645
7	Gordon J BRAND	Eng	68	68	70	72	278	£7500
	Tom PURTZER	USA	69	69	69	71	278	£7500
9	Davis LOVE III	USA	65	73	70	71	279	£5750
	Ove SELLBERG	Swe	66	71	70	72	279	£5750
11	Denis DURNIAN	Eng	73	69	68	70	280	£4796
	Torsten GIDEON	W.Ger	71	70	69	70	280	£4796
	Craig PARRY	Aus	69	71	70	70	280	£4796
14	Rodger DAVIS	Aus	69	69	73	70	281	£4190
	Gordon BRAND Jnr	Scot	73	67	69	72	281	£4190
16	Magnus PERSSON	Swe	67	70	71	74	282	£3680
	Howard CLARK	Eng	66	72	73	71	282	£3680
	Johan RYSTROM	Swe	71	72	72	67	282	£3680
	Peter FOWLER	Aus	66	74	70	72	282	£3680
	Russell CLAYDON	Eng	70	70	70	72	282	£3680
21	Peter MITCHELL	Eng	67	67	78	71	283	£3200
	Keith WATERS	Eng	69	67	75	72	283	£3200
	Carl MASON	Eng	68	71	73	71	283	£3200
24	Anders FORSBRAND	Swe	69	72	68	75	284	£2845
	Miguel Angel JIMENEZ	Sp	71	69	74	70	284	£2845
	Peter SENIOR	Aus	72	71	70	71	284	£2845
	Bryan NORTON	USA	67	73	71	73	284	£2845
28	Mats LANNER	Swe	71	66	70	78	285	£2492
	Paul WAY	Eng	69	70	74	72	285	£2492
	Mark McNULTY	Zim	73	70	73	69	285	£2492
	Des SMYTH	Ire	71	69	72	73	285	£2492
32	Richard BOXALL	Eng	69	69	74	74	286	£2030
	Lyndsay STEPHEN	Aus	68	70	76	72	286	£2030
	Mark JAMES	Eng	71	68	71	76	286	£2030
	Paul CARRIGILL	Eng	70	67	77	72	286	£2030
	Tony CHARNLEY	Eng	72	71	72	71	286	£2030
	David A RUSSELL	Eng	67	72	73	74	286	£2030
	Peter BAKER	Eng	69	73	72	72	286	£2030
	David GILFORD	Eng	72	71	70	73	286	£2030
	Stephen BENNETT	Eng	69	71	72	74	286	£2030
	Derrick COOPER	Eng	69	73	69	75	286	£2030
42	Paul KENT	Eng	70	69	75	73	287	£1497
	David WILLIAMS	Eng	72	69	72	74	287	£1497
	Philip HARRISON	Eng	69	74	72	72	287	£1497
	David RAY	Eng	70	72	73	72	287	£1497
	Vicente FERNANDEZ	Arg	70	70	73	74	287	£1497
	Ross DRUMMOND	Scot	69	71	72	75	287	£1497
	Mark DAVIS	Eng	68	74	70	75	287	£1497
	Glenn RALPH	Eng	72	71	72	72	287	£1497
50	Chris MOODY	Eng	71	70	72	75	288	£1131
	Mike CLAYTON	Aus	73	70	74	71	288	£1131
	Sandy STEPHEN	Scot	71	71	73	73	288	£1131
	Malcom MACKENZIE	Eng	70	72	72	74	288	£1131
	Alberto BINAGHI	It	69	74	75	70	288	£1131
	Eduardo ROMERO	Arg	69	71	71	77	288	£1131
	Juan ANGLADA	Sp	69	74	70	75	288	£1131
57	Jeff HAWKES	SA	71	69	73	76	289	£970
58	Ross McFARLANE	Eng	70	73	75	72	290	£870
	Ruud BOS	Hol	72	71	74	73	290	£870
	Mats HALLBERG	Swe	70	71	73	76	290	£870
	Wayne STEPHENS	Eng	70	73	73	74	290	£870
	Thomas GOEGELE	W.Ger	68	74	75	73	290	£870
63	Armando SAAVEDRA	Arg	71	72	75	73	291	£780
64	David LLEWELLYN	Wal	70	73	75	75	293	£581
	Andrew STUBBS	Eng	73	69	73	78	293	£581
	Greg J TURNER	NZ	69	73	74	77	293	£581

MONTGOMERIE *smashes through*

A so-so season that featured two bitter disappointments ended on a high note for Colin Montgomerie at Quinta do Lago. The former Scottish amateur champion left half a dozen of Europe's Ryder Cup team trailing as he tore up the record book and won the Portuguese Open —Tournament Players' Championship —by 11 strokes.

He need not have worried at all about his credentials to be playing among the world's best professionals. Montgomerie was the tenth first-time winner of the season and none of his predecessors did it more impressively. This was the sixth time that the Championship had been played on the course and no-one had ever got near his 24-under par total of 264. It beat the previous best, by Mark McNulty, by a clear six shots.

His last round of 63 also took a stroke off David Frost's five-year-old course record. A first-time winner has never performed like that before. And he was the first to win by 11 strokes since Ken Brown did it in the Scottish Open in 1984. Only four have won by a bigger margin since the war.

Montgomerie's happiness at his victory was almost matched by Manuel Pinero's pleasure at being able to return to competitive golf. The little Spaniard had not played on the Volvo Tour since the French Open several months earlier because of tendonitis in his left wrist.

He had had injections, laser treatment and acupuncture but none of them seemed to do any good. He was on the point of having surgery when he was recommended to visit a masseur, Alfonse Delgado, who looks after the aches and pains of the soccer players of Real Madrid and Atletico Madrid.

WITH A COURSE RECORD 63 IN THE FINAL ROUND COLIN MONTGOMERIE ROMPED TO A SPECTACULAR FIRST VICTORY

'He is well over 60 but has very strong wrists,' said Pinero. 'I almost passed out unconscious with pain.' But three weeks later he was back on the golf course feeling that a miracle had been effected. To his joy, he played so well that he finished in a tie for fifth place.

After round one Montgomerie trailed the Australian, Rodger Davis, by a stroke. He, Luis Carbonetti and Mark Mouland all had 67s on a day dominated by a bizarre incident involving Mark McNulty, who noticed that the hole on the 16th green did not look the correct size. His playing partners Barry Lane and David Feherty agreed with him and a tournament official was sent for. 'Instead of being 4½ inches wide the hole was less than four inches,' said McNulty. Andy McFee, the Tournament Director, explained that the metal lining of the cup had been inserted deeper into the ground than was usually the case. The bigger area of exposed wet turf had begun to cave inwards when McNulty spotted the discrepancy, although 60 others had already played that hole without anyone else noticing anything amiss.

Montgomerie's second round of 65 for a total of 132 swept him past Carbonetti, Mouland and Juan Quiros. Twelve under par, he led them by four strokes. The third round was the acid test. 'I have been in the lead before and let it slip, so Saturday's round was very important for me,' said Montgomerie. But he broke 70 for the third successive round and remained four shots clear.

Mike Smith, the experienced American, represented the biggest danger to Montgomerie in the final round, especially when he matched the Scot's three birdies in the first four holes. Then Montgomerie birdied the fifth as well, Smith did not and was yet another stroke in arrears. All danger disappeared for Montgomerie on the seventh. He birdied—his fifth of the round—Smith bogied and Montgomerie was seven shots ahead.

Montgomerie completed the round without a bogey, winning by his massive margin when Smith dropped another shot on the last hole. 'I'd have settled for a one-shot win when I started the last round,' said Montgomerie. 'To win by 11 shots was like a dream come true. It proved I can win. I had one or two doubts after what happened in the Catalan Open earlier in the season.' On that occasion he was two strokes ahead with one hole to play but lost when he took a bogey six

Fifth place finish for Christy O'Connor Junior

Torrance sports his new beard

against the eagle three of Mark Roe.

That was a bad start to the season and there was another low point at Royal Troon when the Open was played there. The Scot had every reason for optimism because his father is secretary of the club and Colin has considerable experience of the course. But he failed to qualify and had to sit in the stands and watch.

'It was very disappointing but I was playing badly around that time.' He was missing so many cuts that he went back to Bill Ferguson, the club pro at Ilkley, who had launched him into golf. 'Bill sorted out my alignment and got me back swinging the way I did as an amateur,' said Montgomerie. 'From then on my game began to improve.'

In Portugal he demonstrated just how much it had improved.

Rodger Davis was back after injury

Montgomerie was magnificent

Mike Smith pines for a better lie among the cones

COURSE: QUINTA DO LAGO, ALGARVE **YARDAGE: 7,095** **PAR: 72**

POS	NAME	CTRY	1	2	3	4	TOTAL	PRIZE MONEY
1	Colin MONTGOMERIE	Scot	67	65	69	63	264	£45825
2	Mike SMITH	USA	70	69	66	70	275	£20498
	Manuel MORENO	Sp	71	69	69	66	275	£20498
	Rodger DAVIS	Aus	66	72	69	68	275	£20498
5	Manuel PINERO	Sp	68	70	72	66	276	£10640
	Christy O'CONNOR Jnr	Ire	69	68	71	68	276	£10640
7	Sandy STEPHEN	Scot	71	69	68	69	277	£6095
	David FEHERTY	N.Ire	70	71	67	69	277	£6095
	Gordon J BRAND	Eng	70	71	67	69	277	£6095
	Peter SENIOR	Aus	73	65	71	68	277	£6095
	Antonio GARRIDO	Sp	69	71	67	70	277	£6095
	Peter FOWLER	Aus	69	68	73	67	277	£6095
13	Luis CARBONETTI	Arg	67	69	72	70	278	£4052
	David WHELAN	Eng	72	73	65	68	278	£4052
	Armando SAAVEDRA	Arg	70	70	67	71	278	£4052
	Ove SELLBERG	Swe	73	69	68	68	278	£4052
	Ronan RAFFERTY	N.Ire	73	68	69	68	278	£4052
18	Peter BAKER	Eng	68	72	70	69	279	£3420
	Mark DAVIS	Eng	74	71	65	69	279	£3420
	Jose RIVERO	Sp	68	72	69	70	279	£3420
21	David RAY	Eng	69	74	67	70	280	£2887
	Des SMYTH	Ire	69	72	71	68	280	£2887
	Mark McNULTY	Zim	68	70	72	70	280	£2887
	Wayne RILEY	Aus	74	70	68	68	280	£2887
	Gordon BRAND Jnr	Scot	70	69	68	73	280	£2887
	Sam TORRANCE	Scot	75	70	68	67	280	£2887
	Craig PARRY	Aus	72	70	67	71	280	£2887
	Ken BROWN	Scot	72	69	68	71	280	£2887
	Peter TERAVAINEN	USA	70	71	70	69	280	£2887
30	Mark ROE	Eng	69	68	75	69	281	£2237
	Juan QUIROS	Sp	69	67	72	73	281	£2237
	Emilio RODRIGUEZ	Sp	72	70	71	68	281	£2237
	David WILLIAMS	Eng	69	72	70	70	281	£2237
	Mark MOULAND	Wal	67	69	73	72	281	£2237
	Eduardo ROMERO	Arg	71	70	71	69	281	£2237
	Jose Maria CANIZARES	Sp	73	72	67	69	281	£2237
	Ron COMMANS	USA	69	69	71	72	281	£2237
38	Mike HARWOOD	Aus	69	73	70	70	282	£1952
	Roger CHAPMAN	Eng	74	69	69	70	282	£1952
40	Bryan NORTON	USA	72	73	68	70	283	£1787
	Miguel Angel MARTIN	Sp	75	70	68	70	283	£1787
	Stephen BENNETT	Eng	73	72	68	70	283	£1787
	Ross DRUMMOND	Scot	70	69	70	74	283	£1787
44	Marc PENDARIES	Fr	69	76	71	68	284	£1485
	Daniel SILVA	Port	72	70	72	70	284	£1485
	Martin POXON	Eng	73	69	69	73	284	£1485
	Alberto BINAGHI	It	71	73	74	66	284	£1485
	Bill LONGMUIR	Scot	74	70	65	75	284	£1485
	Paul CARRIGILL	Eng	74	70	70	70	284	£1485
	Peter MITCHELL	Eng	71	70	72	71	284	£1485
51	John JACOBS	USA	70	70	75	70	285	£1100
	Ronald STELTEN	USA	71	71	74	69	285	£1100
	Andrew MURRAY	Eng	71	70	73	71	285	£1100
	Dave LLEWELLYN	Wal	75	68	73	69	285	£1100
	Keith WATERS	Eng	74	68	72	71	285	£1100
	Vijay SINGH	Fij	72	73	68	72	285	£1100
	Steven BOTTOMLEY	Eng	68	73	72	72	285	£1100
58	Magnus PERSSON	Swe	70	70	74	72	286	£825
	Barry LANE	Eng	71	72	68	75	286	£825
	Andrew SHERBORNE	Eng	71	74	69	72	286	£825
	Neil HANSEN	Eng	74	70	71	71	286	£825
	Bob E SMITH	USA	71	74	72	69	286	£825
63	John HAWKSWORTH	Eng	73	71	70	73	287	£727
	Paul KENT	Eng	70	72	74	71	287	£727
65	Ross McFARLANE	Eng	75	68	74	71	288	£482
	David JAMES	Scot	71	72	69	76	288	£482
67	Jimmy HEGGARTY	N.Ire	71	70	72	76	289	£270
	Carl MASON	Eng	70	74	73	72	289	£270
	Denis DURNIAN	Eng	71	74	73	71	289	£270
	Eamonn DARCY	Ire	71	72	75	71	289	£270
71	Magnus JONSSON	Swe	71	74	71	74	290	£264
	Stephen HAMILL	N.Ire	74	71	70	75	290	£264
73	Brian EVANS	Eng	71	72	76	72	291	£260
	David A RUSSELL	Eng	74	71	74	72	291	£260
75	Massimo MANNELLI	It	70	75	71	76	292	£255
	Vicente FERNANDEZ	Arg	73	71	76	72	292	£255
	Robert KARLSSON	Swe	71	73	76	72	292	£255

VOLVO
MASTERS

RAFFERTY *clinches top spot*

IN A THRILLING, LAST ROUND CLIMAX TO THE VOLVO TOUR RONAN RAFFERTY SECURED VICTORY AT VALDERRAMA

It was bright, clear and sunny that last day of the 1989 Volvo Tour, the day when the Order of Merit would be decided and the Volvo Masters won. The season had begun in February when snow blanketed much of northern Europe. Thirty-four tournaments, eight months and several hundred thousand miles later it would be decided with the final stroke on the final hole of the final event of the year. By the time dusk settled over Sotogrande we would know whether European golf had unearthed the key figures of a new generation or whether the old order, still playing at the height of their powers, would remain. Someone would reign in Spain, but who?

The most likely candidates were Ronan Rafferty, who held a two-stroke lead on the last day, and Jose Maria Olazabal, who had led the money list at the start of the tournament and lay second after 54 holes. They had battled with one another in Tenerife, in Holland, in Scandinavia. This was the round that would settle it all.

Should either of them falter then Nick Faldo, the defending champion, was only one behind Olazabal and newly-married Sandy Lyle one behind Faldo and level with Ian Woosnam. The Australian, Craig Parry, 'Popeye Parry' to his cobbers, had an outside chance too. He was only five behind Rafferty.

But before the winner could be determined the ritual slaughter had to go on. Valderrama is unquestionably the best-prepared course in Europe, with fairways so manicured you feel obliged to repair your pitch marks. It is also the most difficult, calling for accuracy and length off the tee, skill in approaching the green to make sure of an uphill putt and a nerveless touch on the putting surfaces.

Only three players could break par on the first day, Olazabal (69), Lyle (70) and Woosnam (71). Faldo began as he had in 1988 with a 74. 'The greens are the quickest in Europe—and the spikiest,' he said. To be sure, every player left a trail of grass specks thrown up by his spikes after each step taken on the greens. It was puzzling that bent grass greens in southern Spain should spike up so much more than those at Muirfield Village, say, or Augusta National. The answer lay in the soil. The grass simply hadn't had long enough to take proper root. If money and labour could solve the problem then it would be solved. When Senor Jaime Ortiz Patino wants something done at Sotogrande, it's done, no questions asked. 'A good vertical mowing programme over the next 12 months should do it,' said Bill Bengeyfield, of the USGA.

Rain swept in on the second day, as if dealing with the course wasn't trouble enough, and only six men beat par for 36 holes this year. They were the old guard of Woosnam, Faldo and Howard Clark and the young Turks, Olazabal, who led on five under par, and Rafferty and Parry both three under. The cut fell at eight over, two strokes better than the previous year. Special medals for courage were presented to Philip Walton and Paul Way who redeemed their opening 81s with 71s, both sneaking through to the third day.

In previous years Rafferty might have slipped quietly from his place near the front of the field in the third round. But having won two tournaments earlier in the year he was a new man, calm, composed and confident. He had a 70 and found himself two strokes in front. His score contained only one bogey, which he regarded as something of a triumph.

Woosnam and Olazabal found it awfully hard. The young Spaniard visited five bunkers in the first eight holes. Woosnam was in countless trees. Olive, umbrella pines, cork, you name them he was in them. Lyle, too, was just as inconsistent. After rounds of 70 and 76 he had a 69 and found himself paired for the fourth round with his oldest rival, Nick Faldo.

By the turn on Sunday Rafferty and Olazabal seemed so intent upon duplicating one another's mistakes that it looked as though Faldo's remorselessness would win the day. Rafferty was out in 39, Olazabal 37, Faldo in a level par 36.

VOLVO
MASTERS
OLAZABAL -2
RAFFERTY -2
SILENCIO
SILENCIO

Rafferty starts his last nine surge

Woosnam carves from sculptured sand

Then Rafferty demonstrated how much confidence he had gained since the Ryder Cup. He birdied the tenth with a 15-foot putt, the short 12th and the short 15th after a lovely tee shot with a metal wood. As Rafferty birdied this hole Olazabal bogied it and suddenly the gap between them was four strokes. Rafferty had beaten Olazabal to win the Order of Merit; now he had to beat Faldo for the title.

But Faldo had kept on taking the lead and he did so again by sinking a good putt on the 16th to go six under par. Rafferty joined him when he holed a 12-foot putt for a birdie on the 17th. A play-off looked likely until Faldo, of all people, misjudged his second shot to the 18th. It clipped a tree and was deflected into a bunker on the right of the green. Faldo had got up and down from this same bunker in 1988 for victory but couldn't do the same this year. He was too far back, perhaps 40 yards from the flag. A bogey five meant he finished on five under par.

All Rafferty had to do now was par the hole and he would win the tournament (prize: £66,600); the Order of Merit (prize: enormous respect, invitations to the three major championships in the US and a season's winning of £400,000) and the Volvo bonus (£65,000).

A five iron found the front fringe. A nervous putt went the perfect length but five feet right of the hole. Without much ado he stroked the putt in to the side of the hole and it fell in gratefully. Rafferty, 25, had beaten the best in Europe in his eighth season as a pro, though it had taken him 25 events to do it, compared with Olazabal's 19.

Not since Christy O'Connor in 1962 had an Irishman won the Order of Merit. Rafferty had done it by sheer doggedness throughout the season and quite brilliant golf over the final nine holes at Valderrama, which he covered in 32. Within minutes of his triumph he was dashing to Gibraltar airport to fly to Japan. The man who had just conquered Europe had other worlds to conquer.

High tee finish from Howard Clark

Faldo fell foul of sand on final hole

Clark chips in at 14th

Ramrod finish from Faldo

Valderrama vista

Blue moment as Olazabal's challenge fades

Have you heard the one about . . ?

'It's all mine'

Mr and Mrs Lyle and their little boy

Left, Rafferty strides towards victory

COURSE: VALDERRAMA GOLF CLUB, SOTOGRANDE **YARDAGE: 7,020** **PAR: 72**

POS	NAME	CTRY	1	2	3	4	TOTAL	PRIZE MONEY
1	Ronan RAFFERTY	N.Ire	72	69	70	71	282	£66660
2	Nick FALDO	Eng	74	68	72	69	283	£44425
3	Jose Maria OLAZABAL	Sp	69	70	74	74	287	£25040
4	Sandy LYLE	Scot	70	76	69	74	289	£20000
5	Peter FOWLER	Aus	75	72	69	74	290	£14316
	Mark JAMES	Eng	77	70	71	72	290	£14316
	Howard CLARK	Eng	73	70	74	73	290	£14316
8	Craig PARRY	Aus	73	68	75	75	291	£10000
9	Vicente FERNANDEZ	Arg	75	73	73	71	292	£8106
	Eduardo ROMERO	Arg	73	73	74	72	292	£8106
	Ove SELLBERG	Swe	75	74	73	70	292	£8106
12	Andrew MURRAY	Eng	75	71	72	75	293	£6190
	Roger CHAPMAN	Eng	73	72	77	71	293	£6190
	Peter SENIOR	Aus	73	78	68	74	293	£6190
	Ian WOOSNAM	Wal	71	69	75	78	293	£6190
	Jose Maria CANIZARES	Sp	75	73	75	70	293	£6190
17	Tony CHARNLEY	Eng	76	75	73	71	295	£5171
	Mark McNULTY	Zim	72	73	75	75	295	£5171
	Christy O'CONNOR Jnr	Ire	72	74	72	77	295	£5171
20	Luis CARBONETTI	Arg	74	71	75	76	296	£4620
	Peter TERAVAINEN	USA	72	74	78	72	296	£4620
	Richard BOXALL	Eng	78	73	74	71	296	£4620
	Miguel Angel MARTIN	Sp	74	75	74	73	296	£4620
24	Brett OGLE	Aus	75	71	78	73	297	£3960
	Michael ALLEN	USA	76	73	73	75	297	£3960
	Rick HARTMANN	USA	75	77	75	70	297	£3960
	Mike SMITH	USA	72	75	77	73	297	£3960
	Derrick COOPER	Eng	76	69	77	75	297	£3960
	Bill LONGMUIR	Scot	74	77	72	74	297	£3960
	Jean VAN DE VELDE	Fr	74	74	75	74	297	£3960
31	David GILFORD	Eng	79	73	73	73	298	£3420
	David WILLIAMS	Eng	75	73	76	74	298	£3420
33	Manuel PINERO	Sp	74	75	73	77	299	£3240
	Mats LANNER	Swe	73	73	76	77	299	£3240
35	Mark MOULAND	Wal	79	72	76	73	300	£2920
	Mike HARWOOD	Aus	75	72	77	76	300	£2920
	David FEHERTY	N.Ire	74	73	76	77	300	£2920
	Paul CARRIGILL	Eng	73	77	71	79	300	£2920
	Vijay SINGH	Fij	76	72	75	77	300	£2920
	Keith WATERS	Eng	75	72	80	73	300	£2920
41	Philip PARKIN	Wal	74	74	76	77	301	£2600
	Andrew SHERBORNE	Eng	75	74	76	76	301	£2600
43	Bryan NORTON	USA	74	77	75	76	302	£2440
	Paul WAY	Eng	81	71	76	74	302	£2440
45	Sam TORRANCE	Scot	73	78	75	77	303	£2240
	Emmanuel DUSSART	Fr	77	74	76	76	303	£2240
	Bernard GALLACHER	Scot	72	78	74	79	303	£2240
48	Frank NOBILO	NZ	75	75	76	78	304	£2040
	Mike CLAYTON	Aus	76	74	81	73	304	£2040
50	Philip WALTON	Ire	81	71	78	76	306	£1880
	Miguel Angel JIMENEZ	Sp	78	72	80	76	306	£1880
52	Johan RYSTROM	Swe	74	77	81	75	307	£1760
53	Martin POXON	Eng	74	77	79	78	308	£1680
58	Brian MARCHBANK	Scot	76	77			153	£737
	Stephen BENNETT	Eng	77	76			153	£737
	Des SMYTH	Ire	77	76			153	£737
	Neil HANSEN	Eng	74	79			153	£737
	Peter MITCHELL	Eng	76	77			153	£737
	Manuel MORENO	Sp	76	77			153	£737
	Gordon BRAND Jnr	Scot	79	74			153	£737
	Colin MONTGOMERIE	Scot	81	72			153	£737
	Ken BROWN	Scot	74	79			153	£737
	Gordon J BRAND	Eng	78	75			153	£737
	Bill MALLEY	USA	81	72			153	£737
65	Jose RIVERO	Sp	78	76			154	£643
	Ross DRUMMOND	Scot	82	72			154	£643
	Malcolm MACKENZIE	Eng	80	74			154	£643
	Carl MASON	Eng	79	75			154	£643
69	David JONES	N.Ire	79	76			155	£630
	Jimmy HEGGARTY	N.Ire	76	79			155	£630
71	Kevin DICKENS	Eng	79	77			156	£600
	Magnus PERSSON	Swe	80	76			156	£600

VOLVO ORDER OF MERIT

(1)

Ronan
RAFFERTY
Northern Ireland
PRIZE MONEY
£400,311.32

(2)

Jose Maria
OLAZABAL
Spain
PRIZE MONEY
£336,239.44

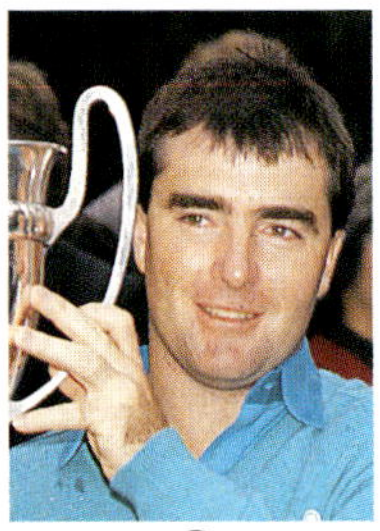

(3)

Craig
PARRY
Australia
PRIZE MONEY
£277,321.86

(4)

Nick
FALDO
England
PRIZE MONEY
£261,552.68

(5)

Mark
JAMES
England
PRIZE MONEY
£245,916.99

(6)

Ian
WOOSNAM
Wales
PRIZE MONEY
£210,100.97

(7)

Bernhard
LANGER
West Germany
PRIZE MONEY
£205,194.52

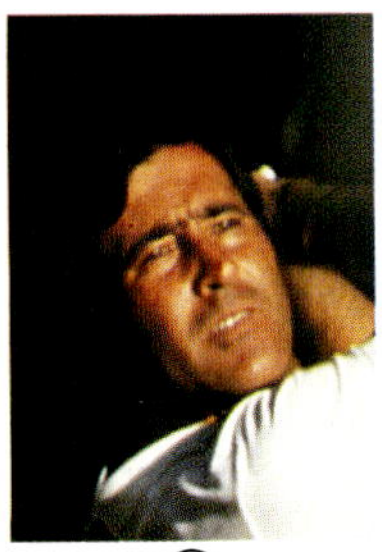

(8)

Severiano
BALLESTEROS
Spain
PRIZE MONEY
£202,762.89

(9)

Mark
McNULTY
Zimbabwe
PRIZE MONEY
£179,693.60

(10)

David
FEHERTY
Northern Ireland
PRIZE MONEY
£178,167.17

VOLVO ORDER OF MERIT

POS	NAME	CTRY	PRIZE MONEY
11	Sam TORRANCE	Scot	£170650.31
12	Gordon BRAND Jnr	Scot	£169890.37
13	Eduardo ROMERO	Arg	£168558.15
14	Mike HARWOOD	Aus	£165059.60
15	Michael ALLEN	USA	£157644.43
16	Peter SENIOR	Aus	£143954.72
17	Philip WALTON	Ire	£135195.33
18	Jose Maria CANIZARES	Sp	£133289.42
19	Derrick COOPER	Eng	£123776.88
20	Howard CLARK	Eng	£123566.34
21	Christy O'CONNOR Jnr	Ire	£122797.41
22	Peter FOWLER	Aus	£119237.16
23	Denis DURNIAN	Eng	£113191.03
24	Vijay SINGH	Fij	£109612.24
25	Colin MONTGOMERIE	Scot	£109084.21
26	Mark ROE	Eng	£107647.95
27	Brett OGLE	Aus	£106002.38
28	Andrew MURRAY	Eng	£101612.19
29	Ove SELLBERG	Swe	£101575.80
30	Gordon J BRAND	Eng	£98914.46
31	Roger CHAPMAN	Eng	£95698.07
32	Mats LANNER	Swe	£95330.67
33	Barry LANE	Eng	£87144.44
34	Jose RIVERO	Sp	£85981.37
35	Eamonn DARCY	Ire	£85041.86
36	Frank NOBILO	NZ	£79325.12
37	Des SMYTH	Ire	£79313.71
38	Magnus PERSSON	Swe	£75087.60
39	Mark MOULAND	Wal	£74829.46
40	Richard BOXALL	Eng	£71093.67
41	Stephen BENNETT	Eng	£70553.38
42	Paul BROADHURST	Eng	£67103.80
43	Jeff HAWKES	SA	£64850.22
44	Rodger DAVIS	Aus	£63396.04
45	Mark DAVIS	Eng	£61362.96
46	Mike SMITH	USA	£60457.11
47	Tony CHARNLEY	Eng	£57417.56
48	Malcolm MACKENZIE	Eng	£57238.69
49	David WILLIAMS	Eng	£55773.43
50	Jesper PARNEVIK	Swe	£55537.57
51	Carl MASON	Eng	£52904.86
52	David GILFORD	Eng	£52337.79
53	Sandy LYLE	Scot	£49408.34
54	John BLAND	SA	£44818.55
55	Philip PARKIN	Wal	£44201.38
56	Peter O'MALLEY	Aus	£43914.59
57	Jerry HAAS	USA	£43841.21
58	Peter MITCHELL	Eng	£43387.06
59	Paul CARRIGILL	Eng	£42588.35
60	Vicente FERNANDEZ	Arg	£42577.35
61	Jean VAN DE VELDE	Fr	£41076.47
62	Grant TURNER	Eng	£40757.31
63	Martin POXON	Eng	£39488.27
64	Andrew SHERBORNE	Eng	£39356.80
65	Hugh BAIOCCHI	SA	£39277.18
66	Luis CARBONETTI	Arg	£38624.62
67	Emmanuel DUSSART	Fr	£38282.54
68	Peter TERAVAINEN	USA	£36915.11
69	Bill LONGMUIR	Scot	£36792.12
70	Bryan NORTON	USA	£36427.41
71	Ken BROWN	Scot	£36338.41
72	Manuel PINERO	Sp	£36250.64
73	Neil HANSEN	Eng	£35104.47
74	Manuel MORENO	Sp	£34484.58
75	Gavin LEVENSON	SA	£34438.92
76	Miguel Angel MARTIN	Sp	£34434.06
77	Kevin DICKENS	Eng	£34332.53
78	Keith WATERS	Eng	£34057.42
79	Rick HARTMANN	USA	£33695.48
80	Alberto BINAGHI	It	£32632.76
81	Johan RYSTROM	Swe	£32285.52
82	Jimmy HEGGARTY	N. Ire	£31161.02
83	Mike CLAYTON	Aus	£29855.14
84	Brian MARCHBANK	Scot	£29833.12
85	Miguel Angel JIMENEZ	Sp	£29348.86
86	Robert LEE	Eng	£29147.21
87	Ross DRUMMOND	Scot	£28585.76
88	Bill MALLEY	USA	£28550.06
89	Bernard GALLACHER	Scot	£28258.12
90	Tony JOHNSTONE	Zim	£27666.82
91	David JONES	N. Ire	£27149.31
92	David A RUSSELL	Eng	£25563.84
93	Ossie MOORE	Aus	£25425.35
94	Antonio GARRIDO	Sp	£25226.79
95	Jamie HOWELL	USA	£23880.34
96	Ross McFARLANE	Eng	£23699.04
97	Paul CURRY	Eng	£23544.90
98	Stephen McALLISTER	Scot	£23403.33
99	Juan QUIROS	Sp	£23230.94
100	Marc FARRY	Fr	£23130.18
101	David LLEWELLYN	Wal	£23116.40
102	Anders SORENSEN	Den	£23007.70
103	Sandy STEPHEN	Scot	£22141.02
104	Peter BAKER	Eng	£22085.90
105	Paolo QUIRICI	Swi	£22073.07
106	Bob E SMITH	USA	£21909.54
107	Ian MOSEY	Eng	£21662.23
108	Philip HARRISON	Eng	£21215.06
109	Armando SAAVEDRA	Arg	£21174.82
110	Peter McWHINNEY	Aus	£21101.50
111	Michael KING	Eng	£20970.51
112	Jim RUTLEDGE	Can	£20759.57
113	Wayne RILEY	Aus	£20174.98
114	Anders FORSBRAND	Swe	£20126.52
115	Chris MOODY	Eng	£19175.43
116	Paul HOAD	Eng	£18450.53
117	Steen TINNING	Den	£18398.85
118	Ron COMMANS	USA	£17932.46
119	Bob SHEARER	Aus	£17926.09
120	Mike MILLER	Scot	£17923.41
121	John MORGAN	Eng	£17839.78
122	Leif HEDERSTROM	Swe	£17736.48
123	Manuel CALERO	Sp	£17461.62
124	Juan ANGLADA	Sp	£17419.05
125	Paul WAY	Eng	£17212.13
126	Glenn RALPH	Eng	£16420.62
127	Lyndsay STEPHEN	Aus	£16342.42
128	Russell CLAYDON	Eng	£16280.88
129	Paul KENT	Eng	£16118.25
130	Ronald STELTEN	USA	£15988.45
131	Jose DAVILA	Sp	£15819.09
132	David RAY	Eng	£15577.52
133	Wayne STEPHENS	Eng	£15277.40
134	Mariano APARICIO	Sp	£15109.61
135	David WHELAN	Eng	£15103.17
136	David J RUSSELL	Eng	£14478.84
137	Marc PENDARIES	Fr	£14261.21
138	Steven BOTTOMLEY	Eng	£14144.33
139	Paul CARMAN	Eng	£13134.45
140	Joe HIGGINS	Eng	£13050.75
141	Charles BOLLING Jnr	USA	£13050.00
142	Massimo MANNELLI	It	£12792.68
143	Jerry ANDERSON	Can	£12311.79
144	Magnus JONSSON	Swe	£12056.61
145	Mikael KRANTZ	Swe	£11941.50
146	Mats HALLBERG	Swe	£11863.61
147	Stephen HAMILL	N. Ire	£10981.35
148	John O'LEARY	Ire	£10326.14
149	John SLAUGHTER	USA	£10075.87
150	Ian YOUNG	Scot	£9991.70
151	David JAMES	Scot	£9727.12
152	Ruud BOS	Hol	£9520.85
153	Michael McCLEAN	Eng	£9175.16
154	Johan TUMBA	Swe	£8407.32
155	Andrew CHANDLER	Eng	£8174.86
156	Robin MANN	Eng	£8043.15
157	John JACOBS	USA	£7923.06
158	Joakim HARGGMAN	Swe	£7582.50
159	Neal BRIGGS	Eng	£7487.43
160	Santiago LUNA	Sp	£7475.82
161	Brian EVANS	Eng	£7283.88
162	Torsten GIEDEON	W.Ger	£7233.40
163	Lee JONES	Eng	£7046.44
164	Ulf NILSSON	Swe	£6955.11
165	Bradley HUGHES	Aus	£6702.00
166	Juan ROSA	Sp	£6676.00
167	Emilio RODRIGUEZ	Sp	£6665.53
168	Andrew STUBBS	Eng	£6576.82
169	Richard FISH	Eng	£6567.59
170	Jeremy BENNETT	Eng	£6472.90
171	Paul MAYO	Wal	£6224.50
172	Jacob RASMUSSEN	Den	£6031.64
173	Martin SLUDDS	Ire	£5826.32
174	Brian BARNES	Scot	£5740.00
175	Tommy ARMOUR III	USA	£5720.00
176	Costantino ROCCA	It	£5255.20
177	Andrea CANESSA	It	£5219.72
178	Giuseppe CALI	It	£5141.95
179	Greg J TURNER	NZ	£4989.67
180	Daniel LOZANO	Sp	£4706.00
181	Magnus SUNESSON	Swe	£4187.50
182	Frederic REGARD	Fr	£4079.82
183	Carl Magnus STROMBERG	Swe	£4014.60
184	Noel RATCLIFFE	Aus	£4010.21
185	Clive TUCKER	Eng	£3562.50
186	John McHENRY	Ire	£3504.35
187	Silvio GRAPPASONNI	It	£3496.56
188	Brian WAITES	Eng	£3305.00
189	John HAWKSWORTH	Eng	£3187.23
190	Michel BESANCENEY	Fr	£2900.61
191	Jose CARRILES	Sp	£2726.67
192	Jonas SAXTON	USA	£2382.64
193	Thomas LEVET	Fr	£2233.20
194	Paul HUNSTONE	Eng	£1920.00
195	Tommy HORTON	Eng	£1877.50
196	Francis QUINN	USA	£1551.33
197	Daniel SILVA	Port	£1485.00
198	Magnus GRANKVIST	Swe	£1474.00
199	Simon BISHOP	Eng	£1373.44
200	Emanuele BOLOGNESI	It	£1361.66
201	Laurent LASSALLE	Fr	£1218.23
202	Marco DURANTE	It	£1211.85
203	Don KLENK	USA	£1084.99
204	Tim PLANCHIN	Fr	£1071.95
205	Alessandro ROGATO	It	£1046.39

contributors

Bill Blighton (Today)	– *Peugeot French Open*
Mike Britten (Exchange Telegraph)	– *Volvo Open*
	– *Credit Lyonnais Cannes Open*
	– *Volvo Belgian Open*
	– *KLM Dutch Open*
	– *Scandinavian Enterprise Open*
	– *PLM Open*
	– *Suntory World Match-Play*
Bryan Cutress (Exchange Telegraph)	– *Lancia Italian Open*
	– *BMW International Open*
David Davies (The Guardian)	– *Peugeot Spanish Open*
Richard Dodd (The Yorkshire Post)	– *Benson and Hedges International Open*
Bill Elliott (The Star)	– *German Open*
Mark Garrod (Press Association)	– *Wang Four Stars National Pro-Celebrity*
	– *Equity & Law Challenge*
Tim Glover (The Independent)	– *Karl Litten Desert Classic*
Robert Green (Golf World)	– *Leading Moneywinner Profile*
Martin Hardy (The Daily Express)	– *Dunhill Cup*
John Hennessy (The Times)	– *AGF Open*
Peter Higgs (Mail on Sunday)	– *Epson Grand Prix of Europe*
John Hopkins (The Sunday Times)	– *Renault Open de Baleares*
	– *Trophée Lancôme*
	– *Volvo Masters*
Liz Kahn (The Independent)	– *Panasonic European Open*
Renton Laidlaw (The Evening Standard)	– *Ebel European Masters/Swiss Open*
Derek Lawrenson (Birmingham Post and Mail)	– *Tenerife Open*
Norman Mair (The Scotsman)	– *Dunhill British Masters*
Jock MacVicar (The Scottish Daily Express)	– *Volvo Seniors British Open*
Michael McDonnell (The Daily Mail)	– *The Year in Retrospect*
Ron Moseley (Press Association)	– *Portuguese Open-TPC*
Nuria Pastor (La Vanguardia)	– *Cepsa Madrid Open*
Chris Plumridge (Illustrated London News)	– *Volvo PGA Championship*
	– *NM English Open*
	– *118th Open Championship*
	– *Johnnie Walker Ryder Cup*
John Redmond (Irish Press)	– *Carrolls Irish Open*
Gordon Richardson (Golf Illustrated Weekly)	– *Jersey European Airways Open*
Mel Webb (The Times)	– *Torras Monte Carlo Golf Open*
	– *German Masters*
Michael Williams (The Daily Telegraph)	– *Bell's Scottish Open*
Ian Wooldridge (The Daily Mail)	– *'Return of the Warrior' (118th Open Championship)*

photographers

CAROLINE OWEN

Marta Alonsa – *pages 31, 33 (top), 48, 49, 50*

Ludovic Aubert – *pages 26, 28 (top), 34, 36 (bottom), 37 (top), 46, 47 (top)*

Eric Avenel – *page 45*

Charles & Margot Briscoe-Knight – *pages 2, 3, 4, 5 (bottom right), 7, 8 (left & bottom), 9 (top middle, middle), 10 (bottom left), 11, 12, 15 (top, bottom left & right), 20, 21, 22, 23, 24 (centre, top & bottom), 25, 38, 39, 40, 41, 56, 57, 58, 59, 60, 61, 62, 63, 64, 65, 70, 71, 72, 74, 75, 76, 77, 78, 79, 80, 81, 82, 83, 84, 85, 86, 87, 88, 89, 90, 91, 92, 93, 94, 95, 96, 97, 114, 115, 116, 117, 118, 119, 120, 121, 122 (top right, middle & bottom), 123, 124, 125, 126, 127, 128, 130, 131, 132, 134, 135, 136, 145, 156, 157, 158, 159, 168, 169, 170, 171, 172, 174 (top & left), 175, 182, 183, 184, 185, 186, 187, 188, 189, 190, 191, 192, 193, 194, 195, 196, 197, 198, 199, 210, 211, 212, 214, 215, 216, 217, 226, 227, 228, 229, 230, 231, 232, 234, 235, 236 (Olazabal, Parry, Faldo, James & Langer), 238, 239, 240*

David Cannon – *pages 98, 100, 101 (top & middle) 102, 103 (top & bottom), 122 (top left), 236 (Woosnam)*

Didier Chicot – *pages 10 (top left), 15 (middle right), 24 (far left), 30, 35, 36 (top left & middle), 37 (bottom), 47 (bottom), 104, 105, 106, 107, 108, 109, 111, 112 (top right), 160, 161, 162, 163, 164, 165, 166, 167, 176, 177, 178, 179, 180, 181, 222, 223, 224, 225, 236 (Ballesteros & Feherty)*

Colorsport – *pages 67, 68, 69*

Peter Dazeley – *Front cover, pages 1, 13, 90 (top left), 138, 139 (top)*

Danielle Fluer – *page 101 (bottom)*

Matthew Harris – *pages 5 (left & top right), 9 (top right, bottom left & right), 10 (top right, bottom right), 15 (middle), 19, 52, 99, 103 (middle), 150 (lower right & left), 170 (bottom), 171 (bottom), 173 (bottom), 174 (right, middle & bottom), 202 (top left and right), 203 (bottom), 213*

Trevor Jones – *pages 146, 147, 148, 149, 150 (top), 151*

Stewart Kendall – *pages 110, 112 (top & middle left), 112, 113, 236 (McNulty)*

David Lean – *page 51 (top & bottom)*

Lawrence Levy – *pages 66, 73*

Sammy Minkoff – *pages 205, 206, 207, 208, 209, 218, 219, 220, 221*

Jack Mirkut – *pages 14 (top), 140, 142, 143, 144 (bottom), 236 (Rafferty)*

Nuria Pastor – *pages 18 (top left), 29, 32, 32/33 (bottom)*

Proserv – *pages 42, 43, 44*

Rex Features – *page 11 (Bush, Thatcher, Faldo)*

Phil Sheldon – *pages 8 (top), 14 (bottom), 16, 17, 18 (top & bottom), 28 (bottom), 53, 54, 55, 129, 137, 139 (bottom), 200, 201, 202 (bottom left), 203, 204 (top & middle)*

Svensk Golf – *pages 15 (middle left), 141, 144 (top)*

Leo Vozelgang – *pages 9 (top left), 133*